What

We

Think

Young Voters Speak Out

Compiled by Dean Robbins and Rob Grabow

Book Publishers Network

03587802

What We Think
Young Voters Speak Out

Dean Robbins is a senior mechanical engineering major at Gonzaga University. He is from Laguna Hills, California, and in his free time enjoys reading and playing fantasy baseball. His favorite movie is *Field of Dreams* and his favorite book is *The Caine Munity* by Herman Wouk.

Rob Grabow will be graduated this Fall *Magna Cum Laude* by Gonzaga University with a degree in business finance. He has an avid interest in politics, and enjoys skiing, basketball, and poker. In the past six years, Rob has lived in: North Pole, Alaska; Port Angeles, Washington; Goettingen, Germany; Livingston, Montana; Spokane, Washington; Brisbane Australia; and Florence, Italy.

This book is dedicated to our families, friends, and any young American seeking a platform for their voice to be heard.

"We have it in our power to begin the world over again."
-Thomas Paine

Table of Contents

OUR GENERATION

Preface
Dean Robbins

I remember the first time Rob and I met to discuss the idea of creating a publishing company which would specialize in books targeting college students. We quickly realized that our knowledge of the publishing industry was limited at best, and thus we sought the guidance and sagacity of a local publisher and author, Tony Bamonte. We met Tony the following Monday in a Starbucks downtown. What We Think was spawned on that day.

Armed with an idea, we set out to make our vision a reality. Our timeline was short, as it was late July and we wanted to close submissions in mid-September. In little over six weeks we had to get the word out to as many 18- to 24-year-olds and college students across the country as we could. We faced an uphill battle to say the least. Rob and I realized that to reach young adults we needed a webpage, yet neither of us had any formal web-design experience. After countless frustrating hours we emerged with a website through which we could accept submissions for the book.

Our first submission came in three days later from a student at Marquette University. We could barely contain our excitement as our friend, Shannon Odell, read it aloud. Bolstered by the knowledge that at least one of our peers shared our vision, we logged the submission in our empty database and with renewed vigor, returned to soliciting our peers.

As colleges and universities started getting back in session the trickle of submissions turned into a steady flow. By the time our deadline passed we had received well over 300 submissions from students at over 100 different schools across the nation in less than six weeks. It was our job to find the first edition of What We Think within those submissions in a little less than one week's time.

After some late nights and a few boxes of frozen burritos, What We Think took form. We were only able to agree on including some of the submissions after lengthy argument, and we sometimes needed input from others to tip the scales one way or another. In reading all the submissions Rob and I began to hear a song in the voice of our generation.

The fundamental idea behind What We Think is to provide a venue for the song of our generation to be sung and heard. This song is an expression of the ideas, hopes, and aspirations of the generation of Americans now entering adulthood. It also provides a forum that permits the exchange of the thoughts and opinions of America's next generation; apart from partisanship, group affiliation, or identity politics, but rather open and accessible to all of our generation as we begin to deal with the major issues we must confront in the years ahead.

Just as past generations of Americans adapted to the times and rose to the challenges presented to them by the good and evil present in human nature, so too, will my generation rise and meet its challenges. While political pundits say that the current demographic of 18-24 year olds is apathetic about politics and more concerned with their selfish world full of technological gadgets, MTV, fashion, and self-fulfillment, than solving the problems in the world around them, Rob and I believe that the perception of an enigmatic silence is wrong. The voices which speak to the nation through What We Think certainly give a different impression – and demonstrate that this new generation just starting to arrive on the national stage is cause for optimism.

What We Think does not claim to be a plenitudinous expression of the feelings and beliefs of my age demographic - it is instead the first strains of the grand symphony which my generation is composing. I ask that you sit back and enjoy the sounds that are my generation speaking. Absorb these melodies, and perhaps, add a few notes of your own.

Preface
Rob Grabow

We stand at a crossroads – A pivotal juncture. Many say we chose the path of apathy. But there are 34 million 18- to 24-year-olds who contend otherwise. We are, in fact, as socially and politically engaged and polarized as the general American populace. Of the more than one thousand American deaths in Iraq, nearly half have been our closest friends and peers; yet, there remains no national forum through which we can express our political and social thoughts, ideas, and reflections.

Dean and I compiled this book in the hope that it would be such a medium. We don't want our voice to continue the long faded trek into the nebulous abstract of what might have been. Many presumed that our voice was never spoken, when in reality, it was simply never heeded. A part of the problem is this: In taking their cues from the polls, the media become that Roman inn-keeper Procrustes, infamous for cutting paying patrons' legs in order they might fit pre-manufactured bed sizes. In many senses, the media cut out the foundational legs of our ideas, cloaking the true substance of what we say. Our complicated message is reduced it to a 10 second-sound bite, a fractionalized vague remnant of the original, and sent back to us. We're then asked how we feel about it. It's in a way the devil and the deep blue sea: Either we accept this bite and are disingenuous regarding our feelings, or we reject it and are bitter and apathetic. After reading What We Think, I hope you come to understand, as I have, that our perceived apathy doesn't represent a fundamental uncaring. Instead, it reflects the fact that we're told how to relate to politics and society without being given a forum to express our views. The fact is that as young adults we neither understand nor perceive the world as the O'Reillys, Matthews, Hannitys, et al…

That said, thematically consistent in the submissions published and unpublished, is a search for truth. Irrespective of political persuasion, these young, talented writers want more than just a hypothetical, dogmatic truth. On the whole, they want a comprehensive understanding of truth on a panorama of issues. In these submissions there is true optimism, a candid yearning to believe in something, be it a presidential candidate, a political system, the media, and so on. In instances, I've found submitters grappling with whether they can believe in something while disagreeing with some of its superficial or foundational components.

    What We Think captures 18 to 24 year olds in their ideological chrysalis. The writers, while they have articulated beliefs and political persuasions seem to be intellectually synthesizing, rationalizing, and reflecting on what they have been raised and told to believe. It's difficult to make palpable, but on the whole, the trend of my generation is one of an optimistic, assertive dialect, in which the bottom line is ideas. It's the most inspiring thing I've been a part of. Imagine one day realizing that your generation, those responsible for the world's future, are everything you hoped they could and would be. I've realized it.

    The submissions in this book are but a tangible reflection of what has always existed. Long before they were anthologized, these ideas, these truths, and these passions, they found residence in the hearts and minds of those published and unpublished. Here I am reminded of a Michelangelo axiom. He claimed to create nothing. Instead, he said he simply free what already existed. In that same sense, I think all of us who have participated in this book have created nothing. We have simply given what already existed its fated right to do so.

    This book doesn't speak for 34 million 18-24 year-olds, maybe not even a majority. There are many remarkable submitted insights not included in this compilation. And I understand the futility in generalizing about the thinking and rationale of our demographic; only as a collective can we accurately speak our many minds. However, What We Think is an opportunity for us, in our own words, to tell America and the world how we care, that we care.

    This is a remarkably well-written, young-adult treatise on America. Read it as you wish; take from it what you can. Realize, as you read, there are dozens of worlds, realities, and truths in these pages. Allow them to sink in before moving on. If you do, I'm confident that you will realize, as I have, that we are the next great generation. We are the reason the U.S. and world has always existed, for embedded within us are the truths past. Here is our voice, do yourselves a favor, give it a listen.

The Presidency and Public Policy

"The American presidency will demand more than ringing manifestos issued from the rear of the battle. It will demand that the President place himself in the very thick of the fight, that he cares passionately about the fate of the people he leads."
-John Fitzgerald Kennedy

"Freedom is a fragile thing and is never more than one generation away from extinction. It is not ours by inheritance; it must be fought for and defended constantly by each generation, for it comes only once to a people. Those who have known freedom, and then lost it, have never known it again."
-Ronald Reagan

"The same war he protested now forced him to be its soldier. Though opposed to the brutality of war, what choice did he have now?"

A Call-Up
Brian Fanelli
West Chester University, West Chester, PA

"No war," Paul Johnson shouted to a middle-aged man who called him unpatriotic. Their debate had lasted ten minutes, until the man finally departed and walked down the end of the street. When the man left, Paul felt his anger melt as he stood with a few other protestors on a bustling street corner.

Paul Johnson, twenty-two years old, stood on the same corner daily to protest war, with a group that could be as large as thirty or as small as five depending on the day. He was tall, lean, and had strong upper-arm muscles that pressed against any T-shirt he wore. He also had a shaved head but brown hair naturally. His eyes were wide and brown, and they burned with hope, that fire that often burns in the eyes of youth. He was against death through the merciless hand of war, so he made a sign nearly a year ago in bright red letters that said, "War is not the answer." Those who passed, usually men and women in business suits coming and going from work, would often look at the signs and give a thumbs up and a smile. Others would use words as brutal weapons and try to belittle the cause. Still, Paul felt as though some type of message was rattling the conscience of the town. The Pennsylvania Peaceniks, the group Paul was a part of, had made their local paper several times. Today, the group was small, consisting of a father and his son and the founder of the group, Jane Harden. Jane was middle-aged, with black-framed glasses, curly brown hair that fell to her shoulders, and a thin figure. Like Paul, she also protested on the corner daily, always wearing a white T-shirt with black lettering that read, "Peace is patriotic." Paul kept a secret from Jane and the group, a secret that influenced him even more to protest the conflict in the Middle East because he had more at stake. Yet he hid the secret from the group, fearing their reaction.

"We did well today. We opened up a few more minds" Jane said, smiling, deciding to close the rally after an hour.

Paul bade farewell to the small group of people. The corner had become a home to Paul, a space that allowed him to practice free speech and state what he believed.

When the small crowd dispersed, Paul walked home, leaving behind spacious, large houses, businesses, and the center of his town. His neighborhood was in the northern part of town, which had cracked sidewalks, old, rusty street lamps, and mostly rows of apartments for homes. He lived with his father in a white row home. Though space was tight, it was enough for the two of them. His father was a mechanic, often coming home from work with black, greasy hands and dark half-circles stretched under his eyes from exhaustion. Though only fifty, most of Mr. Johnson's hair had faded to gray. When Paul was younger, his mother divorced his father, believing Mr. Johnson wasn't providing enough money.

When Paul returned home, his father was sitting on the dark green couch in the cramped living room, sighing as Paul entered the room. Paul looked at his father, a tall, thin man who usually returned from work in a blue mechanic shirt and matching work pants, as well as heavy brown boots, all stained with spots of grease and dirt. His brown eyes peered at his son, shaking his head.

"You've been called up to go to Iraq," his father stated in a low and shaken voice.

Paul's eyes widened, and what he feared for the last months had come true. He could feel his stomach twisting and turning in knots. He would have to go to a war-torn country of chaos to fight in a war he opposed. His father rose from the couch and wrapped his arms around his son.

"I'm sorry," Mr. Johnson whispered in his son's ear, hugging him, closing his eyes to hold back tears from such a dreadful surprise.

That night, Paul wrapped himself in the navy blue sheets of his bed, shrouded in silence and the shadows of his bedroom. Yet he couldn't greet sleep. Images of war danced in his mind, bombs, gunfire, and casualties. He knew when he joined the Army he could be called up, but he hoped he never would be. He desired to use the armed forces only to pay for a college education, since his father couldn't afford it.

The following day, Paul greeted Jane, the founder of the peace group, with the heartbreaking news. They met on the corner where the peace group protested before the war even began for over a year. Tears swelled in Jane's eyes as she was faced with such tragic news. She hugged Paul, wiping tears from her eyes.

"We'll still be here protesting this war, hoping that you come home soon, that all the troops come home soon," Jane said, before releasing Paul from her arms and a tight hug.

Paul's visit to the corner of protest was brief because he had to return home and pack clothes and other items for his trip overseas. The same war he protested now forced him to be its soldier. Though opposed to the brutality of war, what choice did he have now? He didn't have the financial luxury of several young people his age to attend college without the Army's help. He could only hope that he'd return home safe and secure, untouched by war's deadly hand.

"Without war, we would still be under British rule. Without war, America would be split into two separate entities. Without war, the first language of Europeans would be German. Without war, communism would remain a powerful entity to this day."

A War of Uncertainty
Graham Cawthon
Radford University, Radford, VA

"There's a storm coming," the grizzled Mexican translated.

"I know," she responded firmly as the engine of her rusty Jeep started.

She knew he was speaking only of the dark clouds high above the desert sky. In comparison, the weather didn't matter. She had bigger things to concern herself with. Only she knew of the dire situation on the horizon – the potential fate of all mankind. Only she knew what the future had been and what it could be still.

Then, like a moth to the flame, she defiantly drives into the brewing storm to face her untold future.

That, for the movie illiterate, is the final scene of The Terminator – James Cameron's futuristic look at a post-apocalyptic Earth where nuclear holocaust has paved the way for machines to control the world. The scene has been one of my favorites for years but recently it has gained relevance. As international tensions continue to rise on a daily basis, I can't help but be reminded of the words of that Mexican gas station attendant.

The world has drastically changed over the past 18 months. The United States is not the safe haven it once was. Terrorist attacks are no longer something exclusive to Ireland or Arab nations. While it's true that the 1993 bombing of the Twin Towers and the 1995 Oklahoma Federal Building explosion predate 9/11, this most recent attack was on an unprecedented scale.

Despite the notion of some to downplay or discredit the long-term significance of the attacks on New York and Washington, the course of world history has been forever changed as a result. After all, had the events of September 11, 2001 not taken place, would we be in this international staredown we find ourselves in today?

Over the course of recent history, there has been a modus operandi by heads of state to treat hateful regimes with benign neglect. Adolf Hitler's rise to power is a perfect example. He transformed war-torn Germany into an unstoppable juggernaut while under the watchful eye of Europe. France saw no reason to take action until they were invaded and easily conquered by Hitler's forces. By the time England entered the battle, London had been reduced to rubble as a result of German air raids. The United States – due to many within the country that saw the incidents overseas as simply a European issue – did not become involved until we ourselves were caught off guard by the Japanese.

Had Hitler not been allowed to build such a strong army, had he been dealt with before half of Europe was under his control – would World War II have occurred? Would a third of all European Jews have been deliberately slaughtered? Would Hiroshima and Nagasaki have been laid to ruin – a result of the atomic bomb? Needless to say, millions of lives would have been saved had action been taken against the German Chancellor earlier.

The issue of preemptive action is more important today than ever before. For the first time, the average American has firsthand knowledge of terrorist capabilities. We know for a fact that there are a great many people scattered throughout the world that want us and our way of life destroyed.

Germany was a visible threat. Allied forces knew exactly where they were and, for the most part, what they were planning. This is an entirely different situation. Although American and international surveillance has intercepted a great deal of information, we are a long way from putting all the pieces together.

Although the road to making America safe is a long and winding one it must begin with the expulsion of Saddam Hussein from Iraq. A ruthless tyrant since 1979, Hussein has systematically exterminated his own people in mass quantities, invaded neighboring countries, rewarded the families of homicide bombers, given financial aid to Al Qaeda, violated the Geneva Convention, and defied the United Nations for 12 long years. UN weapons inspectors have been held at gunpoint, denied vital access and information, and illegally ousted from the country. The consequences of these actions have resulted in 18 UN resolutions against Iraq, none of which has been acknowledged by Hussein or enforced by the council. Iraq may not be the most powerful threat to our country – but it is the most visible.

Many may argue that North Korea is a more important situation and must be given priority over Iraq. While it's true that the recent admission of Kim Jong-il to possessing and building a nuclear arsenal cannot be taken lightly, it's important to understand the motive behind these threats rather than taking them at face value. North Korea is a communist country run by an egomaniacal leader. Its people are starved and malnourished due to the poorly run government and fledgling economy. It's much more likely, given the circumstances, that the North Korean leader is not out to initiate nuclear war but simply attempting to blackmail his way into receiving American aid. An attack on America or Asian allies would be devastating; however the retaliation to such an act would result in the complete annihilation of North Korea. Unlike the masterminds behind 9/11, Kim Jong-il has yet to show any signs of having a death wish.

None of us knows for certain what the coming weeks and months will bring. There is a threat of a nuclear attack. Our nation dealt with that issue during the Cold War and survived. There is a threat of further terrorist activity. The American government has clearly shown that the war on terror continues, as evidenced by the recent apprehension of Al Qaeda director Khalid Shaikh Mohammed.

While war in itself is destructive and merciless, United States history proves that the result of war can benefit many. Without war, we would still be under British rule. Without war, America would be split into two separate entities. Without war, the first language of Europeans would be German. Without war, communism would remain a powerful entity to this day.

The future is uncertain; it always has been and always will be. There may be a storm coming but we'll get through it. We always have.

This work or portions of this work have previously been published in **The Tartan.**

A-Day
Brittny Nielsen
Seattle University, Seattle, WA

Sirens wailing, breath abating
First flash, missiles exploding
Bombing over Baghdad began.
I watch from so far a distance,
And weep as the city burns.
Each bomb is a loss that I understand is personal.
This moment was not supposed to happen
People are not supposed to die because of their leaders.
I move to the streets to walk with others
Who feel the pain as sharply as I do.
Some girl at Starbucks is screaming that we disrupt her life
As bombs fall and disrupt the lives of innocent people.
They say we should stop the protests because it does no good
The war has started
But I choose to be an active bystander,
I may not be listened to
But I cannot stop speaking.
A-Day began and the President did not watch
Yet my eyes are scarred from the visions
Ear drums echoing with the detonations
The west bank of the River in flames.
As the troops occupy Iraq,
The war occupies my thoughts
A child, injured by bombing, sobs in pain,
First deaths reported.
Few casualties, they report,

And those people are merely a number
A symbol that he is doing the right thing.
I know they were people too,
With families, homes, dreams
All forgotten on A-Day
When victory cannot be measured while there is destruction.

"'The Have and the Have-mores' is the dumbest, most ignorant thing that I have ever heard in my entire life. Karl Marx is rolling over in his grave."

America is Fighting the Invisible Man
Jason Walter
Clemson University, Clemson, SC

I want to see George W. Bush imprisoned for his crimes and Al Gore rightfully put in office.
I want people to quit talking shit about Ralph Nader for trying to change the fraudulent two-party system.
I want to hear "Hadda Be Playin' On a Jukebox" every evening on the radio.
I want to quit having to worry about whether or not the Earth will cease to exist.

I want there to be a new mythology that we abide by instead of the old one...the Biblical one.
I want people to be exposed to the Quran.
I want people to realize that Middle Easterners are humans, not savages.

I'm sick of all of the conformity and all of the questions being answered by unanimous benefactors.
I'm sick of everyone thinking that they know all of the answers and all of the answers being the same answers that the congregations and the government are supplying the frenzied masses with.
I'm sick of people tuning out through drugs, and I'm sick of people tuning into the evening news.
I'm sick of all the Jessica Simpson Ashleigh Britney bimbos being role models for American females.
I'm sick of everyone wanting to be Republican.

Conservatism is righteous, and being liberal is evil.
Well, let me tell you something, the Garden of Eden has always been the state of affairs. Humans have not left the confinement of ignorance.

The snake and Eve are intellectuals.
After clothing, shelter, and water, what is there?
There is protest art, poetry, and music that tries to give the minorities what they need to survive.
Zack de la Rocha and Allen Ginsberg strive for equality.
Rage against the political machine.
Religious fundamentalists want to take over the world.

I'm sick of being sick of being.
Punk and hip-hop are being killed off by punk pop and phony rappers.
Eating from the tree of knowledge does not free on from the festering wasteland that is the Dead that is Thebes that is America...it only makes you sick...everyone else is healthy because they are dominant over nature and women.

I'm sick of all of the children not knowing what good music or good presidency are.
I'm sick of all the politicians, pigs (I'll cut to the chase like in all of the toxic actions movies), and mindless authority figures.
I'm sick of the government arresting marijuana users while corporate crack smokers pollute the minds, bodies, and arms of America.
I'm sick of America being a monster whose tentacles stretch overseas.
I'm sick of things never changing.
I'm sick of music not being bullets.
I'm sick of the fact that Jesus brought a sword for us to kill our father.
I'm sick of Utilitarianism.
I'm sick of Puritanical Oedipus Tyrranus.
I'm sick of having to be blunt.
I'm sick of the Puritan foundation of us.
I'm sick of the United States of Corporations.
I'm sick of elitist collectivism and altruism.
I'm sick of children sniffing glue and paint to get a buzz.
I'm sick of frat boys and the military mentality, and compassion being extreme to the point at which it's demeaning.

I want people to start listening to their souls by reading LITERATURE.
I want the American people to wake up instead of being sedated by patriotism.
I want people to support our poets.
I want every musician to hold off on making love songs until there are enough political tunes to sway the masses to get rid of the two-party system.
I want to get rid of the electoral college.
I want the situations in Iraq and Northern Ireland to be resolved once and for all.
I want peace everywhere.
I want Africa to be what it once was, before it was by the "heart of darkness" from the west.
America is the new "heart of darkness."

America is committing the crimes of yore by striving for empire.

Bush wants to make everyone poor except for himself, his family, and his friends.

"The Have and the Have-mores" is the dumbest, most ignorant thing that I have ever heard in my entire life.

Karl Marx is rolling over in his grave.

I want everyone to stop thinking that anti-patriotic sentiments are Communist or Terrorist.

The man is the system.

I want there to be a new political manifesto.

I want weed legalized or at least decriminalized.

I want the military to be downsized.

I want corporate power to be eradicated.

I want there to be an increase in the liberal media.

I want the drinking age to be sixteen and the driving age to be eighteen.

I want science and math marginalized to the point at which the arts are equally important as science and math.

I want church and state to be separate.

I want women to get paid equally as men.

I want the minimum wage to increase to the cost of living wages.

I want there to be budget cuts for the middle class rather than for the upper upper class.

I want pills and medication to be affordable and easily accessible for senior citizens.

I want the government to focus on social policies rather than spend money on the military.

I want the government to adopt Mexico's take on the War on Drugs.

I want there to be a decrease in the number of churches.

I want there to be an increase in the number of high-quality schools.

I want police brutality to end once and for all.

I want affirmative action reinstated.

I want reparations given to African Americans for slavery.

I want the Green Party to rule our nation.

I want our country to adopt the social policies of Canada.

I want our country to act like Amsterdam.

I want us to stop using the French and the Middle East as a scapegoat for our superficiality.

I want an increase in healthy food options, vegetarianism, and veganism.

I want other nations' histories and foreign languages taught early in school.

I want foreign countries to respect the U.S.A. once again.

I want schools and teachers to be paid more money.

I want our government to stop sending work over to foreign countries because of their lower minimum wage and lenient child labor laws - Americans need these jobs.

I'm sick of the thought that if Bush is reelected, he'll kill off all of the artists and label their work as "degenerate art".

I'm sick of thinking about the world's problems when I'd rather just run.

I'm sick of the PATRIOT Act.

I'm sick of actors and competitive athletes being overrated.

I'm sick of the literary community and the noncompetitive athletes being underrated to the point of oblivion.

I'm sick of the fact that "The Tragedy of Eddie Profit" by Jason Allen Walter is not taught in schools and colleges.

I'm sick of greed.

I'm sick of apathy.

I'm sick of arrogance.

I'm sick of brutality and racism and ethnocentric worldviews.

I'm sick of cigarettes and the K.K.K.

I'm sick of zoos and cages.

I'm sick of Africans and the porn industry being infected with AIDS virus.

I'm sick of malpractice.

I'm sick of existentialism.

I'm sick of Christian philosophers and scientists.

I'm sick of reading philosophical conversations on bathroom walls instead of hearing them live via the news.

I'm sick of people hating on Michael Moore and *Fahrenheit 9/11* and thinking that his movie is propagandist and that it is on the liberal left.

The liberal left is Fascism, which is the compassionate conservatism.

Politically, Michael Moore is a social democrat - which is what liberalism is, and that's right in the middle of the political spectrum.

I'm sick of college students being disenfranchised.

I'm sick of the Anglo-Saxon WHEEL OF FORTUNE and GREAT CHAIN OF BEING.

I'm sick of the disillusionment of women that has been instilled by three thousand years of male empowerment.

I'm sick of writing to an invisible audience.

I'm sick of walking to an unknown end.

I'm sick of women's magazines giving women ten-step procedures to be beautiful.

I'm sick of women not realizing that knowledge and character are beautiful.

I'm sick of guns.

I'm sick of bombs.

I'm sick of war and fighting.

I want words to be bullets.

I want words to change the world for the better instead of war technology blowing up the world.

Weapons need to be replaced by words.

I'm sick of receipts and bank accounts.
I'm sick of corporate art.
I'm sick of *American Idol.*
I'm sick of seeing pop stars on the cover of Rolling Stone.
I'm sick of seeing talent die young.
I'm sick of having my rights taken away on a daily basis.
I'm sick of rulers going against the Bill of Rights.
I'm sick of censorship.
I'm sick of 1984.
I'm sick of *A Brave New World.*
I'm sick of people who are slaves to fear.

Americans fear the Invisible Man.

"By invoking a spiritual purpose behind his actions Bush is beginning to resemble those which he wishes to eradicate."

Bush, Religion, and Iraq
Hailey Witt
Lehigh University, Bethlehem, PA

If questioned about the origins of the United States of America, any citizen could tell you that the foundations of this country rely strongly on freedom of religion and freedom from religious persecution. Inherent in these beliefs is the idea that a specific religion should not form the basis for a nation's policies. When that nation is supposedly governed by and for the diverse citizenry, it would seem strange to have a leader who openly admits to basing political decisions on his personal religion, but that is exactly what we have. Oddly enough much of the population seems to view this as a positive attribute, and as such George W. Bush uses his religion to appeal to more voters. Unfortunately, using religion as a political tool is not as advantageous as it may appear on the surface. This is especially evident in the case of Iraq, where President Bush sees it as his religious duty to restructure the country in the shape of the United States.

If a president were to use his personal moral beliefs to help guide his personal decision making, this would not be a problem. Every human being needs some moral base. Martin Marty, a religious philosopher, explains why Bush's use of religion serves as more than just a religious base in an article in *Newsweek*: "the problem isn't with Bush's sincerity but with his evident conviction that he is doing God's will." This causes problems when President Bush's personal view of God's Will, based on his personal beliefs, becomes intertwined with his goals for the rest of the world. He sees the American lifestyle as that which is ordained by God, and should be thus undertaken by Iraqi citizens. "The liberty we prize is not America's gift to the world, it is God's gift to humanity," is a sentiment Bush expressed as he led America into this conflict. According to him it is the United States' duty to spread liberty, or God's gift to humanity, to the rest of the world, whether or not they want it. He has not only set apart the U.S. as God's messengers, but in order to further distinguish this as a religious struggle, he has characterized the opposition as "evil."

Although this may help the president garner support among the religious right in this country, it has negatively affected the United States' relationships with other countries. "Scores of interviews with government officials, political analysts, and ordinary citizens from one side of the globe to the other suggest that the US is now widely perceived as arrogant," reports the *Christian Science Monitor*. Bush's religious aspirations may be shared by other world leaders, but that is not enough to justify religious fervor in policy making. According to Douglas Todd of the *Vancouver Sun*, "Bush's problem is not that he's bringing religion into the public sphere, but that he's being religiously triumphalistic." While other country's leaders may understand and even share the President's religious beliefs, it is his use of God as a claim to American supremacy which sets our leader apart. As demonstrated by past and recent UN hearings, the United States' refusal to do things any way but its own has led to opposition by world powers such as France and Germany. This lack of support will make it difficult for the US to continue its mission in Iraq when other countries refuse to contribute to a cause for which they do not have comparable motivations to endorse. Because neither France nor Germany feel it is their moral responsibility to create a democratic Iraq, it is hard for them to join America in this pursuit.

Iraq is a strongly religious country, and it is absurd to think that they wish to become a party to American politics any further than it was necessary to rid them of a brutal dictator. "We will not have any contact with the Americans," a Shiite religious leader in Iraq was recently quoted as saying. "We don't want them to stay. Now they have got rid of Saddam... they should leave." (Ford). It seems that the current administration's goal of nation building and creating a country willing to submit to the will of the United States is far from feasible. By targeting certain terrorist groups, often those which are led by a religious faction, the President further increases the image of America as unwilling to accept other beliefs. George W. Bush's actions against the Islamic military group, Hamas, are viewed by some as actions against the entire Islam faith. Abd-al-Aziz al-Rantisi, member of Hamas' political leadership, believes that "Bush is declaring a war on Islam, represented by the Islamic Resistance Movement, Hamas." (BBC, June 2003).

President Bush appears especially intolerant to Muslims overseas because of his ties to Franklin Graham, the leader of a religious fundamentalist group who led prayers at the President's inauguration. A close friend of Bush, Graham has been quoted espousing very anti-Islamic sentiment. He referred to Islam as "a very evil and wicked religion." (Wapshott). The spokesman for the Council on American-Islamic Relations, Ibrahim Hooper, feels that this connection "sends the entirely wrong message" to Islamic nations. "It seems to offer government endorsement of the bigoted views of Franklin Graham." (Reichmann). Still, because of the need for help in Iraq, Graham's religious organization, Samaritan's Purse, will be federally supported when it goes to Iraq for mission work.

Much of the support for a war on Iraq came from the fear that Americans have regarding terrorism after the September 11th attacks. Although it has become clear that there was not a link between Saddam Hussein and this incident, many Americans still feel that this was an important step in reducing the threat of terrorism. One would think that by spreading the will of God to have free democracies we would be helping to create a more peaceful world, but the problems that we are trying to solve are being further fueled by the justification of religion. This is commented on by Christopher Hitchens of *Vanity Fair*: "If religion is so goddamned peaceful, then why are we fighting zealots and fundamentalists on so many fronts?"

By invoking a spiritual purpose behind his actions Bush is beginning to resemble those whom he wishes to eradicate. His constant reference to September 11th and our nation's need to stay strong in faith to get through this time is viewed as unnecessary by some. Benjamin Kabak of the *Swarthmore Pheonix* articulates this: "Our president has taken a day that should be a day of memorial and has turned it into a cheap political advantage." September 11th was an act of aggression which sought to bring down a power thought of as "evil" by a group of religious fundamentalists. Because of the use of religion to justify the actions of the United States, it has become clear that the war on Iraq is nothing less than an act of aggression to bring down a power considered "evil" by a group of religious fundamentalists. The only difference is, in America the religious fundamentalists are in control of the fate of the rest of the world.

Even religious leaders see no higher moral ground in our actions based on the strict adherence to a superior faith. "I've yet to encounter the God who counsels preemptive slaughter in the name of peace," wrote a priest in a response to a *Newsweek* article outlining George W. Bush's spiritual agenda. Most notably, the Pope was fervently opposed to war with Iraq and believed that a UN resolution was the answer to this crisis (Boycott). In May, on a trip to Spain, the Pope implored the Europeans: "Dear young people, you well know how concerned I am about peace in the world the spiral of violence, of terrorism and war provokes, even in our days, hatred and death."

No matter how faith is used to support a political move, there will always be a way to use that same faith to attack it. Because the nature of politics is one that is open to criticism, it is unwise to use such a widely interpretable rationale. William O. Douglas, a former Supreme Court justice, believed that "religious experiences which are as real as life to some may be incomprehensible to others." Because religious beliefs are largely dependent on people's unique experiences, it is impossible to invoke the name of God to placate an entire nation when the name of God serves a wide range of ideals which may not all coincide with the national interest. President Bush, however, uses God as a blanket to cover all sins. If there was concern over sending American troops to die in Iraq, he showed his compassion by saying that his prayers, and the prayers of a nation, were with them. If there was concern over causing turmoil in the lives of Iraqi citizens, President Bush insisted that our prayers were with those innocent Iraqis who were going to be affected by the war. By constantly insisting that God would comfort those in need, he managed to avoid the real implications of these issues: people would die. This use of religion does not benefit any countries, and leads to further distrust of the President at home.

It is not a surprise that President Bush recently made what the *Washington Post* described as "a Freudian slip" when discussing the need for a "bridge between church and state." (Greenburg). The separation of church and state is an important concept to Americans and the rest of the world, and now more than ever is a time to make it clear that the American population will not tolerate a violation of this basic principle. Religion can not serve a purpose in modern political rhetoric other than to soothe an uneasy conscience. It alienates other cultures to use religion as a motivation when cultures hold a range of diverse beliefs. If the United States sees itself as being a power great enough to spread democracy to all nations, then it is its responsibility to have respect for the nations it wishes to exert influence over. It is necessary to our nation's welfare to have a leader who understands this, not a president who expresses American foreign policy as "God's gift to humanity." For this reason it is clear to see that it is time for a change in leadership, in order that the United States can begin to act as a world power should.

"What really burns is that some people actually buy this new American value meal, peddled forth by Darth Cheney and Saruman Rumsfeld. Meanwhile, Ashcroft is hacking through your door with a pick-ax screaming, 'Heeeeere's Johnny!'"

Choking the Red, White, and You
Bryan M. Steele
San Diego State University, San Diego, CA

There seems to be something seriously wrong in this country – nay, scratch that, there is something seriously wrong in and with this country. Things turned astray at some distant wrinkle in time and the disjointed semblance of a peaceful American 21st century seems a remote possibility. We have turned in the wrong direction for leadership, blindly swallowing the flags stuffed down our throats in the name of freedom and democracy. We pray for light yet shield our eyes when it finally comes, instead electing to remain in the comfortable confines of Red, White, and Darkness. We have turned our backs on longtime allies, alienated the greater part of the world which we are supposed to share, and eagerly dispense the empty dream that the world community is on our side. Since when did the Cayman Islands become a coalition force? What, are they contributing mangos to the reconstruction efforts?

The simple fact of the matter is, the U.S. government has achieved and sustained a level of disinformation that can only be compared to the plethora of lies about Vietnam spewed forth for consumption by five consecutive administrations. The difference being, in the era of containment, détente, and finally victory, against the Soviets – victory of course being 2 million dead Southeast Asians and 60,000 dead Americans – the clash of civilizations was not as readily apparent as it is at this very moment in history. Civil wars are consuming, ravaging, destroying, and slaughtering hundreds of thousands of people all over the world. But we're not interested in helping those who cannot offer something in exchange – or, at least, something worthwhile we can take by force.

Instead, we play the big brother humanitarian card, making ourselves out to be the savior of mankind for displacing a government and subsequently occupying a country that happens to have the second largest oil reserves in the world. Then, in setting up a "free democracy" for the people whose homes and lives we've pilfered, we quell any opposition to our new rules by shooting religious leaders, bombing communities of innocent people, and shutting down a popular newspaper that opposed the U.S. occupation. Now, it seems to me that shutting down the press en route to setting up yet another puppet democracy seems rather counterproductive as well as counterintuitive. Besides, it's not even our country. The audacity of this administration to conduct world affairs with a total contempt and utter disregard for truth, integrity, and forthrightness is not only staggering, but terribly saddening as well.

It evokes a certain feeling of a drunken cowboy stumbling out of a dusty saloon in the old west with two six shooters in hand, firing at a fart in the wind. Of course he misses, but nevertheless, as they always tend to do, the bullet finds a home in the jugular of a woman crossing the street with a parasol. The townspeople rise up, demanding an explanation for this raucous and irresponsible behavior. But it just so happens this drunken cowboy, even in the farthest reaches of a two-day whiskey binge, has a silver tongue that could talk a mute into a microphone. Within minutes, he has the townsfolk convinced it was for her own good, citing the fact that the fart was made of uranium enriched gas and was headed straight for the coal mill. The sheriff thanks him for his courage in fighting off this evildoer and hands the drunken cowboy a semiautomatic Tech-Nine, begging him to protect and defend the town from these ghosts of fancy. Within a day, 14 people are dead, but at least the town is safe.

And what we're left with, in this contemporary saloon we call America, is a sick and depraved cowboy mad with power and a bar full of patrons too scared to take his guns away.

Something must be done. We are painfully backdrifting the downward spiral, discarding common sense for the intangible hope that we are not being led astray by a lisdexic half-wit draft dodger with a coke problem and a rap sheet.

Wake up, goddammit. There is not one fact that backs up any of these far-fetched and totally unsubstantiated claims Dick, Bush, and the Four Horsemen of the Apocalypse (Johnny, Condie, Wolfy and Rummy) are misrepresenting as truth. And while you lay cowering in your house with the shades drawn, binoculars set to "terrorist," these fascist lying weasels squirm their way into every facet of your life, replacing your freedoms with the new kind of freedom - the kind where they'll protect us because they know everything about us. Shit, that might not even be that bad. Wait, yes it would. But instead what we're stuck with is a completely Orwellian lack of privacy in exchange for "somehow, somewhere, someone will do something…so be ready."

What really burns is that some people actually buy this new American value meal, peddled forth by Darth Cheney and Saruman Rumsfeld. Meanwhile, Ashcroft is hacking through your door with a pick-ax screaming "Heeeeere's Johnny!" But that's all right, you say, so you invite him in for a cup of tea – imported, of course, from some place you've never heard of. He asks if he can have a look in your computer for terrorists. You say, "Have at it, John. Can I get you another bearclaw?" He politely refuses with a stern look on his face. It seems your computer was devoid of any terrorist cells, but there were 140 downloaded music files on your D drive. It seems someone's been busy, stealing from the music industry. You quickly turn in your son for fear of the Dark Lord's condemnation, blathering something about Billy being a bad seed.

So now that the Attorney General has attained access to your computer, poked around for a while and decided to prosecute your 12-year-old son, do you feel safer? Hmmmm, thought so.

The time has come to shirk this cruel façade, this bastion of corruption, and claw our way back to a time when being American instilled a sense of pride and honor. The time for change is upon us. Either we embrace it and evolve or sink helplessly into the trenches of apathy, too lazy to smell what we're buried in.

"Fundamentally, we must shift our understanding of power and relating to one another from a negative, divisive reaction to a positive, creative action. We can do this only by recognizing that, in the face of the other, I can only see my own vulnerability and my own humanity."

Delusions of Sovereignty
Lance David Collins
University of Hawai'i at Manoa, Honolulu, HI

"Not being a power, [it] can't battle with the powers that be, but it fights a war without battles, a guerrilla campaign against them. And it can't converse with them, it's got nothing to tell them, nothing to communicate, and can only negotiate. Since the powers aren't just external things, but permeate each of us, [it] throws us all into constant negotiations with, and a guerrilla campaign against, ourselves.' – Gilles Deleuze

The focus and direction of politics and dominant political movements has been sovereignty. Collective identity has been created and built on the technologies of 19th century 'nationalism' discourse. For these movements, politics is implementing pre-fabricated stories of why we are sovereign. Everything from health care to reproductive rights to same-sex marriage to civil rights is grounded in the history of 'our' sovereign nation. The flares of nationalism again sweep the globe but not because new Hitlers and Stalins are on the rise; rather, it is the death spasms of a dying political reality.

From the ashes of the 1960s emerged a new way of thinking and a new way of being. In a practical reflection of this shift, U.S. President Richard Nixon took the dollar off the gold standard. This was not a cause of that shift, but a consequence of it. Value was no longer anchored in the analog realm of center and periphery. Instead, value was floated and digitized in relation to other value.

But in the wake of this shift, nationalism has surged. This surge is not a celebration or difference within the shift. Rather, it is a denial and an overcompensation for the reality of being. With the current international legal arrangements of the institutions like the World Trade Organization, the role of business and nations has seemingly reversed. In the height of nationalism, nations would attempt to build business and make wealth for themselves – leading to extreme forms of this in Mussolini's fascism and Hitler's national socialism. The beneficiary of this arrangement was the nation, the nation's rich and the leaders of the nation (the latter two sometimes being the same people). Borders existed to inscribe upon bodies an ethnos, a culture, an identity.

But the legal arrangements of 'free trade' render nations to be simply a method of organizing labor and capital for the benefit of business. Borders, for instance, variegate the organization of labor and experiments in how much of worker organization is compatible with profit margins. Business, recognizing the lack of universal solutions of increasing profits, turns to these archaic forms of 19th century nationalism to zone and reserve local areas of experiment – to maximize profit locally, accumulating globally. Capital, which is much more flexible than language-speaking bodies, needs no visas to visit or to work. Easily mutable, it may flow across borders and zones and laws with little exception.

The post World War II distinctions of the First and Third Worlds become more and more irrelevant as accurate descriptions of much of anything. The shift from analog value to digital value has brought with it a re-zoning or re-carving of the world. The rich of the First and Third World live in gated and patrolled communities in every World. They go to higher education schools which teach critical thinking and self-governing along with the rudiments of working in a well paid job. The reward of going to these schools is the name of the school.

The next group of schools are where the name of the school mean much less, and so a bit more focus on specialized vocational training is necessary, and less emphasis is put on critical thinking and self-governing. The last group of schools, where most people in the First World go, must be financed in such a way where the curriculum is centered around which skills are necessary for being a well-paid worker. The first two skills to atrophy are critical thinking and self governing. Well-paid workers do not need to think critically, they merely need to do a good job.

This criticism is not a call to the worker or a call for the International. This should not lead anyone to believe that a binary opposition of capitalism and communism should be resurrected. 'Free trade' arrangements are the blending of communist ideas to promote capitalist profit. In one sense, it seems as there is no escape from capitalism.

The only axioms of capitalism are profit and stability (stability in the sense of the system preserving itself). Experiments can be made in appropriating and disposing of different institutional structures and thought regimes – and they have. When public assistance was only accessible to white middle-class and working-class mothers, welfare was a meaningful element of the economic system. But, when the concept of substantive due process and equal protection were expanded to include women of color to public assistance, a campaign was waged against welfare and then gutted it.

What are our options? Fundamentalism of every variety has its own cable network proselytizing about the truth. Even the most 'liberal' and 'progressive' of political movements are still framed in terms of sovereign subjects, sovereign nations, and 19th century nationalism.

The Third World is plagued by massive macro-debt in which whole nations are prevented from ever 'having money.' Likewise, the First World is plagued by massive micro-debt in which nations of individuals are prevented from ever 'having money.'

There are no answers. While we can partially identify the problem, how we think of ourselves and of our thinking is part of the problem. Like the horizon, realizing the whole problem can never be attained by thinking about it. Critics of this perspective attack it as hopeless and totalizing. There is no room for movement in a system that includes the opposition. Political resistance is commercialized. Images are eviscerated of meaning and brought about to represent the next consuming desire-to-be.

But there are potentials waiting to be created, waiting to be discovered, waiting to become. The problem before us is not how to best resign to the fate of a totalizing system. On the one hand, this sort of resignation leads to political paralysis, cynicism and stoicism; on the other hand, it can also lead to suicide bombings and other non-negotiable acts. What way lies between these two extremes?

First, we must make a commitment to abandon transcendence. We must abandon the thought of escape from this reality, in this present moment. We must meet the world in a state of immanence. A better way of living is not a reaction to how we live. Rather, it is a creative movement into the unknowable – it is constantly becoming the next thing without regard to the thing now or any ideas about what the next thing may be.

Fundamentally, we must shift our understanding of power and relating to one another from a negative, divisive reaction to a positive, creative action. We can do this only by recognizing that, in the face of the other, I can only see my own vulnerability and my own humanity. As the nation-state model of sovereignty withers away, we must be able to make conscious choices about how we wish to live – and become critical and conscious of the histories which help us make our choices.

Second, we must abandon the luxury of moralism. We must abandon any thought of certainty about the truth. We must adopt an ethical position towards one another. That is, we must understand that the truths we hold to be self-evident are a political choice, contingent on the context – which is always changing. Nothing is self-evident. We must accept that others are not another ourselves participating in a common existence.

We must end our commitments to envisioning a world in quantitative dimensions. The evils of this world begin by eliding difference with common standards of measure and determination. Fundamentally, we are not the same. We bring to life a complex web of historical circumstances layered on different ways of knowing. This is not a call to cultural or moral relativism. Different people at different moments understand reality and the events in it differently. When we begin to make community, we must fully appreciate the choices we make. Democracy is the refusal of prepolitical notions of what the truth is. Things which are different in kind cannot be compared on a scale measuring difference in degree. When this process occurs, one (or all) things must suffer the fate of their appearance.

Finally, we must abandon all hope of future ideas. Utopias are not real. If we can only abandon hope of our perfect fantasy, we may be able to move, just enough, to make change. Without hope, we are free to create and fail and learn.

Suicidal bombings are events motivated by deep hope. Because we will not listen, they write their message directly onto the body and deliver it without regard to who is guilty and who is innocent. We all must listen. But these events are driven by hope. It is the hope that after listening, we will do something and the context in which they leave will change. Hope spawns fundamentalism and it spawns nationalism. We must abandon these fantasies and future expectations in favor of becoming, in the now, in the present.

Rights, as a tributary of contract theory, are a negative understanding of power and relating. Rights are an instrument that an individual has to ward off the power of the state. In other words, rights are something that gather power by limiting the power of the state. In the United States, rights discourse has been successful in creating a Black middle-class and spawning white supremacist groups that use these same legal technologies to prevent state-sponsored programs which help poor and working-class people of color. Political action must tap the creative, in the present moment. Reactive and fearful political acts have no life, but are parasitical to the life which they attempt to divide and conquer. If liberation is merely replacing one prison warden for another, it is no liberation at all.

George W. Bush

Scott Raven Tarazevits
Rutgers University, Newark, NJ

Four more sheers.
Four more sheers?
Four more sheers! Four more sheers!
Get our your hedge clippers
I'm living on the edge with these 'read my lippers…'
No new taxidermists stuffin' muffins made of myopic
  mis-owed promises of mowed lawns with 3rd world landscape scrapes
  of returning slow
  soldier pawns as
      I-raq
  a triple word score
  seven point bonus by b-u-r-n-i-n-g the oval office so that we may
  better see
  a g-u-a-r-d-e-d garden of Eden eating
  'strength and wisdom'
while beating seedy soon to be up-seated re-pub-lickings
  at their own games of nonsense.

Now don't get me wrong. I like George…
Of The Jungle… Its catchy theme song and toga clad warrior
  was always amusing and fun,
  and even though he was basically a moron at least he wasn't running the country.
I also like the George Foreman Grill. Its mighty cooking power may cut the excess fat,
  but all in good taste, leaving behind a most delicious and satisfying meal.
I like George…
Hamilton who probably spends a great deal of time at the beach or on the golf course,
  but then again where would 'he' be without his tan
And George Harrison he made everyone just wanna hold hands.
I like George…

Washington, George Plimpton even Boy George.
And of course I'd feel most comfortable moving towards the future with
George Jetson.
Not to mention,
I also like 'w'...
I gotta give it up to the only multi-syllabic letter in the English alphabet and for it being
   such an individual among 25 of its supportive counterparts.
More importantly w's surprisingly clean hands, despite being associated with such
   scandals as Watergate, the Whiskey ring, Whitewater and war.
At least 'w' has a purpose in the position in the word war.
Without a 'w' we'd still have war but with W., we could have four more.

Now summer is ending and it may be just getting colder outside, but I'm a little scared
I may be catching a draft
So, as a rule I generally stay in-doors.
Cuz if there is one thing I do despise
   it would be all flowering plants and shrubbery-
   and not just any shrubbery,
   but
   burdensome bushes
   that have gotten out of control.
Not even Edward Scissorhands himself could sculpt a masterpiece from this
   Malarkey.
If we put the creator behind Chia Pet, a winner of the Banzai Championship
   and Emeril Lagasse with an enchanted oven mitt
   there still is no chance
   of making chicken soup
   from chicken sh*t
Now you see at this point, I'm sorry to say, just a simple trim won't do.
A new bush is no good either. We already had an old one and it just scared
the neighbors.
We need to uproot the entire garden and plant some new seeds
So all in all,
I like George.
I love 'w' and
I'm voting for John Kerry.

"No Christian can argue with the fact that we are called to love our fel-low human beings. Well, love does not just extend to our family or our personal nation; it encompasses the entire world, including the people who are dying defending our freedom and those they are killing."

Is God on Bush's Side

Lanni Alecia Lantto
University of Michigan Graduate

"We Americans have faith in ourselves but not in ourselves alone…placing our confidence in the loving God behind all of life, and all of history. May He guide us now. And may God continue to bless the United States of America."
-George W. Bush, 2003 State of the Union Address.

The historical and overwhelmingly mainstream idea that Christians should accept religion and patriotism uniformly is perplexing to me. When George W. Bush pledges allegiance to God while supporting big money domination and big wars, I can't help but feel that he is a hypocrite. Immediately thereafter, my mind races to my early years in religious education classes and nightly Bible readings. For years I'd been read-ing about how Jesus professed unconditional love for all his children and preached the human characteristics of humility and compassion. Even within my own personal relationship with God, I just can't see him justifying man's use of unbridled power coat-ed in greed to dominate another race of human beings, especially in His name. Of course, in history books there are a plethora of examples where men have conquered, killed, and raped on their own accord, and unfortunately even the Catholic Church is guilty of these sins. My uneasiness with accepting Bush's holy war had created a nag-ging annoyance in my subconscious, but it was after reading an article by Peter Meilaender entitled "Christians as Patriots," that I really began my ardent assessment of the subject.

In this article he states that there are two main reasons why people love their country: because it is good and because it is our own, and that neither reason can stand without the other. The essay concludes by making two stringent declarations. The first is that, as Christians, our loyalties should not be divided between the church and the state but rather that they are multiplied to incorporate both. In the second statement Meilaender believes that Christians are the model for any polity to have as its citizens

because they know the true meaning of loving unconditionally. Basically, his essay
declares that religion and patriotism together can and should be accepted by Christians.
It's apparent that Bush also takes this stance and that a majority of Americans blindly
accept his rhetoric, precisely because they are both - religious and patriotic.This rhetoric
includes our need to love our society because it is God-given.

This is especially apparent by the signs that have popped up everywhere saying, "God bless America." I can't help but question this logic and ask myself, "Is this
society God's gift, or is it now so completely man-made that secularization and post-
modernization have completely taken over any sort of sacred plan? Are we truly loving
something that is still in God's image?"

Theorist Emile Durkheim believed that social cohesion was threatened by the
breakdown of small communities and the rise of modern urban life. Whereas religion
used to dominate all facets of society, it has now become autonomous in a society currently controlled by capitalist social organizations. A shift has occurred from communal
religious life to industrialized self-fulfilling prophecies. When the church became an
isolated sector of society and the government became the official voice, man's quest for
his own good may have superseded that of God's.

Marx believed that religion was used as a tool by the state to maintain its capitalist goals. Throughout history societies have been constructed with religious under-
tones, making it easier to get an already religiously socialized mass to obey a newly
formed state structure. The Founding Fathers mirrored their political dogma to that of
the church's by using familiar forms of symbolism. The Gettysburg Address used
imagery that likened death by patriotism to the death of Jesus on the cross: "Those who
here gave their lives, that the nation might live." Abraham Lincoln was considered a
martyr for the abolitionist cause as Joan of Arc was for liberating the people of France.
The American flag flew from every doorstep as a symbol for our newly fought independence as the cross hung from wall to wall as a symbol of our rebirth in Christ. The
church had days to commemorate past saintly heroes while the state created Memorial
Day to celebrate its past uniformed heroes. These nationalist symbols were done for a
reason: to make it easier for religious Americans to indubitably accept the political agendas of our leaders.

We are being told that we should love our country even with its imperfections,
and that those who speak out about fighting wars, foreign policy, or a need for peace are
unpatriotic. Now, if religion and patriotism are to be accepted uniformly, that must
mean that Christians must accept these wars, ballistic missile defense plans, patriot acts,
and whatever grandiose ideas are next from our leaders. This is where the problem lies:
religious teachings call for open communication, non-violent resolutions, human rights,
and peace. So, religion and patriotism cannot be accepted uniformly anymore. Our
leaders have strayed away from these teachings but are leading us to believe they are, in
fact, devout Christians. So far it has been a very strategic and beneficial move.

One of God's most important messages is to love your neighbor as yourself. It
seems to me that currently this means our neighbors are strictly within the boundaries of
the United States. We justified our patriotism after 9/11 because Christians should love
their home, that which was destined to them by God. Yet, we ignored that this thing that

we loved was acting on its own behalf, for its own goals, and not within the teachings of God. Our nation is retaliating at our enemies and not at the Taliban, the real terrorists of 9/11, through war. This is a war that is killing our earthly neighbors and invading another's homeland for our own personal economic profit. If it is not about money, then I urge the Bush Administration to relinquish control of all oil fields to the Iraqi people. Surely this will not be done.

Some Catholics may be aware of just-war theory wherein war under certain circumstances is acceptable. The Catechism of the Catholic Church limits just-war to cases in which "the use of force must have serious prospects for success" and "must not produce evils and disorders graver than the evil to be eliminated." In fact, just-cause is interpreted as a means of preventing wars and should be avoided at all rational costs. At a U.S. conference of Catholic Bishops in November 2002, they released this statement: "We fear that to resort to war, under present circumstances and in light of current public information, would not meet the strict conditions in Catholic teaching [for just war theory]. We hope that our moral concerns and questions will be considered seriously by our leaders and all citizens. We pray for President Bush and other world leaders that they will find the will and the ways to step back from the brink of war with Iraq and work for a peace that is just and enduring."

I don't believe this has been the next prophetic "American Crusade." As Christians, how can we justify a country that acts in an un-Godly manner as we sit around idly with all this love, knowing that our fellow men are suffering? God's commandment of loving your neighbor as yourself means standing in solidarity with him/her, no matter our origins of birth. We all have a social contract that binds us to the society where we were born because that is the nature of citizenship. I believe that God wants us to respect and love our societies here on earth as much as we strive to live with Him in Heaven. However, modernization and capitalism have played a huge role in leading our country away from religion. Our society has become a product of man-made desires for individualistic goals, and the current administration is furthering our spiral away from God's sincere desires.

No Christian can argue with the fact that we are called to love our fellow human beings. Well, love does not just extend to our family or our personal nation; it encompasses the entire world, including the people who are dying defending our freedom and those they are killing. As the saying goes, "If we assume that life is worth living and that man has a right to survive, then we must find an alternative to war." I don't understand how we can applaud and vote for a man who chose preemptive war while completely ignoring resolutions of true peace. There is nothing wrong with being a Christian or a patriot, but we do not need to be forced to incorporate them both when our religious identities are being used as tool for deception.

God does not take sides when terrorism and wars are pitted as rich versus rich for control over the poor. God is not on the side of Saddam Hussein or George W. Bush. We must stop killing in the name of religion and patriotism overseas and return our troops to their families. I like my country, but I cannot truly love it until it stops masking its social policies with religious overtones.

See to it that no one captivate you with an empty, seductive philosophy according to human tradition, according to the elemental powers of the world and not according to Christ (Colossians 2:8).

"Rather, the very mention of the world invokes images of terrorism while neglecting to isolate the group of people who represent its constitution."

Issues of Palestinian Identity
Samantha Vinograd
University of Pennsylvania, Philadelphia, PA

In recent years, the local and global effects of the current conflict over the land of Palestine is evident in newspapers, literature, magazines, and other modes of cultural expression. As Jewish Israelis consistently fight with their Arab countrymen and neighbors, the consequences of the incessant bloodshed and turmoil are illustrated in various manners of expression. The Palestinians, as a political and cultural entity, have had a vast influence on the culture of the Arabic world in its entirety. In the years preceding the termination of hostilities between the Axis and Allied powers in World War I, the Arab residents of Palestine began to form into a more cohesive and defined unit as a means of counteracting various obstacles that they saw forming. In order to adequately represent the opinions, feelings, and objectives of their people, a definition of identity was necessary. This definition process, while fluid by its very nature, has had long lasting effects on the region and on Muslims worldwide. Thus, scholars have endeavored to clarify this formative period as a means of understanding how to proceed in future negotiations. In order to effectively comprehend the conflict at hand, a thorough examination of what is Palestinian identity is necessary. As a means of evaluating the very bases of this identity, an assessment of the cultural impacts that the Palestinian question has had on the Arabic world as a whole proves beneficial to the path towards understanding and eventual peace.

Attempts to concretely classify how and when a collective sense of identity began to be espoused by what modern historians refer to as the "Palestinians" have produced varying results reflective of the various perspectives from which scholars have approached the question itself. At the very foundation of this question lies what superficially appears to be a simple task: defining what it veritably means to be considered a Palestinian. As Islamic fundamentalist groups from all over the world identity themselves with the "Palestinians" on newscasts and in speeches, the public is presented with a barrage of associations that fails to deliver a lucid expression of whom the term really applies to. Rather, the very mention of the world invokes images of terrorism while neglecting to isolate the group of people who represent its constitution. Scholars aiming to ameliorate these detrimental misconceptions have tended to use the term "Palestinian" to refer to the group of Arab Muslims and Christians indigenous to the Land of Palestine.

The very term Palestine, a name which in its present form derives from Greek, became an administrative term during Roman times and during the reign of the Syrians denoted a region in the province of Damascus. The term reappeared in Europe during the Renaissance and became part of the political language of the West in the 19th century. Eventually, the British came to use the term to denote the territory from the southern-most districts of the Ottoman provinces of Damascus and Beirut and the unattached district of Jerusalem. Only British imperial policy made Palestine the name of a defined territory in the late 19th and early 20th century. It was at this time that the formation of an identity, espoused by the Arab Muslim and Christian inhabitants of the area, began to blossom.

In essaying to conquer the next task and to define the very term "Palestinian," a larger problem arises. Rashid Khalidi explains this dilemma in asking, "what in Palestinian identity is specific and unique, and what must be understood in the context of broader historical narratives?" While trying to understand the Palestinians as a people with their own unique set of values, traditions and narratives, the academy has tended to concentrate on the relation of Palestinian narratives and identity to Zionism, the state of Israel, Arabism, and Islam. Scholars have argued that identity "is partly the relationship between you and the Other." Veritably, various overlapping senses of identity play a major role in how Palestinians define themselves as a people. Ties to family, to religion, to town, and to the Arab world play an integral part in the manner in which Palestinians define themselves. Yet originally, these overlapping forces existed, at the conception of the Palestinian identity, in concert and not in conflict with one another.

While considering the rise of the Palestinian identity as a result of interrelated narratives and forces is helpful in certain capacities, a successful examination of a unique and separate Palestinian identity is also expedient. In pursuing such an examination, the context in which the Palestinian identity was birthed and matured is important. At the end of World War I, a process of identification with new political entities, namely in the guise of the nation-state, had become popular in the Middle East as foreign powers proposed and imposed boundaries that would supposedly delineate new units of identification. As Bernard Lewis explains, "Palestine and Jordan, as denoting state entities, are both 20th century innovations." Yet, while Egyptians and Syrians, Lebanese and Iraqis developed a sense of loyalty to their own respective nation-states, the Palestinians were forced to solidify their conception of identity in the midst of domination by a foreign power, the British, while up against the Zionist camp. Whether agreeing with Stuart Hall's theories on the development of identity in relation to the Other or asserting that the development of the Palestinian identity was a unique process, the influence that the Zionists and British had on the Palestinians is impossible to ignore.

In his work, *The Multiple Identities of the Middle East*, Bernard Lewis attributes the very rise of movements like Palestinian nationalism to the Europeans. He writes that, "the recovery of the peoples of the Middle East of their ancient history and, eventually their identity, did not begin until the 19th century. This new interest in the more distant past was provoked by the newly imported European idea of fatherland, of the continuing, almost metaphysical relationship between a people and the country they inhabit." As World War I came to a close, the British shrewdly seized the territory of Palestine and, as common in most colonial histories, imposed "national" borders on local inhabitants. In doing so, the British hoped to create and encourage a sense of solidarity and unity among the Palestinian population.

Thus, out of the British Mandate and a growing Zionist ideology, expressions of a largely unheard of Palestinian voice began to be heard. All too soon, neighboring Arab countries seized upon this voice to manipulate both regional and world views. Instead of allowing the Palestinians to develop a cohesive sense of identity, the media and political entities instead chose to mold the Palestinian people into what best suited their interests. In doing so, the Palestinians were forced to confront an amalgamation of narratives and histories that they were supposed to espouse. Before meaningful reconciliation between the Israeli Jews and Palestinian Arabs can be obtained, an acceptance and comprehension of the multiple facets comprising the Palestinian identity must be obtained.

***This work or portions of this work have previously been published by** American Enterprise Magazine.*

"These issues are all so freighting that the mainstream press has hardly touched this topic and how it relates to the war on terror."

It's Selective Service, Not a Draft, People
Aaron Deakins
Eastern Michigan University, Ypsilanti, MI

A couple of years ago while watching the second debate between George Bush and Al Gore, my best friend had an epiphany. He blurted out in no uncertain terms that if Bush won the election, we were going to war. Not just a little proxy war, but a massive, no-cluster-bombs-barred military action. Even though Bush blasted the Clinton Administration during those debates for using the US military for what he called "nation building," we could see Bush's real intentions by the way he held himself. Almost four years later we have realized we didn't even see the shock and awe coming that has grasped the American public.

One only needs to read the document that defines the Bush pre-emptive dogma of war to understand what the future still holds. It is entitled "Rebuilding America's Defenses" and was published by The Project for the New American Century in September of 2000. They are a right-wing think tank that boasts Paul Wolfowitz (current Deputy Secretary of Defense) as a member. The pages describe where the military should be in the coming decade and discuss the need for a new, more technologically advanced war machine. This force should be capable of fighting numerous proxy wars, while also being able to exchange blows in two major large-scale theater wars. But there is a catch in this text that is repeated quite often: there needs to be some solution to the military's shrinking enlistment rate.

In the last couple of months we have seen unprecedented shake-ups in the military bunkers around the world. There have been extended tours, disheartening rotations, massive troop shifts, and call-ups of former personal that have long been removed from combat situations. Senators including John McCain have questioned the strain that has already been put on our under-staffed defenses. This has led some lawmakers to do the inevitable, start to talk about a draft.

About a year ago draft boards across the country started to fill vacant spots. It was a subtle event that slipped under most citizens' noses, and people who did start to talk about it were quickly labeled as having "tin-foil" under their hats. Within that time 28 million dollars was added to aid the process, known as the Selective Service System (SSS). That's not all that is happening though. As this article is being written, there are two separate pending issues in front of the House and Senate that have the attention of Pro-Peace groups across the country. These proposals (S89 and H163), shockingly enough, are for reinstating a draft, and will be debated around early 2005. Many see it as the only ways the military can sustain the quagmire it has gotten itself into.

Think college will save you this time around? Guess again. Moves are being made that would eliminate college undergraduates from being exempt for service. Now you could be drafted and would have to start your training at the end of your semester. They would be a bit nicer to college seniors though, they could defer for a full year.

What about running for Canada? Wrong again. Homeland Security and the Canadian Government have instituted a "pre-clearance agreement" that would keep prospective draft dodgers stateside. This "smart border declaration" is one in the many steps that the US government has made in insuring that the draft process goes as smoothly as possible.

With recent chatter surrounding Iran and what role they play in the war on terrorism, and nuclear proliferation, the case for a draft coming to be a reality grows stronger. In order for the US to remain the only hegemonic power in the world, groups like The Project for the New American Century state "presence of American forces in critical regions around the world is the visible expression of the extent of America's status as a superpower and as the guarantor of liberty, peace and stability." In order for this to happen, we are going to need to send more of our boys and girls (the new legislation states that women will be treated equally) to war.

Many think that Democratic forces in Washington are growing stronger with the negative press that the Bush Administration is receiving because of the war. If the Bush Administration is out, Kerry/Edwards and the Democrats are in. But the verity of the matter is these bills are the work of a bi-partisan group and are being supported by many Democratic lawmakers. They were the ones that brought up the draft before we invaded Iraq. Shocked yet? Here is the kicker: John Kerry has said that if intelligence was sound, he would be all for pre-emptive war too. So one may wonder if Kerry had received the same information that Bush was getting, would he too invaded Iraq?

These issues are all so frightening that the mainstream press has hardly touched this topic and how it relates to the war on terror. Reports have been sporadic at best, with little emphasis on what is actually going on in the SSS system. The biggest problem is that this declared war on terrorism seems to be one that the US has now unwaveringly settled into. While this war can realistically only be one of containment, the US preaches one of utter victory. In order for this to happen, the envisioned military of right-wing policy makers would need to become a certainty. So get your SSS cards out kids, it is time to count heads.

"Carnage is often spoken of with the same intonation as students here would discuss the past weekend: apache helicopters shoot rockets at suspected militants in cars and destroy houses."

Metamorphosing Hours in Ramallah

Eamon Aloyo
Lehigh University, Bethlehem, PA

My new found Palestinian friend, Ra'ed and I were sitting in a stationary air-conditioned car, seemingly in another world, insulated from the hot, dusty outside air and the harsh reality that existed on the other side of the muting cocoon of glass. We were waiting in a line of traffic to pass through Calandia checkpoint into Ramallah, a journey Ra'ed makes twice a day since he lives in Ramallah, but works on just the other side of Calandia, a ten-minute drive before the 2nd intifada began. Now, it can take half an hour if the taxis are unimpeded on both sides of the checkpoint and, critically, if the Israeli soldiers at Calandia let Ra'ed through. If either is impeded, it could take hours, or, not uncommonly, it might be impossible to commute to work. This military checkpoint is the fickle door that controls Ra'ed's life, over which Ra'ed has no control, despite the physical and emotional proximity to his life.

An unspoken tension pierced the day not only because it was less than 24 hours after a suicide bomber killed 22 people in Jerusalem (August 20, 2003), which, as the twisted world of violence dictates, soon after Palestinian violence, Israel will return in kind. But an internal tension was also growing because I too had been reading the news, and did not know what to expect of Palestine. The scene outside was one I had never seen before: a constant flow of taxies ferrying people to within a 25-meter walk of the check point, driving partway down the (now empty) oncoming traffic lane that was boxed in by piles of pained debris that lined the road. I was later to learn that the Israeli Defense Forces (IDF) piles the refuse there to prevent drivers from circumventing the checkpoint. After a short wait, Ra'ed's senior colleague, whose car sheltered us, suggested that since the line of perhaps 15 cars had not moved in 10 minutes, we might want to walk today. Thanking her as we stepped out of the false protection of the crisp air in the clean car into the outside's dry, dusty atmosphere, we fell in line with the other Palestinians carrying on with their daily lives, passing into the concrete road barriers that, irreversible once entered, thrust us toward a pair of easily identifiable, green clad Israeli soldiers. They determined who did, and more importantly, who did not pass through, like lines in the grocery store, only this time the forged smile of cashier was replaced by a harsh glance from a young man you thought should be at home with his friends, or just beginning college. I thought about joking with him or smiling until the M16 slung across his front jolted me into answering his terse questions. Three years of green fatigues is mandatory for Israeli men, and one and a half years for Israeli women, normally starting directly after high school. Young children, hand in hand with their mothers, skirted around old hobbling men garbed in traditional Arab headresses. Perched above the the checkpoint on a small hill 50 meters away, like a brutal prison guard post, was a machine gun nest overlooking the dirty operation.

Partially down the 25 meters separating the two ends of the checkpoint, a small but caustic intermittent blast infiltrated my ears. It was not the pervasive, deeply reverberating noise of a train whistle, but a sharp, hollow bang.

"They're shooting," Ra'ed nonchalantly said, giving a warm but wry smile I saw too often assumed on the face of Palestinians, expressing so much suffering in a single glance.

Now I was scared. What are they shooting at? Why are they shooting? Questions poured out. Should we continue? Maybe it's not the best idea to go on at the moment. But there was little choice; I seemed to be the only one at all worried about what was happening (the West Bank is not frequented by foreigners, nor, after the second intifada began, Israeli Jews, except for the some 230,000 settlers who remain segregated from the Palestinian population). In a strange resignation, everyone, outwardly, seemed to be reacting as if a peaceful evening sun was starting to lose its intensity for the day. What actually was happening 75meters down the road where an Israeli military jeep was parked was one soldier periodically squeezed his finger, which released a deadly metal object toward another human, down an alley. Ra'ed explained: the young man was shooting in response to Palestinian youths throwing rocks at the IDF jeep. It was probably an older teenager shooting at younger ones. Reason has no place in this conflict. Are they shooting back? Of course not Ra'ed assured me - they're just kids with rocks. Men in small groups, taxi drivers waiting their turn, were watching the scene.

Unemployment in the West Bank and Gaza, according the World Bank, is over 50%. Looking on, two Israeli soldiers, from inside the construction area of the new wall segregating most of the West Bank from Israel proper (according to a 2003 U.N. report, the wall will annex almost 15% of the territory of what consisted of the West Bank prior to the 1967 war), stood lazily, leaning forward with their hands clasped on the chain link fence on either side of their heads, rested against the dividing, unforgiving metal. Ra'ed, still smiling, offered for us to get into the front seat of a mini van, which are widely used as taxis. Pulling away I realized I was in the front right seat of the van that had to pass 10 meters behind the Israeli jeep - and soldier. Adrenaline coursing through me, I didn't know if I should duck or watch, as I did. Silence, a collective, tacit understanding, flowed through the van after we passed. I was in Ramallah.

Closer to the small city center, passing under a traffic light, Ra'ed explained that currently none of the lights are functioning in this beleaguered city because of the destruction that has been inflicted over the past three years. Yet the drivers, if a bit crazy, are excellent. Law enforcement, by the means we have come to expect of uniformed police officers, is inconspicuously absent, yet crime remains unrealistically low. During the last intifada, 1987-93, the police force was almost dissolved as well. Despite the lack of police, crime rates in the West Bank and Gaza decreased even while poverty was increasing; it appears the same is happening today, with crime almost nonexistent and poverty soaring: 60% of the Palestinians in the West Bank and Gaza survive on less than $2 per day. Imagining the chaos that would exist in any city in the States if it were known that there were no police gives you some sense of the unremitting solidarity that Palestinians feel; its palpable thickness, instead of weighing down, seems to be a rising force, like hot air off the pavement during an oppressive mid summer's day.

Every Palestinian has stories that are beyond the scope of the mind that has not been exposed to such a life. We unconsciously eschew cruel thoughts from our minds despite the knowledge that cruelty is practiced in numerous countries, in all reaches of the world, every day. Allowing life to be bearable, the active and passive negation of these unsettling thoughts also allows atrocities to continue since because we do not acknowledge them, a necessary step to correcting them, amelioration does not occur. During my first dinner in Ramallah, Ra'ed and a young woman were intense, flinging me their thoughts on the "situation" (a common noun that Palestinians used to describe everything from oppression to occupied cities), and what they had been through - when another student got a call on his cell phone: there were helicopters over another part of this small city. Carnage is often spoken of with the same intonation as students here would discuss the past weekend: apache helicopters shoot rockets at suspected militants in cars and destroy houses. One or two people from our 10-15 person group quietly quit dinner early to return home. But this is life in occupied Palestine. The conversation resumed, the hookah filled with strawberry flavored tobacco was passed, and but a moment was lost.

Continuing our discussion, the young women passionately related the difficulties of life under occupation. For two full days she and her sister did not leave the floor of her room since the IDF was conducting operations in her neighborhood, and anyone who showed themselves in the windows, for fear of sniper fire, would be shot. Their house bears witness: it is scarred with bullet holes, as is she. This young woman, just out of college, was hit once in the back, but is now, visibly, in good health.

Distressingly, these incidents are not unique. Another time she was expecting a friend, as she and her girlfriends had planned a small party. Instead, a knock at the door produced a cadre of young heavily armed Israeli soldiers, faces smeared with paint, yelling at her to open the door. Courageously, she countered that only she and her female friends were there, and that they had no right to enter, refusing them admittance, until a soldier put his automatic weapon to her temple. Adrenaline, a slip, a bump from the other troops pouring in, and I could have never even known that she existed. The young soldiers found nothing, but destroyed the interior of her parents' house. Lastly, a piercing story of what the children of occupation endure: her young nephew who is just learning to speak has never known life except that during this intifada. The first word he was able to articulate, in Arabic, was "tank".

A peaceful cat backed into a corner, Ra'ed later explained to me as we were having a beer at a local bar, is a metaphor for Palestinians, who just like the cat will by nature, eventually lash out and scratch back at the more powerful aggressor. Being earnestly sincere, in contrast to many Americans, is a way of life that is inescapable because of the demanding circumstances. In this typically Palestinian and Israeli means of discussion, the weight of life's experiences oozes through, not as resignation (although clearly some people are resigned), but stoically, as ever-present. The vast differences in the scope of difficulties of life in Israel and Palestine, compared to here, are blatantly ubiquitous in the people there.

Before dropping me back at my hotel for the night, around 11 p.m., Ra'ed stopped at a local bakery to buy pitas, a staple that is eaten three meals a day. Taking our place at the back of line that was overflowing out into the street, Ra'ed explained that since incursions and a curfew were expected in response to the suicide bombing, most people (everyone in line was male) were buying extra bread in case they and their families were confined to their houses.

I had been in the West Bank for less than 8 hours.

"Civilian Tutsis from one village prayed and prayed, and were told to leave their homes, seek refuge at a church...a short time passed, whimpering passed through the thin walls of the church sanctuary, and less than two hours later, there were only ashes left."

OPERATION STAND-BY
Letisha Beachy
Virginia Polytechnic Institute and State University, Blacksburg, VA

Lying in bed, I watch the stars through my open window
and feel the warm spring breeze wash through little wisps of hair
that flutter away from my head. April 6, 1994 -
the day before my huge test in science, oh and I hate science.
As I pulled the veil over my window,
even science could not explain to me why
the night sky swiftly shaded sanguine, or why

The stars suddenly shrieked...

Infant cries silenced by machetes slicing through the cruel darkness.
A Tutsi woman falls to the ground moaning over the dead bodies
of her husband and daughter - a footstep - her Hutu neighbor
hovers over her corpse with a bloodied machete.
Synchronized marching invades village after village
until each is left dead. Just dead.

April 11, 1994 - "Thousands massacred in Rwanda
following President Habyarimana's fatal and mysterious plane crash,"
reads U.N. Ambassador R. H.
"Remove the troops from this area," says U.N. Ambassador B.W.,
sipping from his third cup of coffee and pointing to a map of Rwanda.

Twenty-five hundred faces - mostly Tutsi, but some Hutu spouses, relatives,
and mixed children - huddle together in a school

hearing the end of their refuge break down the doors…
"Mercy! Please! Peace! Peace!" cried several Tutsi civilians -
no place to run, no one to turn to,
wailing and pain
as men, women, and children are
beaten, raped, and slaughtered by Hutus and machetes.

April 12, 1994 - "2,500 civilians killed in a school
after Belgian troops left the area," reads U.N. Ambassador M. F.,
rocking back and forth in his desk chair.
"How's your daughter doing in school?"
U.N. Ambassador B. W. asks the secretary.
"Good! Very good. We're so proud!"

Civilian Tutsis from one village prayed and prayed,
and were told to leave their homes, seek refuge at a church…
a short time passed, whimpering passed through the thin walls
of the church sanctuary,
and less than two hours later, there were only ashes left.

Booming voices filled a U.N. conference room:
"Ten Belgian soldiers killed!" cried one U.N. ambassador,
"Cut the forces by ten times!"
"What have we decided?" asks another.
"That we condemn this geno-" someone starts.
"Shhtt! Don't use that word! We would have to intervene
if we used that word. We condemn the killings in Rwanda."
Eight hours pass.
"Who's going to pay for troops to be sent? We certainly
cannot afford this endeavor."
Angry ambassadors leave the room…
"Let's rest on it, gentlemen…"

Mountains of bodies - all that inhabit
schools and churches,
villages and homes,
hospitals and camps.
Two million Rwandan refugees,
some missing parents, some missing spouses,
forced to return to Hell.

Mothers clinging to their babies and dragging children,
Fathers push along their wives and elderly parents:
their hopeful horizon is the Rwandan border -

into Zaire, Uganda, or Tanzania.
Families separated during attacks,
men, women, and children -
hunger, filth, and fatigue biting them hard
from lying in hiding in the forests
There is no sanctuary…

Only in church and a tiny newspaper column
did I hear about the events in Rwanda…
I failed my science test, but at least I knew why
the stars screamed that night and the sky shaded sanguine…
but why, I wondered, was it for only that night
while the mass deaths continue?
Then I knew, just as I had pulled the veil
over my view of that night, the world had turned its back
and the sky stayed scarlet only above
a lone little country that everyone ignored.
I could only weep and pray…

"Let's rest on it, gentlemen…"

"I would also like to address the assertion that the 9/11 victims were "American heroes." Now, I don't want to disrespect them, but I hardly think that unwillingly dying is an act of heroism."

Patriot Day
Takeo Rivera
Stanford University, Stanford, CA

Last year on this day, I went around school greeting people with "Happy September Eleventh!" I'm not quite sure why.

Now, if you check most of the calendars of the year of someone's Lord 2004, it's become "Patriot Day." At first I thought this to be a vehement misnomer, considering how it's the anniversary of a massacre. After all, December 7th isn't something corny like "Liberty Day" - it's what it's supposed to be: Pearl Harbor Remembrance Day. But I think in a lot of ways, Patriot Day is pretty appropriate.

I'm sure the official line is akin to something Giulianni (I think) said, which was to this effect: "Out of the rubble of a city was born the unity of a nation." Actually, I'm sure that wasn't the quote, but like I said, it was something to that effect. Out of the death and destruction was a renewed patriotism and unity that swept (most of) the country. So in effect, we find ourselves trapped in one o' them paradoxes that almost seems Catholic in nature: out of suffering, we find hope. At least, that's the inherent logic behind it.

The other line that I'm sure is being spread is that the victims of September 11th were "true patriots," as if they gave their lives for the nation. Bush, after all, called them "American heroes."

I wonder who bought into it...?

It was a Tuesday when I first found out about the attacks in 2001. In our Speech 120 class, we shared our thoughts on the attacks. In the interest of confidentiality, I won't say who said what. I will divulge, however, what my thoughts were. My first instinct, being a reader of Z Magazine and the People's History of the U.S., was that there was something fishy here. I knew that the government now had an excuse to "fight back," to exercise holy retribution in the name of capitalism under the guise of democracy. It wasn't long until our Ingsoc Chairman Bush fulfilled the nagging prophecy in my head.

('Course, I don't think I was alone in my suspicions. I think a good lot of the Progressive community thought that way. The Right may call such thinking cynical - and in the most obvious regard they would be correct. The only thing is that we're optimistic in our cynicism, that in our criticism of the stupidity we see around us, we fight for its improvement.)

Perhaps the government was united for about a year (while the Republicans turned the Dems into their prison bitches), but I do not think that We the People were. Most of us emotionally came together to grieve, to plaster American flags and "United We Stand" bumper stickers on our doors and horseless carriages. But hate crimes went on the rise. If there's anything really reliable about the American people, it's hate crimes, after all. Spy plane goes down in China, and off we kill the Gooks and Japs! A-rabs crash into the towers, and we gotta kill the "towelheads," even if they are indeed Sikhs or Pakistanis rather than bona fide A-rabs. Yeah, America's got that proud history: whether you be black or queer, the lynch mob's near! And thus minorities of subcategories are united in larger, more general categories more convenient for both demographers and lynch mobs. So goes the irony of colonialism, as well.

To the Bush Administration's credit, the government has *kind of* made efforts to stop the hate, coming out in support of the Muslim American community (with Bush praying at the mosque and all). Of course, I don't think that quite does it, since they simultaneously launch another campaign that's entirely contradictory to that idea. Words like "crusade," "Axis of Evil," and "civilized world" strike clear superiority/inferiority and good/evil lines, between US and THEM. Think of the love/hate relationship that exists between Afghanistan and the US now. From our perspective, we're supposed to hate them for being terrorists, and yet we're "liberating" the country. We love them by hating them, and vice versa. And so die thousands of civilians - double or triple the number of 9/11 - to fall on Colin Powell's deaf ears. The same goes for Iraq, though most of us were awake by then.

I would also like to address the assertion that the 9/11 victims were "American heroes." Now, I don't want to disrespect them, but I hardly think that unwillingly dying is an act of heroism. If a little girl gets hit by a truck speeding through an intersection, would that make her a hero or a victim? You may say that the difference is that the terrorists intended to attack, rather than some kind of accident; but I ask, would the "victim" status of the girl change of the trucker was intentionally trying to hit her? I don't think so.

Now, the 9/11 victims should be remembered as victims, not heroes or patriots, and I think this is more honest and honorable to their memories. Should we deify them, turn them into martyrs and crusaders, we give into the martial-nationalist idea that they would endorse any method of retribution, no matter how absurd. Perhaps that attitude lingered among some of them, but I hardly think a majority of those who died so tragically would want their deaths to result in a more violent and fearsome world to live in.

I pose another question: Was Archduke Francis Ferdinand a hero?

His assasination led to a chain reaction of political and military animosities and alliances that in turn led to one of the greatest misnomers of all: the Great War. Or, if you prefer, World War I, one of the costliest, bloodiest, and least necessary wars ever fought in the history of man.

There was a fake-history Onion article I read that said: "Archduke Ferdinand Found Alive! 'How Fares Europe?' he asks."

How fares the United States? We fare just dandy, with a misnomer holiday like Patriot Day "celebrating" the deaths of so many - deaths that our government has shameless exploited in the name of power, control, and profit, though not necessarily in that order. I ask again: Is Patriot Day an appropriate name?

In spite of all of that contradiction, I say, yes. In fact, it's because of the contradiction. We live in fictitious times, after all. Don't we, Mr. Moore? This is the reign of Orwell.

So, I guess the million dollar question of Patriot Day, the holiday formerly known as Happy September Eleventh, is:

Does $2 + 2 = 5$?

Peace
Jeannine Sikora
State University of New York at Albany, Albany, NY

"We need to understand that all violence is terror and that an overhaul of the foreign policy of the world's only superpower is necessary in order to prevent a reoccurrence."

Probing Terrorism
Eamon Aloyo
Lehigh University, Bethlehem, PA

Before proceeding any further, I ask you while reading this to attempt to put aside all biases, cultural ideals, and nationalistic tendencies. In order to understand from as objective a standpoint as possible, our ingrained biases, especially those that we believe unquestioningly, should be temporarily suspended. Below I may provide questions to which you have a visceral reaction, but I will ask, for the sake of truly understanding, to postpone your gut reaction until you have seriously explored the implications of the arguments.

Beginning from this open state of mind, I will probe into what has been the driving force of discussions as well as American policy, both domestic and foreign, since the September 11, 2001 attacks: terrorism. Despite its pervasive affects on our personal lives, as well as the world, we rarely stop to consider what terrorism is. Ludwig Wittgenstein, a philosopher, perspicaciously observed that sometimes there are gaps between the use and the actual meaning of a word. In other words, a word may gain a common meaning that does not necessarily equate with its actual meaning. Terrorism has two disparate meanings, and the actual definition is the one I would like to deal with here. The New Webster's Dictionary defines terrorism as "the policy of using acts inspiring terror [defined as "great fear"] as a method of ruling or of conducting political opposition." Under this definition the September 11th attacks fall within the scope of the definition, as do Palestinian suicide bombers, both of which are generally accepted as terrorism in United States society's common conscience.

Yet because of our traditionally limited point of view, we dismiss acts of violence sponsored by states, including the U.S., as just or at worst, justified. State-led violence is seldom referred to as terrorism, save in the case of those states that are designated by the West as rogue states; not often is it heard or read that the U.S., Israel, or a western European country is committing terrorism. We also know that all acts of violence create great fear in those upon whom the casualties are inflicted, and, as von

Clausewitz noted, "war is an extension of politics by other means." Thus, according to the dictionary and von Clausewitz's definitions, every war, every act of violence (that is used for political ends, since I know of no causes where, axiomatically, violence is conducted against political allies), including all of those sanctioned by state governments, is an act of terrorism. That is, because violence strikes great fear into humans, and state-sponsored government violence is, by definition, politically motivated, all state-sponsored incidents of violence are terrorist in nature.

This is a profound shift in how we generally categorize and interpret our world, calling for a comprehensive reevaluation of how we view both violence and terrorism. From here on I will call what we generally think of as terrorism as rogue terrorism since it emanates from non-official sources. Terrorism will refer to the definition as it stands above: the use of violence, which necessarily creates great fear, when it is a method of ruling or conducting political opposition.

Nevertheless, war and hence terrorism, however terrible, is generally accepted as necessary in rare cases. The circumstances of Nazi Germany are normally cited as an instance where force was a moral imperative, seen as the only means possible to end unimaginable atrocities. Therefore, because all wars are strictly considered terrorism, some terrorist acts can be considered morally just.

We should, then, utilize justice to interrogate what terrorism we should support or condemn. Rather than facilely shrugging off difficult moral inquiries by categorizing violent acts as rogue terrorism and thus not only bypassing all thought on the subject but entirely circumventing the deep rumination that is called for in such grave circumstances, we should consider each act of violence with an inquisitive, open mind. Is violence ever ethical? Why are the perpetrators acting violently? And, above all, is this instance of violence just?

We should prudently consider why many know Palestinian suicide bombers as martyrs, not terrorists, and above all why these acts of violence are carried out. In psychology a theory known as the ultimate attribution error is defined: "positive actions performed by people from a different ethnic or social group are attributed to external causes, such as luck, whereas their negative actions are attributed to internal causes, such as dishonesty." Accounting for this, we should both peer inwardly to ask ourselves difficult questions about why some extremists hate the United States and extend our questions to why foreign groups use violence and whether their use is just.

Being able to take or give (depending on how you look at it) your own life in all probability stems from a deep motive to rectify a perceived injustice that was committed against you, or against the social group with whom you identify. The normal political and judicial means must not be available, or the cleansing pipes through which justice must pass may not exist altogether. Consequently, only extremes seem possible: do nothing and accept the injustice, or use summary violence.

Traditional warfare is backed by states because of aggression toward a group, identified as a nation, and in rare circumstances, because of moral imperatives that extend beyond your self-identified social group (the 1990s' NATO military intervention in the Balkans is, while fatally delayed, another example of this). Many of the reasons states resort to violence are paralleled in rogue terrorism: to protect and defend a perceived group's safety and to seek justice.

We must appraise each violent act under the same light and search for justice, independent of our social grouping, equally across boarders of countries, as well as culture, religion, and other divisions. Only an objective approach to why suicide bombers kill themselves and why aircraft carriers are dispatched will provide answers.

John Rawls, a prominent philosopher, proposes a foundation upon which we can construct our own beliefs. If we were to exist outside of the world peering down on society, says Rawls, and we did not know on which side of the (in)justice wall we would be placed, how would we want the world to change? How then would we consider the changing society?

We can apply this idea to state violence, and thus terrorism, as well as we can apply it to rogue terrorism. If we did not know whose body and mind we would inhabit, how would we then view the world. Only by seeking information that is outside the monolithic mass media can this view be approached.

The September 11th attackers must have profoundly believed an inimical policy was enacted against their group. We need to understand that all violence is terror and that an overhaul of the foreign policy of the world's only superpower is necessary in order to prevent a reoccurrence. No longer can dictators be supported or installed as has been, and continues to be, actual U.S. policy. No longer can the CIA be allowed to support unjust military action, as it did in both Iraq and Iran during their 1980-1988 war. A third offshoot of Wittgenstein's observation, here, would be that many times words that governments use (as well as other sources) simply mean something opposite of either of their two normal meanings, those being of use or strict definition. In other words, no longer should the U.S. lie. No longer should U.S. hypocrisy be tolerated because of U.S. power. For example, states that use torture, such as Israel and Egypt - being the first and second highest recipients, respectively, of U.S. aid - should not receive funding until their human rights are improved.

Every group of people must take full responsibility for their personal as well as group actions, and objective viewing of them must be maintained. For all burdensome issues, such as human violence and terrorism, we should deeply consider what is ethical. We should never unquestioningly defer to any of the reasoning foisted on us without determining for ourselves whether we agree with simply one point of view.

The Bombing

Dheeraj Jagadev
College of William and Mary, Williamsburg, VA

As the heavens thundered through the night skies,
shattering the uneasy calm that cries,
Behold my comrades! It isn't over yet
and what will these nefarious deeds beget?
For days, months and years will it continue,
but it will not bring at all nothing new
except for more deceits, coverups and lies
that inso far has ruined millions of lives.
Hellfire and damnation will be upon
those heads who have decided to go on.
Starvation, misery, death, destruction,
hysteria, tyranny, oppression,
these are but a few of the obstacles
in a path strewn with hatred and its tentacles.

"Nazi Germany, Soviet Russia and Communist China well understood this monopoly. And they demonstrated that if the state has the power to conscript you into the armed forces, then the state has the power to conscript you into whatever folly or wickedness it deems most utilitarian."

The Immorality of Conscription
Jonathan Rick
Hamilton College, Clinton, NY

No matter how one rationalizes it - duty, the Constitution, necessity, practicality, shared sacrifice—conscription abrogates a man's right to his life and indentures him to the state. As President Reagan recognized (at least rhetorically), "[T]he most fundamental objection is moral"; conscription "destroys the very values that our society is committed to defending."

The libertarian argument says that freedom means the absence of the initiation of coercion. Since conscription necessitates coercion, it is incompatible with freedom. The common reply holds that conscription, like taxes, is tantamount to paying rent for living in freedom. In this view, rather than entirely laissez-faire, freedom imposes certain positive obligations.

Put another way, this means that your right to your own life is provisional—which means you don't have that right. This means that you must buy your rights by surrendering your life. Of course, since government's purpose is to protect your rights, it cannot then claim title to your most basic right—your very life—in exchange. Such an idea inverts the state-citizen relationship and establishes the cardinal totalitarian axiom that hinges every citizen's existence to the state's disposal.

Nazi Germany, Soviet Russia and Communist China well understood this monopoly. And they demonstrated that if the state has the power to conscript you into the armed forces, then the state has the power to conscript you into whatever folly or wickedness it deems most utilitarian. (This logic is not lost on the Bush administration, which given the dearth of CIA personnel who speak Arabic, is floating plans to draft such specialists.) Moreover, as Ayn Rand argued, if the state can force you to shoot or kill another human being and "to risk [your own] death or hideous maiming and crippling . . . if [your] consent is not required to send [you] into unspeakable martyrdom—then, in principle," you cease to have any rights, and the state ceases to be your protector. "What else is there left to protect?"

By contrast, with voluntary armed services, no one enters harm's way who does not choose that course. As such, the state must convince every potential soldier of the justice and necessity of the casus belli. But conscription is the hallmark of a regime that cannot be bothered with persuasion. It matters little that you may neither approve of nor even understand the cause, for conscription churns men from autonomous individuals into sacrificial cogs. To a free society, however—one rooted in the moral principle that man is an end in himself, that he exists for his own sake—conscription robs men, as the social activist A.J. Muste wrote, "of the freedom to react intelligently . . . of their volition to the concrete situations that arise in a dynamic universe . . . of that which makes them men—their autonomy."

In this way, conscription exemplifies the "involuntary servitude" the American Constitution forbids. Yet the same Constitution that forbids Congress from enforcing "involuntary servitude" (thirteenth amendment), instructs it to "provide for the common defense" (Preamble) and to "raise . . . armies" (Article 1, section 8, clause 12). Do these powers not amount to conscription? On one hand, they may—though the argument that because something is constitutional, it is ipso facto moral, fails to question whether the Constitution, on the given issue, is itself immoral. On the other hand, the verbs "provide" and "raise" need not entail coercion. Discerns David Mayer, a professor of law and history at Capital University, where the Constitution is ambiguous, we should refer to its animating fundamentals. We should read each constitutional provision in the framework "of the document as a whole, and, especially, in light of the purpose of the whole document. . . . [T]hat purpose is to limit the power of government and to safeguard the rights of the individual." Conscription explicitly contradicts these American axioms.

Even so, some argue, conscription is necessary to ensure America's survival in the face of, say, a two-front war. A government that acts unconstitutionally in emergencies is better than a government that makes the Constitution as a suicide pact. Stability, of course, is neither government's purpose nor its barometer. True, governmental stability provides the security necessary to exercise one's freedom; but a government that sacrifices its citizens' freedom to prop itself up is no longer a guardian of freedom but a tool for tyranny. No matter how grave and imminent the threat, the maxim of Roman statesmen should take primacy. "Fiat justitia, ruat caelum" (Let justice be done, though the heavens fall). Or, as Patrick Henry later declared: "Give me liberty, or give me death."

Yet what if, out of ignorance or indifference, people fail to appreciate a threat before it is too late? Would the sixteen million men and women whom the U.S. government conscripted for World War II - over twelve percent of our population at that time—have arisen, voluntarily, in such numbers, at such a rate, and committed to such specialties as we needed to win the war? Isn't conscription, as President Clinton termed it, a "hedge against unforeseen threats and a[n] . . . 'insurance policy'"? Haven't our commanders in chief—from Lincoln suspending habeas corpus during the Civil War, to FDR interning Japanese Americans during the Second World War, to Bush's Patriot Act today—always infringed certain liberties in wartime? In 1919, the Supreme Court declared that merely circulating an inflammatory anti-draft flier, in wartime, constitutes a "clear and present danger."

We should first distinguish between legal, civil, or secondary rights, like habeas corpus and trial by jury, and natural or first rights, like the right to one's life. While wartime may justify a temporary alteration or suspension of the former, nothing can justify violating the latter, which are inalienable. Second, since the price of freedom is eternal vigilance, if one wants to continue to live in freedom, one should volunteer to defend it when it is threatened. Third, a dearth of volunteers would probably occur because the administration is corrupt or it undertakes to wage a corrupt war. For instance, without conscription, the U.S. government would have lacked enough soldiers to invade Vietnam; an all-volunteer force (A.V.F.) would have triggered a ceasefire years earlier, since people would simply have stopped volunteering. Indeed, rather than deter presidents from prosecuting that increasingly unpopular and drawn-out tragedy - from sending 60,000 Americans to their senseless deaths—conscription enabled them to escalate it.

Still, even in a just war, enlistments might not meet manpower needs. Sometimes quantity overcomes quality. Napoleon, no neophyte in such matters, noted that "Providence is always on the side of the last reserve."

But God does not side with the big battalions, but with those who are most steadfast. As President Reagan put it, "No arsenal or no weapon in the arsenals of the world is so formidable as the will and moral courage" of a man who fights of his own accord, for that which he believes is truly just. This is why American farmers defeated British conscripts in 1783, and why Vietnamese guerrillas defeated American conscripts in 1975. Would you prefer to patrol Baghdad today guarded by a career officer, acting on his dream to see live action as a sniper, or guarded by a haberdasher whom the Selective Service Act has coerced into duty and who can think of nothing else save where he'd rather be?

Furthermore, when private firms, in any field, need more workers, they do not resort to hiring at gunpoint. Rather, they appeal to economics, by increasing employees' compensation. If anyone deserves top government dollar, it is those, who as George Orwell reportedly said, allow us to sleep safely in our beds, those rough men and women who stand ready in the night to visit violence on those who would do us harm.]

Nonetheless, isn't an all-volunteer force (A.V.F.) a poor man's army, driving a wedge between the upper classes who usually loophole or bribe exemptions, and the middle and lower classes on whose backs wars are traditionally fought? Similarly, doesn't an A.V.F. devolve disproportionately on minorities, who, as one former Marine captain writes, "enlist in the economic equivalent of a Hail Mary pass"? In fact, today's A.V.F. is the most egalitarian ever. While blacks, for instance, remain overrepresented by six percent, Hispanics, though they comprise about thirteen percent of America, comprise eleven percent of those in uniform. Moreover, overrepresentation of a class or race stems not from the upward mobility the armed forces offer—training soldiers in such marketable skills as how to drive a truck, fix a jet or operate sophisticated software—but from the inferior opportunities in society.

Still, critics insist the A.V.F. excludes the children of power and privilege, of our opinion- and policy-makers. Isolated literally and socially from volunteers, these chicken hawks can thus facilely advocate military "advisors," "police action," national "interests," and humanitarian intervention. After all, as Matt Damon remarks in *Good*

Will Hunting (1997): "It won't be their kid over there, getting shot. Just like it wasn't them when their number got called, 'cause they were pulling a tour in the National Guard. It'll be some kid from Southie [a blue-collar district of Boston] over there taking shrapnel in the ass." "The war," therefore, as William Broyles Jr. recently noted, "is impersonal for the very people to whom it should be most personal." By contrast, the more people who serve, the more people will seriously weigh the real-life consequences of their opinions. It's much more trying to advocate "regime change" in Iraq if your spouse, friends, children or grandchildren might come home in a body bag (and even more vexing if the government does not censor such coverage).

To be sure, serving in war gives one an essential understanding of its horrors. But that veterans, ipso facto, possess better judgment than their civilian counterparts elides both that Abraham Lincoln and Franklin Roosevelt, who never saw combat, became America's greatest wartime strategists, and that those who waged the Vietnam debacle—including presidents Kennedy, who won a Navy and Marine Corps Medal, and Johnson, who won a Silver Star—were decorated warriors. Moreover, as Lawrence Kaplan, senior editor at the New Republic, observes, Vietnam left Senators Chuck Hagel (R-NE), John McCain (R-AZ) and John Kerry (D-MA) on three divergent paths, with Hagel a traditional realist, McCain a virtual neoconservative and Kerry a conventional leftist. Experience, while invaluable, is neither mandatory nor monolithic.

But conscription will restore the ruggedness today's young Americans sorely lack, critics contend. Complacency cocoons my generation, who depend on anything but ourselves. Maybe they even quote Rousseau: "As the conveniences of life increase . . . true courage flags, [and] military virtues disappear."

Yet soft as we may appear vegging out before MTV, history shows that when attacked, Americans are invincible. As President Bush said of 9/11: "Terrorist attacks can shake the foundations of our biggest buildings, but they cannot touch the foundation of America. These acts shattered steel, but they cannot dent the steel of American resolve." Moreover, the problem is not a dearth of regimentation, but a dearth of persuasion; the administration has failed to convince potential soldiers to enlist. Rather than see this as a sign of pusillanimity, it seems that those with the most to lose think Washington is acting for less than honorable reasons—which should cause the government, not to reinstate conscription, but to rethink its policies.

In his inaugural address, JFK acclaimed the morality behind conscription. "Ask not what your country can do for you," he declared. "Ask what or can do for your country." But our founders offered us an alternative between parasitism and being cannon fodder, between betraying one's beliefs by serving or becoming a criminal or expatriate by objecting or dodging: autonomous individuals pursuing their own happiness, sacrificing neither others to themselves nor themselves to others. The catch-22 goes further, since the prime draftee age, from eighteen to twenty-five, in Ayn Rand's words, are "the crucial formative years of a man's life. This is . . . when he confirms his impressions of the world . . . when he acquires conscious convictions, defines his moral values, chooses his goals, and plans his future." When man is most vulnerable, draft advocates want to force him into terror—"the terror of knowing that he can plan nothing and count on nothing, that any road he takes can be blocked at any moment by an unpredictable power, that, barring his vision of the future, there stands the gray shape of the barracks, and, perhaps, beyond it, death for some unknown reason in some alien jungle." Death in some alien jungle yesterday, death in some alien desert today.

*Awarded first place in the **2004 Dean Alfage Essay Prize** *(Hamilton College).* ***Published by the* Sense of the Life Objectivists,** *September 4, 2004; in the* **Spectator** *(Hamilton College) in three parts, September 10, September 17, and September 24, 2004.***

"He tried his best to fill in the hole where the oak tree once was and tried to clean up the grass. But it was still dirty, and the tools were still broken, and things were going badly."

The Modern Parable
Daniel Falkner
Canisius College, Buffalo, NY

As the spring sun washes over spring lawns, the weeds grow from the dirt in a garden outside of a grey house. They appear from nowhere, growing faster than any other plant in the garden. There are often several shoots stemming from the single trunk, growing nearly two feet tall and spreading, like a tiny forest. Though they might have always been large, they were barely noticed until they suffocated the rosebush.

The man recently moved into the grey house. The house was given to him three years ago when the last resident left. The neighborhood mourned the old tenant's leaving, for he was a wonderful neighbor. He watered the garden and picked the cherries. He helped out the neighbors. He was friendly, and played music. The house had even seemed white while he was there. The neighbors often wish he hadn't left.

The man's father once lived in the house. The neighbors were not as fond of him, but he kept the garden in satisfactory condition. He often fought the weeds or the insects in the front yard, though he always hated the oak tree. One day he attacked the oak tree, nearly killing it. But it managed to survive, and quietly stood after that.

As the days warm up, from fifty to sixty to seventy, the man makes his appearance outside as well. He emerges from the grey house, wearing his ragged jeans and his "Union Steel Football" t-shirt. He walks outside with a bottle of General Pow's Weed Spray and soaks the budding plants, trying his best to kill their roots. With his bare, southern hands, he sprays the chemicals as much as the bottle instructs. He waits twenty-four hours to see whether or not the spray has worked as the commercial says. If it doesn't, he's out there the next day repeating the process.

The man loves the garden—the green lawn, the cherry tree, the rose bush. He lives alone, and loves to watch the beautiful garden. The brown hair on his head and the white of his teeth would suggest he's in his fifties, maybe a little older. In the hot afternoon of a July day, he loves to sit under the shade of the cherry tree in his ragged jeans and his t-shirt, a small smirk on his face. And every evening, the man picks the cherries and relaxes in his lawn chair as he eats them, a glass of milk by his side. "This milk will give you strength," his dad once said. "I used it, too. It's good milk." The man watches the garden grow and holds a spray bottle in his hand.

"Aside from those weeds," the man says to himself while he eats his cherries, "this garden is beautiful. This yard is perfect."

The weeds weren't as noticeable before the catastrophe that occurred early on in the man's occupation of the grey house. There used to be a magnificent rosebush that the entire neighborhood loved to look at. The man was new to the house, and his understanding of the care for the rosebush wasn't as good as maybe it should have been. On a fateful morning as the man arose from his bed, the rosebush had been suffocated by the weeds. It had shriveled and perished. The neighborhood, and the man, was in shock. Since that fateful day, the man blames nearly everything on what the weeds have done. And the neighbors now hear about them often.

So the man sprays. Every two weeks in the spring and throughout the summer. The chemicals go to war for him and his cause. He wakes up the next morning to see how the weeds have died. If they're sufficiently wilted, he is happy. If they're still alive, he often looks for a stronger chemical.

The man continued this routine for the early months he occupied the grey house. Every spring and summer night, he sat in his lawn chair with his ragged jeans and a t-shirt, getting strength from his milk and eating his cherries. He watched the soil carefully, as if he could stop the weeds by looking at them; through fear. He always held the spray bottle and he always smirked slightly at the wonderful job he felt he was doing on his garden.

During their mid-afternoon walks, some neighbors would commend his work.

"Looks good," they would say.

"Yep. Now she's moving in the right direction" the man would say back to them, turning to see who it was. "I have to make this place beautiful once again."

The neighbors continued their walk, speaking to one another as their arms conducted their words. The man continued his battle; spraying and prodding and ripping.

Other neighbors would pass by as well, more skeptical of all the poison and spray he was using.

"You sure about that?" they would ask.

"You bet. Trust me."

In his second year at the brick and vinyl house, spring and summer came and went without the cherry tree giving any fruit. The man was worried. He sat in his lawn chair cracking his knuckles instead of pitting the fruit. He continued to hold his spray bottle tightly, always wondering what to do. All summer he waited for the tree to flower. He stared at the tree, willing it to flower. It never did. As fall and winter came to be and there was still no fruit, he rationalized that it must have been a bad season. But then the bark of the tree was flaking off as well. He felt he must act. Things were going badly and the neighbors were getting upset.

"That tree isn't looking so good," the neighbors said the next spring. "Maybe you should do something about it."

The man thought the people got some delight from his misery. They saw that the man with the perfect garden had a cherry tree that was dying. His garden was sick.

The man hated the idea that the people were mocking him. During late spring, the man bought an axe and began chopping down the oak tree. The people seemed scared. They hadn't seen such harsh action before. They had wanted something done about the cherry tree, but they were confused: why would he chop at the oak tree when the cherry tree was dying?

"Why are you chopping down that tree?" the neighbors asked, slightly surprised.

"This tree is causing the problem," the man said. "My father said it was bad when he lived here, and it's the only way I can make this place beautiful again."

"Really? Did you ask anyone else?" the neighbors asked. "It's worth a shot don't you think? Instead of chopping it down?"

The man didn't listen. He chopped at the trunk. The tree was old. It had been there as long as he had occupied the house. It had been in the neighborhood for a long time. The man told the neighbors it was bad though, and the neighbors were impressed at how quickly the man took care of it. The trunk only took a few hits before falling. What few leaves were on the tree seemed to wither away quickly. The man brushed off his hands and hauled it to the back of the house.

"Was it really such a bad tree?" the neighbors would sometimes ask. "It's too bad that was the only thing that you could have done."

"The garden will be beautiful once again," the man told them.
The man brought a pick axe from the garage. He began to impale it vigorously into the ground; pulling out chunks of earth with every thrust.

"What are you doing?" the neighbors asked.

"I have to get the roots. I have to get it all if I want this garden to be beautiful again."

"Are you sure?" the neighbors asked. "What about the cherry tree? What about the weeds?" But the man didn't listen. He thrust the metal into the ground. He ripped and tore for many days. The roots of the tree grew deep. The people watched him as he ripped at the earth. They even lent him their tools. He eventually asked for more and more tools.

"You should be careful," the people said, "you don't want to rip up any of the other roots."

But the man was content with all the ripping he was doing, and finally he got all the roots out. The ground was hardening with the fall cool, and the yard was torn and overturned. The grass had dirt on it. The weeds had grown once again while the man's attention was on the roots. There was a large hole where the oak tree once was. But the man was happy. He had ridden the oak's stain on his beautiful garden. It was October now, and the snow fell early. The cherry tree wilted terribly. The neighbors were dreadfully sad.

"But the cherry tree is now safe and free," the man told the neighbors.

"But the pick axe is dented and you broke many of the tools that we lent you," they told him.

The next spring came and the man sprayed the weeds that had made such great roots while he hadn't paid attention to them. He tried his best to fill in the hole where the oak tree once was and tried to clean up the grass. But it was still dirty, and the tools were still broken, and things were going badly. He sat on his lawn chair in his grubby jeans and his shirt, eating cherries he had bought from the market. A small smirk was on his face as he looked at his yard. He wanted to convince the neighbors of what a good looking garden he had. One day, as the man admired his yard, a neighbor passed by.

"Isn't this a great yard?" the man asked the neighbor. It was the summer of the man's fourth year now, and the neighborhood was wondering whether or not they should ask him to leave.

"I mean," the man continued, "The weeds aren't that bad and the cherry tree is getting a little better, don't you think? And look at the hole from the oak tree, it doesn't look so deep. Right?"

The neighbor looked into the man's eyes; eyes that seemed stronger now than when the neighbor first met him. The neighbor tried to look around the man, who seemed to be blocking the yard.

"I don't know," the neighbor began. "I remember when the cherry tree was giving great fruit. I remember when the oak tree was standing there, not harming any-one. I wondered why you never asked for anyone's opinion on the matter. So much like your father. I worry now too much about those weeds, that they might affect my house. I used to be happy in this neighborhood. I used to feel safe and not feel scared. I just don't know."

With that said the man turned around and walked away. The man watched him pass into the distance. The man looked to the cherry tree and the weeds. He looked at the hole from the oak tree and the broken tools. He looked at all these things and remembered how it was when he moved in. He was angry, and he lied to himself. He handed out letters to the people about his beautiful garden. The letters spoke of how the cherry tree was getting better. And how dark times are now behind the neighborhood. The letters spoke of safety and hope, and freedom. The man talked about how much better the garden was now. The letters said that since the rosebush fell, the man has had to take drastic measures. But those measures have helped restore what was once there. The letters always talked about the rosebush. And how the rosebush's falling was some-how linked to the oak tree.

Despite all his work to convince his neighbors, most of the people no longer said hello to the man on the street. They looked onto the garden with anger and regret. They had great disdain for the last few years. They wanted change. They wanted change badly. Some wanted their tools back, though they knew it would never happen. Some wanted the cherries to grow. Still, some even felt badly for the oak tree, which they still weren't sure was so terrible. They missed the rosebush as much as the man, if not more, but they knew that all this wasn't because of the rosebush. They wanted change.

These were some of the points that were brought up when the man asked to remain in the neighborhood. After all, it was a privilege to stay at the grey house, and the neighbors ultimately decided whether or not they wanted him to stay. There were some neighbors that believed him, and felt that removing the oak tree and killing the weeds was necessary for the audacious downfall of the rosebush. They exalted him. They wanted to let him and his glass of milk stay at the white brick house. But they would not have their way. There were now young neighbors with new ideas and fresh eyes. There were now old neighbors who were infuriated with what was happening. There were even blind neighbors who now took notice. There were poor neighbors, outcast neighbors, and homeless neighbors who all wanted their voices to be heard. And they were.

It's a year later and the grey house is now occupied by a new man; a man with a hope and a vision to guide the house and the neighborhood. The neighbors are very happy and excited about him. He works hard on the garden, trying to fix the damage done to the cherry tree and the oak tree hole, the weeds and the grass. He works hard and inspires the people. They look back on the days of their old neighbor with sadness, though they know that future days may be better. And they have hope.

The Wall
Eamon Aloyo
Lehigh University, Bethlehem, PA

"The world, with the United States included, stood idly by while Nazi Germany rose to power. Desperate pleas were heard from those targeted for extermination by the evil fascists of yesteryear. For far too long, those cries were ignored. Now, the civilized people of the world have an opportunity to stop another ghastly catastrophe before it escalates any further."

This IS World War III
Eric Kohn
Millikin University, Decatur, IL

There is a tired cliché that seems as ancient as the topic to which it refers: those who do not learn from history are doomed to repeat it.

If I send my high school world history text book to the leaders of Russia, Spain, Germany, and France, will you guys promise to read it?

We are reliving history right now. We find ourselves in a time warp, back sixty some years. Only this time, the circumstances seem to be inverted. Sixty-plus years ago, a horrible tyrant rose to power in Germany. He was bent on world domination and the extermination of entire segments of the world's population who didn't measure up in his eyes. Years of appeasement and disregarding the problem only escalated the situation further.

Finally, the line was crossed when the nation of Poland was invaded. Immediately, threatened nations implored the rest of the world, most specifically the United States, to join their cause and defeat the fascist regime of Nazi Germany. Sadly, for years the United States resisted entering the war, desperately clinging to a failed ideology of isolationism and the faux-safety that it provided. That illusion was shattered on a bright December morning in 1941, when America was attacked on her own soil.

Now, change the names of a few nations and reread the last couple of paragraphs making a vital substitution: replace the December, 1941 morning with a September, 2001 morning.

Does it look frighteningly familiar?

What's the only major difference? Now, it's the United States that is begging the rest of the world to wake up to the reality of this grave and unimaginably horrific state of affairs.

And, tragically, it's the rest of the world that has been slow to recognize the demon of Islamic fascist terrorism beating down our door.

The Spaniards and the Spanish government have assumed the World War II role of the French. When two hundred innocent civilians were slaughtered in the rail yards of Madrid, they opted to roll over and surrender. But, as the kidnapping of two French journalists in Iraq has shown, appeasement will buy no favor with this inhuman scum. The election of new pacifist socialist leaders will not keep Spain safe.

We watched in horror as a several tragedies befell the people of Russia. For years now, the region of Chechnya has been warring with Russia in an attempt to break away and form a theocratic Islamic society. Shortly before elections in the Chechen region, militant Islamic separatists brutally attacked the nation of Russia.

First, two planes were brought down shortly after leaving Moscow. Next, several car bombs exploded in the streets of Moscow. But, sadly, these were only preludes to the horror that would befall a school in southern Beslan.

Islamic terrorists – not "Chechen rebels," as they are so euphemistically dubbed by the partisan liberal American press in an attempt to disassociate this event from the greater war on terrorism – invaded and took 1500 men, women, and children hostage. In the end, they would slaughter over 350 people. Of those, over 150 were children.

This is all part of the same war the United States has been fighting since September 11th. Now, it's just been brought to a new front.

The United States finds itself in the unfortunate role of having to point to these horrific tragedies in other lands and convince the rest of the civilized world to join force with those that have already been fighting to rid the world of a new breed of hatred and malevolency.

The world, with the United States included, stood idly by while Nazi Germany rose to power. Desperate pleas were heard from those targeted for extermination by the evil fascists of yesteryear. For far too long, those cries were ignored.

Now, the civilized people of the world have an opportunity to stop another ghastly catastrophe before it escalates any further. September 11th should have been the final wake up call, but it was not. The Madrid bombings should have been the final wake up call, but they were not. We can only hope that this inhumane slaughter in southern Russia will awaken the rest of the world to the regrettable reality of our times.

The rest of the world can not afford to wait any longer. It's time to wake up to the lessons of history. They need to learn from our past mistake of delaying our seemingly inevitable involvement in the Second World War.

We are fighting World War III. And losing is not an option.

"The amazing and swift successes of the campaigns in Afghanistan and Iraq, coupled by the astonishingly quick turnaround time for establishing the road to free democracies, demonstrate the U.S.'s ability—under President Bush and his coalition of the willing—to work toward regional and world security."

Unilateralism, Multilateralism, and the War on Terror
Gregory P. LaVoy
Kalamazoo College, Kalamazoo, MI

All Americans wish that the country could live with the sense of security and harmony experienced prior to the terrorist attacks of September 11, 2001 - this is a given. Rather dangerously, however, many liberals have adopted this naïve and now obsolete worldview as the foundation for which to base the direction of American foreign policy, a policy they wish would make room for international consensus. This concept has been absorbed by liberal talking heads and many in the Democratic Party as an argument against war, but particularly against strong action by President Bush in his battle against Islamofascism.

As with most of the illogic that the left spews into American political culture, these ideas not only promote a brash misunderstanding of world politics, but also fail to provide a necessary plan for securing America's future. These politicians need to come to an understanding of some rather simplistic observations: the nature of our "traditional allies" has drastically changed; many of whom we thought were our allies are not our allies in the War on Terror; having broad support outside of these traditional barriers is not "unilateral" or "unacceptable" in any manner; and America cannot depend on other countries or international organizations for protection.

Much has been made over the past year of President Bush's "rush to war" without America's "allies" on board with the decision. Led by their Presidential nominee Senator John Kerry, the Democratic Party has seized this portrayal - however undeserved—as a major talking point in order to expose apparent "flaws" in the President's foreign policy.

Why do liberals and other pundits place an emphasis on who is willing to partake in military campaigns or who supports whom? What significance does it lend to whether or not America should act to protect itself from foreign threats? Why does it always seem that our "oldest" and "dearest" allies include everyone except those countries assisting the U.S.?

The straightforward solution to creating a foreign policy aimed at ensuring world security is to offer the world the opportunity to defend itself and preserve its security. However, a coalition of countries should not be prohibited from pursuing such security when others choose not to partake; this composes the logic behind President Bush's "coalition of the willing." Bush's policy and willingness to recruit and work with other states through international organizations (particularly the U.N.) has been grossly mischaracterized into something of the Lone Ranger who shoots at anything that moves. The positive response by dozens of nations during the buildup to the Iraqi invasion, as well as many nations' proportional efforts at aiding the coalition's efforts in Afghanistan and Iraq lends credence to the argument that America has not "gone it alone" or pursued policy far removed from what should be considered commonsense.

Anti-Americanism has been fraught in Europe and elsewhere, and thus it should not surprise anyone if many nations and cultures around the world are not overly-willing to aid Americans in their epic battle against terrorism. The only perceptions with which we should be concerned are those attached to people who desperately want to kill us—they must be stopped. At the same time, the U.S. government should not blindly allow an anti-American trend purported by our "allies" to prevent action; after all, America was hated before Bush, and America will be hated after Bush. The process to change the non-lethal "hearts and minds" should commence as soon as America's security is ensured.

After all, this desire to be well liked and create a policy that is accepted by foreign leaders is an idea better suited for junior-high cheerleading gossip than that of ensuring American security. In order to guarantee America's national security, the U.S. cannot submit to the desires of appeasement or be unwilling to act because of foreign leaders' national interests. The attempt to govern the world by international consensus through institutions like the U.N. has been a fruitless exercise executed in a state of sheer inadequacy for handling emergencies and security threats. Instead of belittling the determination and sacrifices of our true allies who responded to the President's call to ensure security while also bemoaning the absences of those who did not, liberals (and all Americans) should laud the accomplishments and focus on what America can do in the future to help these newly-reorganized states. When the U.S. sees a direct threat, it must be willing and able to respond with direct action; that is, action that is unimpeded by foreign special interests.

As the undisputed world hegemon, the U.S. will naturally take the lead and bear the biggest costs of fighting world terrorism, particularly when action comes as a response to a devastating terrorist attack and a preemptive attempt at preventing future attacks. This reality further becomes apparent in the realization that the battle against Islamofascism is the battle for the preservation of Western culture, ideology, religion, et cetera—all of which the U.S. gloriously and unrepentantly represents. The amazing and swift successes of the campaigns in Afghanistan and Iraq, coupled by the astonishingly quick turnaround time for establishing the road to free democracies, demonstrate the U.S.'s ability—under President Bush and his coalition of the willing—to work toward regional and world security.

The Democrats' plan to secure America consists of "returning to America's traditional allies" and other structures of world government - dubious strategies that promise neither to secure America's future of have any impact on the reality of world politics. President Bush has presented a doctrine - he has given America a plan. It says: "you screw with us, and we are going to mess you up big time - we are no longer going to tiddle around and lay waste to an aspirin factory, but rather we are going to roll through your streets and overwhelm" - shock and awe at its best. The President has given America a system that has been twice implemented against two of (what were) the greatest threats to American security, and now offer two of the greatest opportunities to showcase American goodwill. This type of action that is inclusive of - but not run by - world concerns while obtrusively showing America's demands for security compose the only type of policy that will enable a continually prosperous and safe America.

The bottom line - however unilateral or nationalistic it may sound - remains that the United States must look out for her own security, and decisions regarding such a vitally important issue cannot be delegated to a Gallup poll of foreign leaders or collective world thought. International relations in the anarchic system in which we find ourselves is burdened by power-struggles and threats where alliances must be formed to ensure a future of freedom. As such, the U.S. government has the responsibility of ensuring America's security, and if that means stepping on political toes, further enraging so-called allies, or acting outside of accepted diplomatic perimeters, by all means, please get started.

Waiting

Brittny Nielsen
Seattle University, Seattle, WA

Holding hands and breath, we wait...
Long to hear the news that we know is not coming
Closing our eyes, just listening to the words
Stumbled over by a leader
We whisper, the word is "nuCLEar."
If he can't say the word, should he be making the claim?
My grandma calls and she is afraid too,
She's seen several wars in her lifetime.
Why is this one different?
It's the bombs, the bombs used against people
People like us...
He justifies the pain with threats
But we know, we know they are just like us
Did we forget that it happened to us?
How we felt when we were attacked?
We have not solved the problem with more violence
The hatred and pain still exist, perpetuated by revenge
War does not make peace, trite, but true
Little sister, oh little sister,
The world is not safe for you.
We tried to make it safe for you
I wanted to make it safer for you
But they didn't listen.
I walked down streets with my heart in my hands
And they turned their backs on us,
They said we were just a focus group.
You say you don't understand the world
Don't know what's going on here
But the people there are just like us

Remember they are people. just. like. us.
Preemptive strike or religious war
War against terrorism or war against people who are different
What is the difference?
People who are people but believe in different things are murdered
Under the name of freedom.
We were made fun of, called un-American,
Called un-patriotic while they ate their stupid freedom fries
Looking for someone else to blame, someone else to hate
Until they realize they now hate themselves
And peace could've been the first option.
We will still be here, listening, waiting for them to understand
What we said made sense in the first place.
Soon it will no longer be his problem
But will we still be alive to tell them
We knew that they were people like us,
We knew that they were people too.

Social

Reflections

"But what do we mean by the American Revolution? Do we mean the American war? The Revolution was effected before the war commenced. The Revolution was in the minds and hearts of the people; a change in their religious sentiments, of their duties and obligations...This radical change in the principles, opinions, sentiments, and affections of the people was the real American Revolution."
        -John Adams

"Many Americans continue to ask, is the race still on? Are minorities still at the same disadvantage, or has equality been reached with American universities? I believe that the race is still on, and predominantly middle to upper class Caucasian students are still being given systematic priority."

Affirmative Action and the University of Michigan: Will it Stay or Go?
Jenica Mariani
Santa Clara University, Santa Clara, CA

W hat can be done in order to preserve the purpose of affirmative action? I believe that affirmative action, specifically in light of the *Grutter v. Bollinger* case, will need to be redefined into a race-conscious economic form of affirmative action. In this policy both conservatives and liberals alike will be able to compromise and come to constitutionally supported agreement.

Former President Harry Truman predicted that equal opportunity education would become a pivotal issue in the lives of Americans, more than fifty years before it happened. The President stated, "If college opportunities are restricted to those in the high income brackets, the way is open to the creation and perpetuation of a class society which has no place in the American way of life" (Kahlenberg, 9). Although Truman might not have envisioned the implementation of affirmative action, he was able to recognize that education, and thus power and money's unequal distribution could not ethically become a lasting characteristic in American society.

From when the ideal of affirmative action was first referenced in 1961 under President John F. Kennedy, race-based acceptance policies in American undergraduate and graduate competitive institutions have received a wide range of responses, from intense enthusiasm to strong opposition. Now, twenty-five years after the monumental *Bakke v. The Regents of California* case that changed the face of affirmative action permanently, particularly in California, race-based admission policies are being threatened at the University of Michigan in both the undergraduate and law school programs. This time, if the University of Michigan loses and is unable to continue utilizing affirmative action policies, it will undoubtedly affect how policies are run in universities nation-wide.

It was only fifty years ago that *Brown v. Board of Education* (1954) overturned *Plessy v. Ferguson* (1896), which had legalized segregated school systems in the United

States under the assumption of "separate but equal." This ideal was recognized as unattainable due to the nature of separation once it was overturned. Chief Justice Earl Warren spoke for the court in the ruling of *Brown v. the Board of Education*. Warren explained: "[Education] is a principal instrument in awakening a child to cultural values, in preparing him for later professional training, and in helping him to adjust normally to his environment. In these days, it is doubtful that any child may reasonably be expected to succeed in life if he is denied the opportunity of an education. Such an opportunity, where the state has undertaken to provide it, is a right with must be made available to all on equal terms" (Krugler, 117).

In the spirit of equality, affirmative action was formed. This form of equality that affirmative action was intended to represent was symbolic of America's long overdue response to racism and discrimination, as it had inhibited minority groups in the fields of education and employment since the birth of the Constitution. President Lyndon Johnson was the first to speak specifically about affirmative action. On June 4th, 1965, he spoke at the Howard University graduation. The President stated:

> *You do not wipe away the scars of centuries by saying: 'now, you are free to go where you want, do as you desire, and choose the leader you please.' You do not take a man who for years has been hobbled by chains, liberate him, bring him to the starting line of a race, saying, 'you are free to compete with all the others,' and still justly believe you have been completely fair...We seek not just freedom, but opportunity – not just legal equity, but human ability – not just equality as a right and a theory, but equally as a face and as a result (Timeline of Affirmative Action...)*

Many Americans continue to ask, is the race still on? Are minorities still at the same disadvantage, or has equality been reached with American universities? I believe that the race is still on, and predominantly middle to upper class Caucasian students are still being given systematic priority. It is worth mentioning that significant improvements in increasing diversity on U.S. campuses, particulary in the public state university systems have been made. Most diversity problems are present at private universities, such as Santa Clara, where the university has yet to create significant growth in the economic and racial diversity of their student body.

At the University of Michigan, the undergraduate admissions policy makes a conscious and successful effort to offer admission to African-American and Latino applicants due to their historical lack of representation in American universities. During the undergraduate admissions process students are assessed on a 150-point scale. Twenty points are added to students who are part of a racial or ethnic group that has minimal representation at the University. There are two opposing arguments to the advantage that these students receive. President George W. Bush responded in opposition to Michigan's affirmative action program, specifically to the grading criteria. During his televised reply concerning the case, the President stated "...the method used by the University of Michigan...is fundamentally flawed...At the undergraduate level, [underrepresented minorities] receive 20 points out of a maximum of 150, not because of any academic achievement or life experience, but solely because [of their race]."

In the definition of "life experience," the President ignores a crucial notion that one's particular race most often is intertwined with one's understanding of life, or "life experience." What race, ethnicity or culture one belongs to greatly affects his or her perceptions, opportunities, and treatment in American society. President Bush's proposal of percentage plans as a race-neutral solution is also fundamentally defective, essentially because these programs are dependent on segregated K-12th schools. It is not representative of a progressive or long-term plan to support the advancement of American minorities.

Kweisi Mfume, president of the NAACP, a strong supporter of affirmative action, responded in opposition to Bush's speech. Mfume has observed how privilege in education has been granted to other groups (or specifically Americans of European descent) for decades before implementation of minority supportive affirmative action programs. Mfume states, "Affirmative action has been enjoyed by various groups for three centuries. As a lawful means of remedying present and past discrimination...it is still the right thing to do to level the playing field and a proven way to increase diversity."

The judges of the simultaneous cases against the University of Michigan in its undergraduate and law school admissions programs are also in disagreement. U.S. District Judge Patrick J. Duggan sustained the University's affirmative action policy in *Gratz v. Bollinger* in December of 2000. Jennifer Gratz, who was a white 1995 applicant to the undergraduate program, claimed that, in light of *Bakke v. The Regents of California*, she had been rejected because of Michigan's racial quota policy and reverse discrimination. Lee Bollinger, the represented of the University of Michigan, and the defendant, was able to maintain the policy under the guidelines that "race as a plus factor" had been recognized as constitutional. The University "argued it was not a quota system because there was no fixed percentage of minorities to be admitted to the school." (Kjos) They also referenced Justice Lewis Powell from the Bakke case, who found it constitutional to use a "plus factor system." Powell stated:

> *The experience of other university admissions programs, which take race into account in achieving the educational diversity valued by the First Amendment, demonstrates that the assignment of a fixed number of places to a minority group is not a necessary means toward that end... In such an admissions pro gram, race or ethnic background may be deemed a "plus" in a particular appli cant's file...(Backgrounder...)*

When the University was again sued for discrimination by another white female applicant, Barbara Grutter, after she had been denied admission to the law school when she applied in 1996, they were alarmed by Justice Bernard A. Friedman's ruling that their policy was unconstitutional. Suddenly, two separate branches of the University had come under scrutiny and two opposite rulings had taken place. As of this writing, both cases have been appealed and are the headed to the Supreme Court for a final decision. The decisions that will be made this summer will be pivotal in the future of affirmative action on campuses nationwide.

A new phenomenon that has been observed is the role of economic status of the applicant as well. Richard Kahlenberg of the Century Foundation, a research organization that investigates major economic, social, and political issues, has suggested the possibility of economic-based affirmative action program, rather than strictly race-based policies. Kahlenberg states:

> *Racial preference, by contrast, is not a reliable proxy for disadvantage. While it is true that blacks and Latinos are disproportionately poor, racial affirmative action currently benefits the most advantaged minority students disproportion ately, and does little help poor and working class students of color. (Kahlenberg, 3)*

During the Civil Rights era, President Johnson described that societal "chains" had been placed on American minorities, inhibiting them from having access to all of their civil rights. As society changes, the constitution must also progress. If affirmative action was originally designed to help minorities during a time when being a minority could have a parallel of classification of having an economic disadvantage, and this phenomenon is changing, this change must be observed. I am not suggesting that race-based affirmative action policies be removed; I am merely suggesting that students who are of a minority background and are also economically disadvantaged should be recognized as the main beneficiary of affirmative action policies. Not only have these students lived the experience of a racial minority in the United States, but also have economic backgrounds that need the support of affirmative action, as well as financial aid, in order to make college possible. As Chief Justice Warren said, "…it is doubtful that any child may reasonably be expected to succeed in life if he is denied the opportunity of an education." (Kugler,) Now, fifty years later, education, particularly college education, is a needed tool for access to at least a middle class lifestyle. If an American citizen has the intelligence, drive, persistence and desire to obtain higher education, his/her efforts should be rewarded by society lending him or her a helping hand, if so needed.

A policy that recognizes socio-economic stance has been backed by liberals and conservatives alike. Conservative Supreme Court Justice Antonin Scalia has been a supporter of economic affirmative action for decades. In response to *Bakke v. The Regents of California*, Scalia, who was a professor at the University of Chicago at the time, endorsed an economic-based affirmative action policy. Scalia stated:

> *I am…opposed to racial affirmative action …I do not, on the other hand, oppose – indeed, I strongly favor – what might be called… "affirmative action programs" of many types of help for the poor and disadvantaged. It may well be that many, or even most of those benefited by such programs would be mem bers of minority races that the existing programs exclusively favor. I would not care if all of them were. The unacceptable vice is simply selecting or rejecting them on a basis of their race (Scalia).*

Many parts of Scalia's 1978 assertion would not be valid - for instance, the assumption that programs aimed at helping the "poor and disadvantaged" would exclusively help minorities. He also adamantly dismisses the plights of minorities in American society, and for this reason I believe that his overall argument is flawed. It is ignorant and racist to ignore the repercussions of past injustices incurred by targeted minority groups as a result of their skin color as a direct result of American government and societal policies and practices. As Kweisi Mfume stated, "Affirmative action has always been seen as a lawful means of remedying present and past discrimination." (Kjos)

Forty years ago, affirmative action was implemented in order to combat discrimination and social constructions that did not treat white and minority citizens as equals. Those forty years have now passed, and in light of the University of Michigan case, American society, university leadership, politicians and justices have been forced to examine its progress once again. Although lives of minorities have arguably improved with the implementation of civil rights and affirmative action, there is still a parallel racial and economic divide. Until these two factors can no longer be seen in American universities, workforce, media, entertainment and overall society, policies making up for the economic and racial advantages that some of us are born with should be afforded to others who do not receive them at birth. It is the government's moral duty to offer all American citizens equal opportunities as much as possible. Until equal access is reached, programs like race-conscious economic-based affirmative action should be designed, and strictly race-based policies, as a secondary solution, should be left intact.

"Perpetuating this hypersensitivity will not find Osama bin Laden, will not aid the war on terrorism, nor will it prevent further attacks from penetrating our borders. These are the preeminent issues that need to be dealt with, rather than wasting energy to police the open-forum for "treasonous" statements."

America Is Under Attack
Galena Mosovich
Temple University, Philadelphia, PA

America is under attack. Bolded on the top of every newspaper and flashed at the bottom of every television screen for the past month, this broad statement denotes more than the obvious threat to our nation. In reality, the repercussions of the Sept. 11 attack resonate further than New York and Washington. The principles that are the foundation of our country have been defaced.

One of the greatest American liberties is the First Amendment, which guarantees freedom of speech, freedom of the press, and freedom of association and assembly.

Some recent occurrences can be considered an indubitable violation of these rights, and thus a breach of American democracy.

ABC's *Politically Incorrect with Bill Maher* stirred some serious controversy over a Sept. 17 broadcast. Following a vague discussion of President Bush's characterization of the terrorists as cowards, two major sponsors, a dozen affiliates, and even the White House denounced the late-night talk show ironically as both incorrect and unacceptable.

In this disputed discussion with the evening's four panelists Maher said, "we have been the cowards, lobbing cruise missiles from 2,000 miles away. That's cowardly. Staying in the airplane when it hits the building, say what you want about it, it's not cowardly."

This type of dialogue, however, is typical for the fast-paced show in which provocative thoughts are barely completed before other challenging topics are introduced.

In order to clarify Maher's initial statement, he released an apology to those who misinterpreted his point and expressed gratitude to ABC for its unconditional support.

Among other consequences, Federal Express and Sears pulled their advertising, and the White House press secretary, Ari Fleischer warned that "people have to watch what they say and watch what they do."

Alexis de Tocqueville is officially rolling over in his grave.

This statement from the government calls for immediate attention. Americans have the right to address issues and express opinions without fear of losing sponsors. The second that the country is told, in not so many words, to execute this scary kind of political correctness, it is obvious that a serious problem is in the making.

Perpetuating this hypersensitivity will not find Osama bin Laden, will not aid the war on terrorism, or prevent further attacks from penetrating our borders. These are the preeminent issues that need to be dealt with, rather than wasting energy to police the open-forum for "treasonous" statements.

As Maher said on a recent broadcast, "you can be in opposition and not be committing treason."

Regardless of whether an opinion is pleasing to the ear or not, Americans are still guaranteed the right to speak their minds. The ability to disagree is the foundation of our country; it is the beauty of our nation; it is what we are fighting for. If censoring this beauty is a priority, then we should take notes from our enemy.

"I believe we all looked at the world and each other differently after the attack. When hate was directed at us, we retaliated with hope and love for each other."

An American Bond
John Teresi
Southern Illinois University, Carbondale, IL

1 098 days have passed since dual airplanes ripped through the translucent New York skyline and crashed into American history. Approximately 26,352 hours ago I realized what it was like to feel patriotism.

September 11, 2001 was a day when all of our families grew larger. Many started the day thinking of their neighbors, friends, and acquaintances as "them" and ended the day realizing that "them" is actually "us."

On that disheartening autumn day, all Americans had emotions in common: pain, anger, and loss. Many did not realize the extent of the horror until days after it happened. For others, like myself, the realization was immediate.

A friend of mine watched the towers fall from the windows of her New York City high school and fell to her knees when she witnessed the second plane collide with the 100,000 ton steel tower. The azure sky was reshaped and polluted with a palette of black, gray, orange, and red fire racing towards the sky.

On 9/11, Americans found more in common with each other than ever realized. We traded in our political affiliations for unity. Our ethnicities and backgrounds were ignored. We traded in our differences for the commonality that we were all American. As Americans, we realized that the people who died in the World Trade Center were not just New Yorkers. They were Americans. They were patriots. They were our brothers and sisters.

Although we may not be related or may not have known the victims of that horrible event, we saw ourselves in them. We felt the pain that a woman on the 102nd floor felt when she phoned her husband for the last time to let him know that she wasn't going to make it, but that she was going to be OK. We found ourselves hurting with the man on the other line that told her he loved her and that she shouldn't be scared. We had the angry feeling deep in our stomachs that our soldiers had when they said, "Someone is going to pay for this."

Many of us sped in our cars to give blood, donate money, or send cards and letters to the families that had the deepest losses of all. When all blood centers were full, we had no problem being put on a waiting list, and coming back the next day. We would have done whatever we had to do.

The weeks following September 11th were barraged with patriotism. Many stores were sold out of American flags as soon as the shipment was delivered. Cars drove down the streets displaying red, white, and blue flags, signs, and artwork. One car that I passed had a sticker that read, "I am a proud Muslim, and I am a proud American." I believe we all looked at the world and each other differently after the attack. When hate was directed at us, we retaliated with hope and love for each other.

After the tragedy of 9/11, we can all agree with the philosopher George Santayana, who said, "A man's feet must be planted in his country, but his eyes should survey the world." A strong stance has been taken and we have been safe. There have not been any attacks on U.S. soil since September 11th. I am overwhelmingly thankful that our great country is still safe and confident. No matter what differences we have, there is a common bond that we all share that is more important than any other: we are American.

"Commodity has also taken hold of how we see ourselves - bodies ready for tightening, a mind ready for education. Yet we can run going nowhere and go to school without learning."

Before I Sleep
Christopher Continanza
Villanova University, Villanova, PA

Before sleep I lie down and watch a little television. Nothing special, just the same old History Channel show trying to sensationalize bulldozers. Then we cut to commercial. Suddenly my boredom turns to fantasy and fetish. The SUV commercial shows me just how far to the ends of the earth I could drive should I so choose (and find a road). And as I laugh at how stupid the marketing campaign is, I begin to fantasize about driving off-road in the backwoods of wherever. That could be interesting. I could build a whole new self - I could be the rugged man who drives on whatever road he pleases because that's just what he does. Then people would notice me...but before all this happens I catch myself and wonder - just what have I become? Is it true? Could I be just another victim of consumer culture?

The oft-lauded consumer culture is a system of beliefs that is at worst destroying all meaning and at best eroding it. But why and how? And do you even care? Essentially, consumer culture can allow you to read this discourse (if you've made it this far) and go away unchallenged in your daily life.

It is this disconnect - driving a wedge between theory and practice - that consumerism has created. It is not a different ideology in which people value materialism or hedonism compared to the "truer" values and the "greater good." Rather, it is a disposition towards values in general. It is a way in which we engage all as things removed from a history, from a context, and treat them as they are without any question as to how they got there.

Take a trip to the music store. In front of the eyes lie myriad choices of CDs to choose from. What informs this epic decision? What "jumps out" at us in the store? This is where all that money invested into advertising pays off. The plastic-wrapped women (and men) are highly sexualized and provoke other desires than what music we like - we're no longer buying CDs, we're purchasing our self. The glistening aisles promise acceptance and renewal, sacrifice and salvation. And as much as we love to hate pop music, the "hard core" bands are wearing just as much makeup. Their muted or offensive packaging is marketed to those who don't want the corporate nonsense, shrink wrapped by the very corporation you hate, I hate, and the artist hates so much he wrote a song about it. The CDs the store wants to sell are placed at the front and ranked from one to ten so you can walk away and feel like you bought a winner. They are disseminated into genres to the point where if you want something that doesn't fit into one you get to play guess-the-closest-genre until you're at it. There is something wrong going on here.

The problem with consumerism is not Britney Spears. It's that the same people (the corporations - who if they don't own the label own the store or maybe the venue you caught the show at) sell me my NOFX, whose last album's political dissent would have made the Dixie Chicks blush. The problem is that all choices, even dissent, become consumer choices. Even the multitudes of genres, which attempt to cater to different tastes, are still just using taste to generate sales. Yet all hope is not lost. With the widespread availability of home recording devices, the price for making your own original album doesn't have to cost more than a paycheck. This provides the consumer with an unprecedented chance for authorship and resistance.

But resistance to what? The goal, of course, is to sell the platinum record. Any success at home will be bought up, re-recorded, re-mastered, and re-mixed. Maybe some lyrics will get edited or maybe they won't so it's still "edgy." Either way a core essence of what made the original original will be lost in the name of repetition. And let us not forget those who cannot afford to play the game. While I figure out my new Tascam US-122 home recording solution, someone is starving. Yet I don't go out to give this Other anything - I wouldn't even know where to start. Already capitalism has me chasing new toys - the home recording device. And that's how it wins. Were we originally searching for meaning here? Soon the autonomy of music-recording becomes a fetish to build the best studio. Soon my pity for the starving Other is subsumed in my fickle desires and I become at first distracted and then just disinterested - I'll donate extra on Sunday.

This process is erosion. Desires for profundity are soon made flat into an insatiable desire for more. Every time I watch the commercial or I go shopping for music or I buy anything I employ these consumer methods of engagement. Desire, then, is no longer something that can take root and grow into a passion. Instead its roots never gain hold, constantly told to buy, not use, and then buy more. What is bought becomes inconsequential to the act of purchasing itself. The self becomes an empty slate in which new sensations can entice and seduce but never foster a commitment even if commitment drives the desire.

And as bad as this all seems to be, it is too easy to assume that people are just going along with this blindly. The truth is that this potential for the loss of meaning is affecting all of us. We see it with the "seeker": trying on religions for size but with the jury ultimately out. Do we conceptualize this person as just a mere mark capable of being duped by simple sleights of hand? Isn't this person really looking for something more in which they can identify themselves? The problem, then, is not with what the seeker is seeking, and not with the seeker himself. The problem is the disjointed insertion of consumerism between the two.

In our engagement of everything as commodity, we forget about its history. Most people shriek at the task of servicing their home computer, yet we all own one (and they're really not so bad). The ability to secure income has replaced our ability to do; we can all too easily pay for it to be repaired or have tech support tell us what to do rather than actually figure it out. The ability to have money becomes the only ticket to safety and security so long as it is the only skill we have. Even if you mastered the computer, you still have to pay the electric bill to keep it running. Thus a steady income becomes the foundation for security and as we rush into these jobs to pay these bills and establish security, we develop a false sense of loneliness. Not only are the traditional avenues of help eroded (we're no longer summoning neighbors to raise the barn), the new system has everyone so locked into wage-dependency we cannot afford to part with our own paychecks to help someone in need. So alone we sit in a house full of our own stuff - wanting to do more in a real, concrete way but deprived of the means and methods of doing so.

Yet this deprivation of methods is not "the man" trying to cover it all up under lock and key (unless you're George W.); the corporations are working in their best interests. Our inaction is just as much an effect of our own changing formulation of desire. In an arena where want is constant and the choices are innumerable, a Hamlet-esque paralysis can almost be a safe haven compared with the consumer fear of losing choices or "missing out" on the better lie. There is, after all, an unprecedented social mobility in consumer culture. Now is the time where in just one generation a family can go from poor to affluent, but this is not without a price. In the end, the social ladder has become this every-man-for-himself-as-we-run-from-a-flaming-city-while-clutching-our-worthless-earthly-possessions rat race. We see tax cuts as liberating us to spend more freely while the programs keeping homeless off the streets get thrown aside. As good as autonomy is, it is useless without a community in which to be autonomous. Consumer culture sidesteps some of the tougher issues of community by giving us symbols to use instead of practices to adhere to and places in which to do so. For consumer culture the only community is the mall: an ocean of individuals each motivated for his or her own purchases amidst a sea of advertising promising just about everything. This is just an afternoon; this becomes everyday life. Although consumer desire for more is a profound insatiability, it is never a concentrated desire - it never finds a place to grow deep. Consumer desire is not Augustine's call to God, for there is a certain freedom in the commitment to one. Rather, there is merely the desire for more which is manipulated by the controllers of mainstream distribution in order to turn a profit. Commitment becomes eroded as we slowly turn to more commodities for more fulfillment. The self as molded by these forces is a poor fighter against them: easily duped into commiditying his or her own rebellion. Where are the great college protests of my day? Where are the great traditions I can embrace? At first it seems that we are doomed to the shallow end of the pool of existence. This writer, however, finds hope in that real people are smarter than that.

It is hard to highlight the problem and even harder to pose a solution. I don't have the solution to end all, but I think the right start begins in acknowledging the Other, and I mean really seeing someone as a person. Commodity has also taken hold of how we see ourselves- bodies ready for tightening, a mind ready for education. Yet we can run with going nowhere and go to school without learning. The Other, too, can be engaged as an instrument to self-fulfillment. We view mates as composite lists of pros and cons, and love becomes an equation. We see ourselves as moldable clay, but most New Year's Resolutions fail - we have the desire, but we lack the follow-through. This is another example of how our methods of engagement spill over into all practices, facing us with the chance to have all meaning evaporate from right beneath us.

Instead, we have to regain our sense of mystery. There is a certain respectful curiosity in trying to figure out what something really is as opposed to just figuring out what elements of it are useful. And we also owe it to ourselves to realize we are in the process of history-making. There is no thing that appears from nothing. The commodities we see have histories and as consumers we can make informed choices or even choose to produce things ourselves. We have to stop seeing this as a problem but as our problem. We have to take a personal stake in these matters. We have to care.

But this is just a suggestion pointing towards a different way of looking at the world. Any step out of consumer choice will still start from consumer choice, and the danger in new ideology is reaction - in creating something different for the sake of having something else to believe, leading us to commodify our ideals. We have the autonomy to take an active decision in all choices we make, and once aware can begin to see how deep consumer culture penetrates. The repose and peace that our radical human freedom should allow us to have is replaced with the ever-seducing myth that just over the edge of the next flaming piece of trash is happiness. This writer, however, finds hope in that real people are smarter than that.

"One could say the arrangement of the room itself was a reflection of our democratic ideals, a government where the power resides, theoretically among the people, not polarized in one man."

Citizenship Project
Patrick Sciacchitano
George Mason University, Fairfax, VA

While most of my college colleagues were cavorting on various beaches around the sunny sides of the world and sacrificing their brains to the god of Spring Break, alcohol, my fellow classmate, Bryan, decided to go with me to the Capitol to pay a visit to Congress. Although nothing out of the extraordinary, the two hours we spent watching the top brass of the military high command sweat under the scrutiny of their congressmen (and congresswomen!) were a most interesting and informative experience. What I shall describe will focus mainly upon the interactions and group dynamics among the principle figures, their relations and contacts with the observers, and a short description of the subject of the hearing. All of these observations will be in the context and relation with the democratic theory, and process of our government.

Before I speak of the group dynamics among the government officials themselves, I think it is necessary to illustrate the setting in which these interactions took place. My somewhat ignorant picture of a congressional hearing always (somehow) occurred on the floor of Congress, with the leading speakers from either party giving impassioned diatribes to whoever was there. I suppose that it is quite a popular view as well, given that is what we often see on CNN, and I suppose as well that is why CNN chooses to cover these dramatic gatherings. One instantly recalls Republican congressman Tom Tancredo lecturing an empty House chamber on C-SPAN – quite an incredible piece of acting. It seems that the real work is done in the committees, while the House and Senate floors serve as soap-boxes.

What we instead found was a nondescript, though rather large committee building next to the Capitol – the Rayburn. The room itself was quite grand and dignified, with plush trappings and fine oak. Equally grand and dignified were the enormous portraits of various congressmen around the room, who I suspect were former heads of this particular committee. The congressmen's seats were arranged in such a way that no one position remained in glaring prominence, the portraits were arranged in a similar manner; in fact, only one spot was truly a focal point, the wall directly behind the middle seat of the upper row, on which hung our flag. One could say the arrangement of the room itself was a reflection of our democratic ideals, a government where the power resides, theoretically among the people, not polarized in one man.

Before I had been admitted into the actual chamber itself and been awed by its resplendent trappings, I amused myself by watching some of the army officers outside griping about their duties. One could tell these were desk-jockeys, some who were old war-horses nearing their retirement. They were all part of the generals' (or admirals') entourages, taking scrupulous notes and perhaps finding loopholes in the congressman's statements when his attention lapsed. In fact, there was a great sense of camaraderie and fellowship among these officers, especially, it seemed, among the higher-ranking ones.

While the army buddies caught up with each other about the old times, the other observers, various staffers, aides, or gophers from government or private agencies were not as congenial. One female staffer went so far as to move a seat away from me for no apparent reason. Am I that repulsive? Is it so hard to say hi? It seemed like these robots were the ones on leave from the front lines. Apart from the robot staffers and the armed forces, there was not a single, patriotic, freedom loving, citizen of America attending the hearing besides Bryan, myself, and an aged lady in the back who, judging by her ruffled dress, which was covered with numerous political buttons and stickers (they were on her hat also), seemed to spend quite a lot of her time in these meetings. Something about her demeanor and appearance made me suspect she was a third-party gopher. Perhaps the candidate herself!

Though somewhat troubling, the absence of my fellow citizens was not shocking; we are after all rather apathetic and elected these people to run the government for us so we could concentrate on getting rich – the "important" stuff. It seems that most of us have chosen to elect trustees rather than delegates, though how many of us have the time to observe the full mechanics of Congress? I think what is more important is that we need to realize that much of what we are fed on TV or read in the papers has undergone much transformation, meddling, polishing, and media posturing. The great Athenian leader Pericles once said in his famous *Funeral Oration*, "we do not say that a man who takes no interest in politics is a man who minds his own business, we say that he has no business here at all"

So we come at last to the actual dialogue, though as you probably have already noticed, observing the preliminaries was interesting itself, especially to one who has never seen such a proceeding. The congressmen came in at different times, (most almost 45 minutes late!) sometimes in pairs, usually alone. You would think that allocating money for the defense would be a somewhat greater concern than whatever else they were bothered with at the moment. What I found quite touching was an unexpected warmth and congeniality between the congressmen and the officers. During the introductions, both sides frequently thanked each other for their help, and praised their achievements. It was a genuine exchange of compliments between the people in whom we place our trust. They were there to work together to lead our nation to a better future, not to squabble for power (though inevitably, they did squabble over other things, but not for the sake of squabbling itself or power). If they were, I could not detect it; for once, it seemed that partisan bitterness could be set aside. It instilled hope in me, that with good, honest people the system could work, and could cooperate to solve the challenges facing them.

The challenge at hand was indeed of utmost importance; the future of the armed forces and its new role in relation to the war on terrorism. This subcommittee was but one microcosm of this burgeoning transformation – the allocation of the money to propel such a change. Essentially, the Generals were asking Congress for more money to convert their troops into more mobile units that could be rapidly deployed throughout the world. In addition, such a transformation would allow the military to maintain more deployments and missions abroad with less troops. Such a proposal was designed and long sought to alleviate a significant problem the military has been grappling with since the end of the Cold War: how to maintain a potent presence abroad with a diminishing pool of troops. Personally, I think that these new "mobile" divisions are a band-aid treatment, a good start, but a temporary treatment nonetheless. Until more of us are willing to pick up the rifle, this problem isn't going to go away.

One particular aspect that utterly astounded me was the abominable cost to equip and maintain our army! Adding three brigades alone would cost $2.9 billion dollars, with all the logistics and supporting units included. Training an additional 30,000 troops for three years would require a mere $74 million each year. I find it quite ironic that our Republic places supreme importance on our military, as evident by the unimaginable sums we spend on it, yet complain when the government increases its surveillance powers at home. Both are for our protection, yet it seems that when such protection infiltrates our living rooms, and is not conveniently at a far away place, like Bosnia or Azerbaijan, then we demand the luxuries of our freedom over security. The price of our liberty is indeed a hefty one.

One particularly charming congresswoman was quite intense in her inquiries. While the men seemed content to split hairs over costs, there seemed an almost implicit agreement between the congressmen and generals (all men) not to press and delve into the more fundamental questions. I felt that though they were concerned, they were more interested in passing the inquiries through and leaving the debate for a later time. The congresswoman thought otherwise. She pressed her questions, especially on the readiness of the troops in Iraq, and in particular if they were prepared for a civil war. Her foresight has been proven fairly astute, especially in light of the recent turmoil instigated by the firebrand Moqtada al-Sadr. However, the generals deftly deflected her questions with ambiguous and convoluted responses ("collateral damage" = innocent casualties). She was especially concerned with the treatment of women, and how the military treated female soldiers who were sexually abused. Sadly, the generals delivered the same deflections; one would think that this a "safer" zone where they could admit unpreparedness or inadequacy – God forbid such failings – yet, he convoluted himself out of the question again. It seemed to me this was a ritual that occurred often, and not just in this particular hearing. In fact, much time was spent by the officers explaining their terminology and jargon to the panel. However, as I think in retrospect, it may have been that particular subcommittee hearing was not the proper forum to voice the concerns the congresswoman had; perhaps another hearing was already in place for those other problems;

still, for whatever reason the congresswoman chose that time and place. Whether or not such a decision was expedient I shall never know.

There was an interesting commotion though during the break. but it failed to excite life into the robot staffers: a class of middle-schoolers from Missouri (so said their nametags) arrived to be bored to death. They had the look of children who would be interested temporarily by the new settings and would probably be amused while they had to sit through the field-trip. Really though, they would much rather have been in the Air and Space museum. I could tell. The officers were very friendly to them of course, what would excite a general more than potential recruits? I even recall one asking a student half-jokingly "when are you going to join the marines, son?"

If I have learned anything from attending this hearing, it is realizing the enormous amounts of revenue we spend for our defense. Never did I truly realize it until I heard these people speak of creating $500-million-dollar armored mobile divisions as if they were merely calculating the cost of their groceries. I cannot help now but see a price tag attached to every piece of equipment, and every division or unit insignia I see on TV. Such it seems, is the price of waging death. Indeed it should be expensive, or we would grow too fond of it, as Robert E. Lee once said. Our trip to Congress was quite enjoyable, interesting, and enlightening. There are times when the citizen feels distant from one's leaders – being close to them brings one closer to one's country as well. Perhaps that is why the staffers/robot gophers are so lifeless.

Dear World Leaders:

Allison Ranae Richardson
University of Kentucky, Lexington, KY

Dear World Leaders:

I just wanted to thank you for not recognizing the pandemic problem of AIDS. I suppose you thought, 'If we do not recognize HIV/AIDS then we do not need to do anything about it,' right? At the global level the number of people living with HIV continues to grow. The last time I checked the world was surpassing 38 million reported cases. Now how can that be true? HIV does not lead to AIDS, or so our nations are telling us. Why doesn't AIDS exist in YOUR world? Is it because you are too embarrassed to discuss sex, or can you not bring yourself to recognize homosexuality? Although how could I have forgotten that homosexuality doesn't exist in YOUR world either. Well I am here to say AIDS is real. AIDS exists in OUR world. It thrives within the world in which YOUR children play. Remember when you tuck YOUR children into bed at night that someday YOUR little girl or YOUR little boy may become infected with HIV. Then this tirade will be apart of YOUR world. Only at this point it will be too late. So while you stand over your children's grave, always know that you put them there. You turned YOUR back on them when you turned YOUR back on OUR world. William Lloyd Garrison once said "My country is the world, and my countrymen are mankind." My countrymen and I are not asking for war, genocide, or anarchy. We simply want some recognition.

Sincerely,

Our World

P.S. While you were reading this letter 3 people have died from AIDS and hundreds have become infected. I just thought you should know.

"His systemization defines white by sanguine, brawny, gentle, and inventive - all positive trademarks. Black, by contrast, has markedly negative implications: phlegmatic, crafty, indolent, and negligent."

Fictitious Image of Race
Zachary Foster
University of Michigan, Ann Arbor, MI

Race, defined by genetically discrete groups, does not exist. Instead, it is a culturally constructed typology invented to subjugate perceived differences (Linnaeus 1758: 425-426). Natural distribution of such traits as skin color, facial features, hair type, etc., occurs gradually rather than abruptly, with the alleged genetic markers inherited independently (Kottak 2004: 232). Cognitively, 'blackness' varies between societies, such as Brazil and the United States (Kottak 2004: 243-244). In other words, if white people are truly 'white' and blacks are in fact 'black' (besides the fact that black and white hues have little to do with actual skin color), than why would an American and a Brazilian look at the same person and conclude positively they are different races? Racialization reduces immensely contrasting peoples to cultural equals. Foraging bands in the tropics of Zimbabwe and wealthy capitalists in Johannesburg, for example, have little if anything in common. Race, therefore, has nothing to do with its assigned colors (white, black, red or yellow). Rather, it is the projection of ideas, characteristics, and roles illuminated by Max Weber in the Protestant Ethic. I must preface my analysis of race and the Protestant Ethic with the appreciation of this interminable fallacy. Thus, taxonomical racism or simply race is a result of the Protestant Ethic insofar as its ability to project the fictitious image of undesirable attributes within ego onto the racialized other is concerned.

It serves as a fitting introduction to mention that White and Black hues have starkly different word associations. A man named Charles Linnaeus's invented a typology of humans consisting of four races—European albus (Europeans), Americanus rubescens (Native Americans), Asiasticus fuscus (Asians) and Africanus Niger (Africans). His systemization defines white by sanguine, brawny, gentle, and inventive—all positive trademarks. Black, by contrast, has markedly negative implications: phlegmatic, crafty, indolent, and negligent. In a general sense, we irrationally connect white with peace, purity, angels, heaven, and virginity, while black is reflective of evil, desolation, sin, sex, and death. These quasi-synonyms are not insignificant. If the Puritan ethic rejects 'non-white' traits, then moral Protestants cannot be sinful, sexual, negligent, etc. The foregoing semantic idiosyncrasies are subconscious causes of the stereotypical images of 'black' people (discussed subsequently) by projecting a shadow of the unwanted self onto other racialized groups.

Beyond this dichotomous oddity yet embedded in the same racist framework is a set of immoral qualities believed germane to 'blacks.' The Protestant Ethic stresses hard work, asceticism, profit seeking, and sexual repression (Weber 1904: 155-183). It further denounces laziness and poverty (Weber 1904: 155-183). Moral 'Euro-American' Protestants, then, must be frugal, hard-working, and inhibit their sexuality. They must also be ethically and monetarily successful. Conversely, they cannot express their sexuality, be lazy, or fail to provide for their family. This is precisely the reason why 'African Americans' are stigmatized. According to Lamont, (2000) 'whites' perceptions of black moral failures center first and foremost on work ethic, self-reliance and socioeconomic status"(60). She continues to argue that a majority of 'white' Americans describe 'African Americans' as lazy and irresponsible. Vincent Marchesi, a technician, elucidates this deep-rooted opinion: "Blacks have a tendency to try to get off doing less…to keep the job, where whites put in the extra oomph…A lot of blacks on welfare have no desire to get off it…" (Lamont: 2000: 61). What's more, 'whites' readily linked 'African Americans' with violence and crime (Lamont: 2000: 64-5). When asked to verbally associate black men with sex, all students in sociology seminar at the University of Michigan quickly came up with the word "rape" (Paige 2003). While the aforementioned moral qualities exist in all groups, racialized or not, it is no coincidence that 'Euro-Americans' prove largely ignorant of this pattern. So, if race doesn't exist, then what is it? It is the projection of these attributes deemed unacceptable by the Protestant Ethic onto 'blackness.'

This projection is a colossal paradox. Euro-Americans were empirically the rapists. Plantation owners were infamous for having mistresses and raping slaves. Lynching often involved sexual atrocities. Black males frequently had their genitals heinously cut off (Paige 2003). The 'whites' devalued the African Americans' moral code; they beat them into subservient roles throughout the course of American history - slavery, semi-serfdom, segregation, and poverty (Paige: 10). By the barrel of the gun and the leather of the whip, white southerners violently coerced slaves to labor. In this sense, Euro-Americans were the lazy ones. While this characterization hardly speaks for all Euro-Americans, it aptly identifies the bedrock of American racism. These projections stem directly from the Protestant Ethic that compels 'whites' to attribute their own impulses (sex, violence, laziness etc.) onto African Americans.

What about those 'whites' who themselves demonstrate immoral and disliked characteristics of the proper Puritan ethic? Predictably, they are not considered white, but white trash. White trash is distinctively not white. It is disgusting and useless. White trash is, in fact, a racial identity in itself. "She [a woman living in Detroit] quite purposefully asserted that the term white trash conveyed a class-based divide between "people" and "trash" that was the same across the black/white racial divide" (Hartigan

Jr. 1997: 48). The term white trash is additionally reinforced by individuals "just above" this fantasy class divide (Hartigan Jr. 1997: 52). This trend irrefutably demonstrates the need to objectify other racialized factions of society. Just like skin pigmentation, 'white trash' and 'poor whites' form a continuum (Hartigan Jr. 1997: 53) that must be divided by those who believe so resolutely in the Protestant ethic.

Similarly, other racialized groups such as Native Americans and Asians experience the same fundamental consequences of racism. The basis for US citizenship was determined by race up until the mid 1960s (Lopez 1996: 37). In fact, in 1935 the U.S. was the only other country in the world aside from Hitler's Nazi Germany that limited naturalization to certain races (Lopez 1996: 44). Throughout the late nineteenth and early twentieth centuries, the US Supreme Court was unable to definitively determine who was white (Lopez 1996: 79-107). Asians are not white, but yellow. After all, they do not personify the White Protestant Ethic. According to Linnaeus, the man who invented race, Asians are melancholy, rigid, haughty, and covetous (Linnaeus 1758: 425-426). Native Americans, alternatively, originally were considered 'white' (Vaughan 1982: 917-921). While their cultural practices were labeled deplorable, they simply required the 'white man' to enlighten them (Vaughan 1982: 923-931). They were supposedly choleric, obstinate, content, and free (Linnaeus 1758: 425-426) - simply unacceptable Protestant values. As Linnaeus's racial typologies became well accepted, however, they turned from white to red. If race exists as biologically discrete groups, than how do the genetic codes of entire Native American tribes change from 'white' to 'redskin' in just a few decades? Moreover, how do Asians change the color of their skin from 'yellow' to 'white' by Supreme Court decisions?

In short, races are merely constructions of perceived differences that exist in the mind of the racializer, not in reality. Weber's Protestant Ethic amplifies these (violence, rape, laziness) and whites project these qualities onto African Americans. In turn, 'blacks' are then blamed for being poor because of the very reasons they lie in poverty in the first place: they are disproportionately lazy, criminals, drug and alcohol abusers, rapists, etc. Historically, however, the 'whites' (or racializers) acted on these ethical transgressions. Other racialized groups, such as white trash, Native Americans, and Asians are similarly stigmatized. Consequently, in order to eradicate the root cause of American Racism, we must promptly dismantle the social and moral implications of the Protestant Ethic.

"The intelligentsia in America's universities and the liberal elites in the media also bristle when Bush mentions evil. But these people are not reflective of the rest of the country."

Good and Evil

Jason C. Miller

Michigan State University, East Lansing, MI

P RAGUE – Nestled between a McDonald's and a casino – two clear signs of the changes since 1989's Velvet Revolution – just a few blocks from Wenceslas Square, one can find the Czech Republic's museum of communism. This is new Europe. The Czechs call themselves Central Europeans – pointing out that Prague is farther west than Austria's Vienna – and would rather not be lumped in with the less developed former Soviet republics. Even though they insist on different names, the Czechs still share a common identity with all of those escaping communism and embracing freedom. They are the prototype for the rest. Having elected strong conservative democrats and embraced a free market, they now enjoy a standard of living on par with Western Europe. The past represented in that museum gives the Czechs a worldview that is different from Western Europe and closer to that of America on many critical issues.

The museum could represent the past of any nation behind what Churchill labeled the Iron Curtain. It documents the bloody early stages of Lenin's and Stalin's regimes and the imposition of this ideology on the good people of Czechoslovakia. The museum continues with stories of life under the secret police and the danger of simply existing in the country after its Warsaw Pact neighbors invaded to crush the Prague Spring. Daring to think or act in support of freedom would land you in prison or worse. The Czechs know that the previous regime was evil.

The recently deposed regime in Iraq was known to abduct children for the pleasure of the leader's family. Dissidents were tortured in amazingly brutal ways. Ethnic minorities were attacked with mustard gas. That too is evil.

Or at least that is how Americans think. When President Bush declares that America is out to get "evildoers" we understand what he means. Some may critique our President's pronouncements as hokey, but Americans generally believe in the existence of good and evil. One of the most religious societies in the west, America is founded on

Judeo-Christian ideas. Even those who are not religious understand the language of Middle America.

The intelligentsia in America's universities and the liberal elites in the media also bristle when Bush mentions evil. But these people are not reflective of the rest of the country. They are adherents to a pseudo-nihilist worldview and denounce any absolute pronouncements except their own absolute (that there are no absolutes) and see the word "evil" as a judgmental term. Calling something evil is the evil thing to do. This postmodern philosophy has a big role in the American media, but it is a minority in American itself. In Western Europe postmodern philosophy is the dominant strain.

Prime Minister Blair of Britain has been Bush's greatest ally since September 11. He did not hesitate to use the word evil to describe the attack or the actions of regimes that support those tactics. But Blair is still an anomaly. An old-style Gladstonian liberal, Blair is reputed to be a religious man. His staunch support for Bush has gotten him into domestic trouble with a people who have, even if not as thoroughly as France, adopted a post-modern view. Though Blair as a leader is an exception to the rule of Western Europe, his people are not.

In the weeks leading up to the Iraq war, Central and Eastern European countries sided with the U.S. and ignored Germany and France's opposition to pre-emptive war. Secretary of Defense Donald Rumsfeld described the diverging camps as Old Europe and New Europe. It was clearly a dig against the French and a comment on the rising relevancy of the post-communist states. But is there something more to this? Do the states and peoples of New Europe share a strong ideological bond with America? Do they believe in evil?

The American Ambassador to the Czech Republic sees the understanding of evil as a critical tie between New Europe and America. Ambassador Stapleton, a close personal friend to President Bush, said the Old Europe / New Europe distinction is "neither temporary nor superficial." He reports that former President Havel told Bush, "The lesson for the Czechs is that you have to deal with evil in its time." A recognized playwright, Havel was a man who used the word evil frequently as a literary device. But he truly believes that there is a real-world difference between good and evil.

Recognition of the concept of evil has significant policy implications because it is a part of an overall anthropological view. If humans are capable of good and evil, then governments must be constructed around that notion. It is the idea of man's inherently fallen nature that inspired our founding fathers to create checks and balances. The foreign policy implications of this worldview are often overlooked by the intelligentsia. If the terrorists are evil and the ideas they believe are fundamentally evil, then no amount of foreign aid will change that. Helping them to get better jobs won't stop their actions. Correcting our foreign policy won't eliminate the problem; it will just make America a less immediate target for their movement. Evil cannot be negotiated with; it can only be confronted. Americans have always believed in good and evil, but are now more conscientious of it in the international sense. For Bush, Stapleton says, evil is about September 11th.

The attacks were not just a loss of 3000 lives. Americans internalized the feelings of that day. September 11th remembrance ceremonies draw tears from Americans with no direct connection to the attacks. But many Americans do have a personal connection, especially the policy and defense community. Stapleton pointed out that nearly every Congressman knew somebody who suffered in either New York or Washington. And though the citizens of many nations died in the World Trade Center, the internalization of the attack is an American thing. We must wonder if the Czechs internalized their own suffering under communism and if it helps them to understand our references to evil in ways that Western Europe has forgotten.

The press secretary of the Czech embassy in Washington seems to think so. Addressing questions from a group of young journalists, he said that the use of the word "Evil" aroused passions in France and Old Europe, but was understood in the Czech Republic...because of our past." France and Old Europe have experienced their share of evil under Hitler's boot, but that past is not as recent as the totalitarianism visited on Czechoslovakia. It is distant enough from their mind to fade from their worldview. To France the word itself is something that the uneducated would use. Having a stated foreign policy objective of crushing evil is just silly and stupid.

Jarosalva Moserova, senior Czech Senator and recent presidential candidate, draws a parallel between America's new aggressive foreign policy against the tyrants of the Islamic world and the tyrants of yesterday. "Europe," she said in reference to the doves in France and Germany and the Franco-puppet state of Belgium, "did nothing to free the old Soviet satellite states." This personal understanding of what it is like to live without freedom has drawn the Czechs closer to America's foreign policy.

Though America did not send troops to liberate the people held behind the Iron Curtain, it was still a stated policy goal of America to help them. Ronald Reagan declared the Soviets the "Evil Empire" and launched an economic, political, and military strategy designed to bring the regime down. Czechs and people throughout Soviet-occupied Europe heard the message of hope and freedom through Radio Free Europe. Though we did not do enough to protect them in the first place, the people of New Europe still have gratitude because at least America cared and did something.

In spite of this, New Europe adopted a conciliatory attitude toward Old Europe after the French President Chirac demanded the new democracies of the east "shut up." This and the recent landslide elections to join the European Union in several Central European countries shows that their economic interests must tie them closer to those willing to sit idly by as evil terrorizes the world and not as strongly to America as we would like to assume.

Perhaps supporting America was only a move to advance their interests. A senior advisor to Czech President Klaus told young journalists "There is no real cultural divide between Old and New Europe." He claimed that vehemently siding with America in the war against Saddam was just "realpolitik" to gain US favor. While Old Europe thinks only of its economy, New Europe still has enough fear of foreign threats to see the need for a transatlantic alliance to protect it from being engulfed again. From the perspective of a resident of Prague, a city whose standard of living is much higher than the rest of the country, the administration official suggested a growing cosmopolitan culture, where the real divide is urban versus rural, not a product of national identity. When it comes to culture, he explained, young people in London, Seoul, and Prague have more in common with each other than their kinsmen in the countryside.

Perhaps New York would have been added to his list of examples prior to September 11th. His suggestion raises questions as to whether the postmodernism and disbelief in value judgments like evil were as prominent among average Czechs in their cities as in Western Europe.

The man on the street didn't seem to share the official view of the Czech government. Bringing up the war issue in Prague pubs didn't generate an anti-American backlash as it might in a Paris cafe, but there wasn't much support for the war. A telecommunications analyst asked me why America even cared and implied it was either oil or Israel or some combination of the two. A food-service worker seemed to think Bush was just a rowdy American. When the conversation was directed to evil, though, the pub goers unanimously agreed that there was such a thing as good and evil. They weren't rabid postmodernists. They could also accept parallels between the regimes of the Middle East and of the Soviet Satellites. But, they wondered, why should the Czechs get involved?

There were bigger things to deal with in life - new girlfriends and gossip about old girlfriends, consumer electronics, new jobs and fears that compliance with EU rules might hurt some old jobs, and other products of the growing prosperity experienced by the people under a new regime of freedom. The prosperous have more important things to deal with than conquering evil.

Democracy may very well produce the seeds of its own destruction. The prosperity of peace and freedom leaves no time to consider the forces of oppression in the world. Many Czechs are forgetting about the brutality experienced in their past as they enjoy the luxuries of the present. This is the first step to the postmodern worldview. The communist party even captured a big block of seats in the parliament as some of the youngest voters acting in rebellion joined with old hardliners.

Americans are not just people who believe in evil; we are the ones with the resolve to act out against it. We share an understanding of the nature of evil with our friends abroad; they because of their past, and we because of our tradition of faith, yet they are now willing to ignore evil just as we were but two years ago. After the fall of communism we turned our heads as the forces of terror grew as quickly as the NASDAQ. We ignored the warning shots in Kenya and Yemen and Saudi Arabia. But when we woke up to evil on the morning of September 11th we changed. We are now resolved to defend the world against it, even if they aren't interested in being helped. Those of us with a vivid memory of September 11th must work to make sure the small children of today do not, like the youngest Czechs who lived through 1989, grow up to forget the past. We must ensure that America will be the force for the next century to "deal with evil in its time."

"Time suddenly had no barriers. Emotions surged through my body. I wanted to laugh and cry simultaneously. The kiss was different than any I'd experienced before, purer, softer, and most of all, right."

Heartbreak
Lianna Cristina Carrera
Randolph Macon Woman's College, Lynchburg, VA

Heartbreak. We've all been through it. There's no magic pill to take away the pain, the utter feeling of destruction which depletes the soul seemingly beyond any agony the physical realm can bring. All the senses that are blessings of God meant for us to appreciate life, turn into Satan's pawns. Touch, can't bear to think of how it used to feel. A kiss, a stroke of the cheek, playing a lovers version of thumb war. Sight, it hurts to open and face your reality and not only that, everywhere you look there's a memory. That couch, that picture skiing, the clouds that she saw as a bunny that really were two girls hugging. It still looks like two girls hugging to me. Hearing, every song seems to be extracted from your heart and sometimes played to a melody that is quite catching. And then there is thought, wasted on a downward spiral that daggers your lungs to the ground, yet has the ability to momentarily fade to thoughts of happier times. It's 11:45 and you can't sleep. It's 2:15 and you can't stop thinking and in return, you can't stop the hurt. The hurt that makes your eyes dry from soreness, the hurt that lays bricks on your already heavy heart. Every night you forget how it was that you finally fell asleep the night before, but you pray it come quicker tonight. You pray you'll toss less tonight, you pray your brain ceases this attack on your wellbeing and frees you from this self destructive path. It's heartbreak. A literal destruction of physical, emotional and mental capabilities, that together make life unbearable and seemingly worthless. You swear to your being you'll never let anyone in ever again, no matter what.

But we do; after time you can't remember pain. Sure you remember what you went through, but the actual pain you'll have no recollection of. My heartbreak is the same as yours.

Despite all the red flags along the way, I can't stop my heart's thought. That feeling I recognized from a time ago yet strangely unique. Just beautiful. She was just beautiful. My heart skips. I forgot it could do that. My heart beats the same as yours.

Sitting at opposite ends of the couch, feet intertwined, an act that barely crossed the line of friendship, we laughed. The entertainment was provided by *Monsters Inc.* The movie ended with a catchy tune, "I wouldn't have nothing if I didn't have you!" Sully sang. Coming back to reality, I felt as if my heart was deceiving me. I felt safe. A feeling my heart hadn't allowed me to feel since heartbreak. She smiled at me as if wondering what my eyes found so entrancing. I melted. Looking out the window, I saw the serene steady fall of snowflakes adding unnoticeably to the snow plains below. Perfect, I thought. Perfect. My eyes are the same as yours.

I looked back at her. I wish my heart would decide on a pace. She had the most intriguing eyes, a mix between blue and gray. And when her eyes looked into mine, from across the couch I felt my heart dip to my stomach. I was afraid, so afraid of being hurt again. My doubts are the same as yours.

Ignoring my inhibitions, I decided to intrigue her further. Using only my hands, I signed with a language, "Two girls, in a house why? Because it's snowing outside." A phrase that seems so insignificant yet would provide the platform for what would happen next. As the moon set sail over the midnight sky, we exchanged signs. With each one I found us playfully moving closer until we were shoulder to shoulder. After hours of anticipation I finally silently signed what my heart had been screaming, "I want to kiss you." I was so afraid. My fears are the same as yours.

And so I kissed her.

Time suddenly had no barriers. Emotions surged through my body. I wanted to laugh and cry simultaneously. The kiss was different than any I'd experienced before, purer, softer, and most of all, right. For those few moments it was she and I, with all our energies concentrated on one another; nothing else seemed to matter. It felt as if my heart had found its perfect fit, the exact crevice it had been looking to safely lie in for a long while. I look for my crevice just like you do.

Now I sit and I think of my future. She is very much a part of it, or so I hope. I think about having kids, and how I'll be a complete mess when he or she is born and wraps his or her fingers around my pinkie. I think about marriage and often wonder if I'll be able to contain my tears at the altar. Because from the time she steps through the door to the time she saunters to my side, I know she will be the most breathtaking woman my senses have sought. I dream of my house, my cars, my job, my white fence, coming home to a family and falling asleep every night with her in my arms. My dreams are the same as yours.

Until then I settle for dates. There's no homosexual hot spot, we enjoy movies, dining, dancing and bowling. There's awkward moments, funny times, and driving in circles in search of something to do. Most of the time we hold hands in the car. My dates are the same as yours.

So if my heartbreak is the same as yours, my heart beats the same as yours, my eyes see the same as yours, my doubts are the same as yours, my fears are the same as yours, my heart looks for a safe crevice just like yours, my dreams are the same as yours and my dates are the same as yours, could it be that my love is the same as yours? Some people think not. They can't fathom two women together, or two men together because it's beyond their realm of comprehension. It's different from what they know, what they are used to, and what they've been taught. It's time to remove the blinders that make it okay to demoralize what they fear, and what they don't understand.

And if they took the time to understand, maybe my girlfriend's dad would be a sure thing to walk her down the aisle, instead of her sobbing in my arms wondering if he'll even be a part of her life. Maybe I'd know for sure whether or not my mother will even come. Maybe then when we walk down the streets holding hands, we wouldn't have to let go because we're afraid that the immature teenage boys will holler names or get physical. Maybe then I could walk into a job interview not wearing a dress and lipstick, but wearing whatever I feel comfortable in and be hired for my ability to do the job. Maybe then supporters of the federal marriage amendment, and especially President Bush, would stop trying to supposedly codify the sanctity of marriage to deny me the chance to ever marry legally. Maybe then no one would be tied to a fence and left to die. Maybe then people would stop saying the word "Faggot," and "that's so gay," both phrases that lynch my soul. Because I am gay, and I do love, and I do have dreams and hopes, just like you. The only difference is that my heart is in your hands because you all truly decide if I can love freely, or if I must hide it in shame. Hide my heartbreak, control my heartbeats, close my eyes, hide my doubts, and hide my fears. If I let others dictate my love, I will settle for a crevice that will never quite fit, dreams that were never my own, and dates that feel as awkward and funny as you trying to date someone of the same sex.

But I can't wait that long for everyone to realize the mistakes that history has time and time repeated. Discrimination demoralizes everybody. So I have to keep living, most of all for my heart. Because I believe the purpose of life is to know and feel love. And I swear to my being I fell in love the night of our first kiss. I fell in love with someone too beautiful for me, too perfect for me. And I'm flying. Because my heart loves the same as yours.

Hey Everybody!
A. Katherine

I called my new fish Cat.
Don't ask me why, I just thought It'd go over better
Cats seem more acceptable these days, don't they?
Well she, the fish, was hard to hide.
Those bright colors always reflecting off the water,
I couldn't fool them with cat for long.
But I tried
Kept her secret for a while
I knew they weren't used to fish
Just cats
They couldn't understand what I saw in a fish
Why did I have to be difficult?
Just buy a fuckin cat, right?
Well, I don't want a damn cat
I want a fish
I don't even want a catfish
I just wanna fish
I don't even wanna call it Cat
I just wanna fish
I want this fish
Cause I love this fish
Her colors match me
We swim the same water

"The hippies in the 1960s had the passion. However, we have the knowledge, stamina, and desire to effect real change. Ours is the generation that will fix the problems of the past. It will be difficult, but we need to do it anyway."

How to Save the Earth from Imminent Destruction
Rebeca Bell
Denison University, Granville, OH

*T*he first metal recycling in America occurred when patriots in New York City melted down a statue of King George III and made it into bullets .

    I have a pretty solid theory on why my generation is so concerned about the environment. It's all because of the Berenstain Bears. The Berenstain Bears are a bear family of four who live in a hollowed-out tree. Brother Bear and Sister Bear have your average sibling rivalries, Poppa Bear is lovable and a bit bungling, and Momma Bear is the wise bear that holds the family together. In a series of children's books written by Stan and Jan Berenstain, the Berenstain Bears explore serious issues from jealousy (*The Berenstain Bears and the Green Eyed Monster*) to homelessness (*The Berenstain Bears Think of Those in Need*).

    In *The Berenstain Bears Don't Pollute (Anymore)*, the Bears learn all about how pollution affects all aspects of their formerly pristine Bear Country home. They have oil spills in the streams, trash on the ground, and smog in the sky. I hate to spoil the ending, but Brother and Sister Bear eventually convince Poppa to be more earth-conscious and the Berenstain Bears live to teach another lesson another day. Meanwhile, children learn that pollution is a problem, and most importantly, that something can be done about it. The Berenstain Bears and other environmentally responsible children's books helped create what I believe to be the most environmentally conscious generation of Americans since the industrial revolution. Not only did we have children's books, but we also are the first generation to live entirely in a time when recycling was mainstream, since it was introduced into culture after the first Earth Day in 1970. The hippies in the 1960s had the passion. However, we have the knowledge, stamina, and desire to affect real change. Ours is the generation that will fix the problems of the past. It will be difficult, but we need to do it anyway.

What will finally inspire our government to get serious about the environment? Some maintain the game theory, which assumes that people and governments are only motivated by their self-interest. Game theory believers will argue that there has to be something in it for them. They do not see this as selfish, just survival of the fittest in a dog-eat-dog world. When discussing environmental issues, game theorists usually look for the economic costs and benefits. They often wait until the economic timing is right. The anti-game theorists put environmental issues above all else. They will sacrifice money and prestige to fix the earth's problems now. They are sad and embarrassed by modern man's selfishness. The anti-game theorists consider themselves altruistic and are unwilling to wait for changes to be made.

When a complex country deals with a complex set of problems, however, neither theory will work. The game theorists are too selfish and slow. The anti-game theorists are too irrational and will give away too much. It will take people who combine the two theories to convince the government to change. Solutions to the sweeping environmental problems that lie before us do require altruistic and pure motivations and thought. We have to sacrifice a little now for the people of the future. But we also have to measure these sacrifices so as to not inhibit current environmental policies.

We are the generation and we are able, with the right frame of mind, to convince the government to address environmental problems now. But what are the problems? That list is long and sad. Some examples include groundwater contamination, glacial retreat, coral reef destruction, deforestation, drilling, wildlife extinction, urban sprawl, disease resurgence, and wasteful materialism. These issues not only reflect a dirtier world, but also actually cause human suffering.

For example, when groundwater sources are contaminated by anything from landfill to septic tank seepage, people that depend on them either get really sick or really thirsty. Glacial retreat also means less fresh water for people to drink. A combination of groundwater contamination and glacial retreat equals water scarcity. Extinction, deforestation and coral reef destruction mean the priceless loss of possible drugs that could save human lives from the diseases caused by lack of fresh water and disgusting urban living conditions.

There is one issue, however, that is truly the mother of all environmental problems. As it gets worse, it actually feeds the other issues in a terrible cycle of global destruction. Its effects will be so long-lasting and obvious that even if it were solved tomorrow, people alive in 200 years would still be feeling it. This massive and scary issue is global warming. And because the issue is so big, it is also extremely controversial.

Global warming is the creative name scientists came up with to identify the warming of the globe. Those who doubt its existence or don't think it is a bad thing call it climate change. There are doubters because, as hard as it is for me to believe, global warming is still a theory. There are, however, some things we know to be true.

First, we know the sun warms the earth. The sun's rays hit earth and bounce back toward space, keeping earth's temperature balanced and constant. Earth's atmosphere, made up of water vapor, carbon dioxide, and other naturally occurring greenhouse gases, prevent all of the sun's heat from bouncing back into space. The heat that our natural atmosphere absorbs and keeps on earth allows life, as we know it, to exist. Without it, we would just be an icy rock in space.

Second, we know that the average mean temperature of earth has increased. In the last 120 years, earth's temperature has increased 0.6°C (1.1°F). Six-tenths of a degree in 120 years does not sound like a serious, life-threatening, and earth-shaking phenomenon. But only a few degrees of average temperature separate today's climate from the climate that existed in the depths of the last ice age 20,000 years ago. In recent years, global warming has meant more than an increased average temperature. There have also been temperature extremes. "During 1997 and 1998, the global temperature set records for 15 consecutive months.... The year 1998 was the warmest of the millennium, topping 1997 by a quarter of a degree [Fahrenheit]." Before these records were set, the 1980s were the hottest decade ever, with five of the hottest years ever recorded. 1991 was even hotter, and 1998 was even hotter than that. The earth is definitely warming.

Third, we know that carbon emissions into the atmosphere have increased. In 1860, one-tenth of a gigaton (billion metric tons) of human-induced carbon entered the atmosphere. By the end of the 1980s, that number reached 8.0 gigatons. Human-induced carbon emissions increased by 13 percent from 1980 to 1988 alone. Carbon emissions come from the use of fossil fuels - when carbon is burned the reaction yields CO_2. Fossil fuels have been our primary source of energy since the industrial revolution. Between 1850 and 2000, human use of fossil fuels grew 500-fold. "The level of carbon dioxide today is believed...to be as high as it has been in at least 60 million years." And our dependence on fossil fuels just keeps growing. We are definitely emitting more carbon dioxide.

So, human-induced carbon emissions have increased and the average earth temperature has increased. Critics say there is no evidence of a connection between the two. That's why it is still called a theory. In other words, even though the average earth temperature is greater every year and greenhouse gases in the atmosphere have multiplied rapidly over the same period of time, it's probably just a coincidence. Most scientists believe there's a direct correlation. Most governments of the world believe there's a direct correlation. But the United States has decided to just wait and see for a while.

While we take the close-our-eyes-and-pretend-the-problem-isn't-there approach to fight global warming, the rest of the world, thankfully, is taking action. The recent chain of international global warming events in which the United States practiced inaction began in 1989. In May of 1989, the U.S. delegation to a multi-national conference in Sweden said more information was needed before beginning the work on an international treaty that would reduce the impact of global warming. In November of the same year, the United States joined with China, the former Soviet Union, and Japan not to support a treaty created at an international conference in the Netherlands that would have cut greenhouse emissions by 20 percent by 2005. China, the former Soviet Union, Japan, and the United States account for over 60 percent of the world's entire output of greenhouse gases. The worst polluters are, of course, the most unwilling to change.

In 1990, President George H. W. Bush gave a speech stating that we needed to better understand global warming before we could do anything about it—which can be

translated as "let's wait and see." Eventually, in 1991, the Bush administration submitted a plan that addressed global warming, but it did not even mention carbon emissions
at all. Bush finally made a commitment, albeit a weak one, in 1992 when the United
States signed the United Nations Framework Convention on Climate Change (UNFC-
CC). The UNFCCC committed us to stabilize greenhouse gas emissions at a decent
level and to create a national action plan to address the greenhouse gas issue at home.
The national plan was to voluntarily lower greenhouse gas emissions to 1990 levels by
the end of the decade.

When President Bill Clinton entered the White House, the United States finally
entered the international environmental negotiations. After several rounds, Clinton
signed the Kyoto Protocol to the UNFCCC in 1998. Hooray! Unfortunately, Clinton
never sent the treaty to the Senate for approval. Boo. Kyoto would have entered the
U.S. into a legally binding agreement to reduce emissions by 7 percent below base-line
years for the period 2008-2012. When President George W. Bush took office, he made
it clear that he wanted nothing to do with the Kyoto Protocol and banished it from
U.S. policy.

Meanwhile, other countries of the world, including the European Union, Japan
and Russia have ratified the treaty. They are reducing emissions; we are waiting for more
information while our greenhouse gas emissions are still increases each year and are projected to do so for another decade. Even the UNFCCC voluntary emissions control plan
failed, mostly because it was just voluntary. It not only failed, it failed big. "Based on
historical data, 2001 emissions were about 13% in excess of the UNFCC goal."

If we do not stop the trend, there will be serious repercussions in the future.
Greenhouse gas emissions take anywhere between 10 and 100 years to exhibit their full
effect on the environment, which is why it is hard for scientists to prove what is going
on right now. But we don't have to wait 100 years to see some of the effects global
warming has had on the earth. Lucky us! Let's begin the tour of destruction with the
most obvious effect of a hotter earth: ice is melting.

A chunk of ice broke off the Larsen ice shelf in Antarctica in 1995. This chunk
of ice was the size of Rhode Island. It broke off because the average temperature in
Antarctica has risen 20 degrees Fahrenheit in the last 20 years. Twenty degrees! Ice is
melting in other parts of the ocean as well. Every year since the Titanic met an iceberg
in the North Atlantic, the U.S. Coast Guard has issued warnings of the 500 icebergs that
float in those waters. In the winter of 1998, "for the first time in 85 years, the Coast
Guard did not issue a single iceberg alert for that area."

Ice is melting at the poles, which is the area scientists think will exhibit the
most obvious effects of global warming. But ice is also melting in the United States.
The glaciers in the Blackfoot-Jackson Glacier Basin of Glacier National Park in
Montana have shrunk from 21.6 square kilometers in 1850 to only 7.4 square kilometers
in 1979. Scientists used two different models to project the melt rate of what is left of
the glaciers. The results of the models predict that, at the current rate, glaciers will be
gone between the year 2030 and 2100. The same kind of glacial melting is taking place
all over the world, from the Andes to the Himalayas.

There are also more serious reasons why melted glaciers and melted ice caps are a bad thing. Glaciers feed mountain and lowland streams. "Fifty percent of the freshwater that humans consume yearly comes from mountains." Without glaciers feeding the streams, serious water shortages will take place and are already taking place in, for example, downstream communities near the Andes Mountains.

As glaciers melt, the water enters a stream, which enters a river, which flows to the ocean. When giant chunks of ice break off the Larsen ice shelf in Antarctica, the ice enters the ocean. The net result is that oceans are rising. "Globally, a 10 to 25 centimeter rise in sea level has been recorded during this century." A 10 to 25 centimeter increase is a lot if you realize the ocean covers 70 percent of earth's surface. This increase is more than the ocean level has changed in the last thousand years. "The sea level is now at its highest level in 5,000 years, and rising."

Global ice melting affects the earth in many serious ways. But the most important aspect is that it serves as proof that something serious and long-term is going on. For example, glaciers respond directly to climatic factors like temperature and precipitation. But, unlike plants and animals, they cannot "adapt behaviorally or physiologically in ways that mitigate the impact of climate change." If the temperature gets too hot, glaciers can't relocate to a colder climate. They respond directly to the environment, which makes them "excellent barometers of climate change," but it takes decades for glaciers to react to the changes, which means glacial retreat "can be attributed to real climatic changes, not to temporary anomalies."

Glaciers cannot adapt to warmer temperatures. They just melt. Insects, plants and animals, however, adapt the best they can. They migrate farther north or to deeper waters where the temperatures are cooler. Areas that were once too cold for certain species are now like paradise for them. This causes changes in ecosystems and habitats. That fact that environments change and animals have to adapt is nothing new. That is how life has survived on this planet. The problem is that the change is happening too fast.

The heat will affect plant and animal life in at least several possible ways. First, the location and density of species may adjust to find cooler climates; for example, fish may live in deeper, colder parts of the ocean where animals that prey on the fish cannot go. Animals may starve because their food source has disappeared. Second, the timing of natural phenomenon such as egg-laying, migration, hibernation, flowering, and malting that are triggered by temperature changes may happen at different times in the year. Animals in the arctic portion of Alaska are shedding their winter coats too early and getting sick because of it. Species may also react physically by getting bigger or behaviorally by hunting differently.

A peer-reviewed scientific study of global warming effects on animals and plants that was published in *Nature Magazine* found that recent temperature changes have already influenced many species. Titled, "Fingerprints of Global Warming on Wild Plants and Animals," the study found that over 80 percent of the 1,468 tested species are changing in ways appropriate to higher temperatures. The authors of that study conclude, "Clearly, if such climatic and ecological changes are now being detected when the globe has warmed by an estimated average of only 0.6°C, many more far-reaching effects on species and ecosystems will probably occur in response to [predict-ed] changes in temperature...."

Ecosystem changes also affect people, in sometimes life-threatening ways. People living in the mountains of Rwanda and Kenya are already suffering from global warming. Mosquitoes that, until recently, did not exist in the area because it was too cold brought diseases with them when they migrated north, including malaria and yellow fever. Malaria outbreaks are happening all over the world because mosquitoes have expanded their territory and are flourishing in the heat. Around 500 cases of malaria occur every year, causing a million deaths worldwide, most of which occur in young children in sub-Saharan Africa.

Scientific studies have found that global warming is not the only cause of malarial outbreaks; population growth, mosquito resistance to insecticides, and the quali-ty of public-health systems also contribute. But global warming makes the spread of the disease more common and more likely. "If tropical weather is expanding it means that tropical diseases will expand."

In the early 1980s, there were only a few hundred cases of malaria a year in northwestern Pakistan. As the mean temperature increased, however, the number of cases also increased to 25,000 in 1990. People living in Papua New Guinea, at an ele-vation of 2,100 meters, used to be considered safe from mosquito-borne disease, but they experienced a malaria outbreak in 1997.

And it's not just happening in lesser-developed countries. Termites, cockroach-es, and mosquitoes combined forces to attack the city of New Orleans in 1995 after five years without a killing frost. Malaria mosquitoes reached Toronto, Canada, by the late 1990s. And dengue fever spread into Texas for the first time in recorded history. Dengue fever, one of the World Health Organization's ten deadliest diseases, is a flu-like viral infection that can cause internal bleeding, fever, and, in some cases, death.

Global warming will melt earth's ice, transform ecosystems, help spread malar-ia, and damage the earth in a trillion other ways as well. It is a very real problem that demands real solutions. President George W. Bush, however, doesn't get it. When he finally decided to stop ignoring the problem like his father did, he came up with a plan that will actually make the problem worse.

I like to think that the idea for the George W. Bush Environmental Plan came from his father's less than perfect environmental policy. And by "less than perfect" I mean non-existent. A perfect example lies in the movie titled *The Greening of Planet Earth*. This movie, funded by the coal industry and shown often in the older Bush's White House, attempts to "persuade policymakers that a warmer, wetter, carbon-dioxide-enhanced world would be, contrary to the alarms of environmentalists, a godsend." The movie says the benefits of global warming are wonderful! Farmers will be able to grow 30-60 percent more crops! We will have enough food to feed the entire world! Deserts will become grasslands! Grasslands will become forests! Global warming will be the best thing ever! Of course, the movie never mentions the trillions of bad, destructive, scary things that may also happen. This movie sums up the Bush family's environmen-tal policy: pretend it's not a problem.

So Bush learned from the best. In fact, I believe his ability to ignore sound science in favor of special interest groups, to alter the public perception of global warming, to limit environmental funding, and to diminish our country's credibility on the world environmental stage surpasses that of his father and every other president that came before him. Combined. For example, when he decided to hide science by altering an important environmental report, the report became so completely ruined that the Environmental Protection Agency pulled the entire global warming section from the report "to avoid publishing science that isn't credible."

Mess with science, and you are going to get some angry scientists. So, in response to Bush's anti-science record, scientists are finally coming out of their labs to let the world know how bad Bush really is. A February 2004 statement from the Union of Concerned Scientists criticized the Bush administration for manipulating "the process through which science enters into its decisions." The statement claims that the administration had done so by "placing people who are professionally unqualified or who have clear conflicts of interest in official posts and on scientific advisory committees; by disbanding existing advisory committees; [and] by censoring and suppressing reports by the government's own scientists."

Not only did the administration change the information in the environmental report, the scientists report, "The administration also suppressed a study by the EPA that found that a bipartisan Senate clean air proposal would yield greater health benefits than the administration's proposed *Clear Skies Act*, which the administration is portraying as an improvement of the existing *Clean Air Act.*"

When he is not hiding science, he is cutting funding for science. The President's proposed budget for the 2005 fiscal year cuts the Environmental Protection Agency's budget by about $600 million, the smallest EPA budget since 2001. If approved as is, the cuts would destroy a program that provides loans for local communities to fix wastewater infrastructure problems. The President's proposed EPA budget would also hurt the Superfund program, which cleans up the nation's most hazardous waste sites. Perhaps most terribly, the President's proposal would cut scientific funding by $100 million, which is part of his campaign to reduce non-defense research from multiple federal organizations.

From Bush's point-of-view, I guess it makes sense to cut funding for research if he is just going to hide the results anyway. This way it saves a step in the process. While he wants to cut funding, he continues to make the argument that there is not enough information on global warming to make the necessary decisions. I don't know how Bush expects more information to develop if he continues to cut research funding! Thankfully, Bush is wrong. There is enough information out there to make informed environmental decisions. The Pew Center on Global Warming, a non-partisan organization dedicated to the use of credible scientific information, states on their website, "We accept the views of most scientists that enough is known about the science and environmental impacts of climate change for us to take actions to address its consequences." The Union of Concerned Scientists thinks there is enough information. The Environmental Protection Agency thinks there is enough information. Peer-reviewed, nationally accepted research states there is enough information. Bush just doesn't like what the information says.

There is, however, only so much Bush can do to hide, ignore, and cut funding for information, right? Eventually he had to make some actual policy decisions and these decisions were based on actual scientific research and what was best for the earth, right? Wrong! Bush is so great at being the worst environmental president ever that even his plans to fix the global warming problem have made or will make it worse!

I submit to you Exhibit A: the *Clean Skies Act*. The *Clean Skies Act* is the Administration's answer to the question of what to do about emissions from coal-fired electric power plants. It would replace requirements established in the *Clean Air Act* with a national cap and trade program for sulfur dioxide, nitrogen oxides, and mercury. It ignores carbon emissions entirely, however, which is stupid because carbon emissions are the real problem. They are responsible for half of the atmosphere's human-induced heat blocking. Since carbon is such a big problem, why didn't Bush include it in the bill? Maybe you should ask the fossil fuel industries, oil companies, and mega-corporations that will benefit from the omission. According to the Union of Concerned Scientists, *Clean Skies* would be less effective in cleaning up the nation's air and reducing mercury contamination of fish than proper enforcement of the existing *Clean Air Act*.

Exhibit B: the Kyoto Protocol. The Kyoto Protocol is an international treaty designed to attack global warming on a global level. Twelve years in the making, Kyoto is the current stage in international emissions law. When voluntary emissions reductions failed, the countries agreed that any treaty had to have binding agreements in order for it to work. In 1997, in Kyoto, Japan, the countries began negotiations that lead to an agreement to reduce their overall emissions by 5 percent by 2012.

There were some rough spots during final negotiations and some analysts were skeptical that Kyoto would ever come together. To make matters worse, before the meeting to set up compliance mechanisms, Bush withdrew U.S. support for the treaty. National Security Advisor Condoleeza Rice stated that Kyoto was "dead." Bush et al. assumed that without the support of the United States, the countries would never agree. True to form, however, Bush was wrong. By the end of 2003, all aspects had been agreed upon, and the major countries, including those in the European Union and Japan, had ratified the treaty. Russia ratified the treaty in the summer of 2004, which finally established Kyoto as international law. (Fifty-five countries responsible for 55 percent of emissions had to ratify the treaty in order for the treaty to go into effect.)

Kyoto is not perfect. It will not completely stop the warming of the earth, nor will it reverse the effects that are already happening. Kyoto's main weakness is a concession made to the rich countries that allows them to buy emission credits from countries that do not need all the credits they were allocated. In theory, a country would not have to reduce emissions at all if they could buy enough credits from other countries. Some critics also think that it sets emissions standards too low to really do any good. Kyoto is not perfect, but it is a start.

So why didn't George W. Bush want the United States to be part of this historical, groundbreaking treaty that takes the first steps in the worldwide reduction of emissions? Because of industries that rely on fossil fuels, of course! "[T]hree days after a

New York Times front-page story reporting that the administration was planning to cut carbon dioxide emissions, intense lobbying by fossil fuel interest groups led to a sharp change in policy by President Bush...." Not only did he withdraw from Kyoto, but he also committed to producing 1,300 new power plants over 20 years!

Bush also did not like the fact that, although developing countries are included in Kyoto, they are not required to substantially reduce emissions. Their development is considered more important. The Kyoto countries decided that it does not make sense to require the same reductions from countries that are struggling to exist. Besides, developing countries are not big contributors to the global warming problem. The average person living in North America will use the equivalent of 10 tons of coal a year. The average Bangladeshi uses less than 220 pounds. Isn't it just like Bush to make the poor pay as much as the rich? Sounds just like his tax policy. At least he's consistent.

Exhibit C: the greenhouse gas intensity index, my most damning piece of evidence of Bush's environmental failures. The greenhouse gas intensity index is the George W. Bush Environmental Plan. With all of the resources at his disposal, including some of the smartest people in the country, and all the power to create an entire environmental plan the greenhouse gas intensity index is what he came up with.

Greenhouse gas intensity is a brand new measurement that measures the ratio of greenhouse gas emissions to economic output, so it basically measures the efficiency of the economy in terms of greenhouse gas emissions. The more efficient, the fewer emissions per dollar of economic output and the lower the intensity level. Bush explains this concept on the White House website: "The new approach focuses on reducing the growth of GHG [greenhouse gas] emissions, while sustaining the economic growth needed to finance investment in new, clean energy technologies." He states that his greenhouse gas intensity measurement will help us slow the growth of emissions, then, "as the science justifies," it will stop and eventually reverse that growth.

Bush admits openly that his new measurement system will only slow the growth of emissions. But that is almost giving him too much credit. Using the intensity measurement, he predicts the "183 metric tons of emissions per million dollars of GDP that we emit today will be lowered to 151 metric tons per million dollars GDP in 2012." That is an 18 percent decrease by 2012.

Without more information, Bush's intensity measurements actually seem viable. Take a closer look. The intensity rating has been decreasing naturally since 1990. Without any involvement from Bush, the intensity rating would decrease 14 percent through 2012. So Bush's big plan will only improve the situation by 4 percent. If we had signed Kyoto, by 2012, we would have lowered emissions by 7 percent. Bush's plan is definitely a step in the wrong direction.

Finally, if the greenhouse gas intensity measurement is a ratio of emissions per million dollars in GDP, then doesn't the number decrease as long as the GDP continues to increase? Does that mean we can pollute as much as we want as long as there is a booming economy? The greenhouse gas intensity measurement is a weak alternative to Kyoto, which is a pretty embarrassing reality.

There is absolutely no easy way to fix the mess we have created. Any real solution is going to be a combination of several options and will also require some serious sacrifice. The first, most important step to solving the problem is to vote Bush, the most environmental unfriendly president ever, out of office. Once that is taken care of, some (preferably all) of the following need to happen:

Decrease emissions. Using real measurements, the total number of bad things we pump into the air has to decrease, not just grow slower. Voluntary cut programs, like the FCCC and Bush's plan do not work on the national level. Voluntary reduction programs, however, have been successful for some companies, including British Petroleum, Toyota, Sunoco, IBM, and DuPont.

Increase research funding. The only way we can find more and better solutions to this problem is through diligent, unbiased research. Such research is responsible for inventions like biodiesel fuel and hybrid cars. When scientists invent a new environmentally sound product, use it. The EPA website, for example, ranks cars according to how "green" they are. Check the ratings out before you buy. Most important, research is needed to figure out a way to decrease our dependence on fossil fuels. There will always be a global warming problem as long as our factories are addicted to the source. Harold Bernard, the author of a book on global warming called Global Warming Unchecked, started his book with this passage:

> *'You doomsayers are always wrong,' one critic of the greenhouse effect railed at me as we discussed global warming. The critic was unwilling to concede that maybe 'doomsayers' are 'always wrong' because forestalling actions are taken based on their warnings.*

If we respond to the warnings now, we can prove the doomsayers wrong. Being "wrong" is much better than the alternative.

We can always do a little bit to make the earth a cleaner place. The Berenstain Bears taught us that much when we were four years old. But because older generations, those not exposed to those earth-loving Bears, have made a mess of things, it is our responsibility to do more than ever. We can no longer just recycle and turn off the water while brushing our teeth. We have to invent a cheaper way to use recycled goods and we have to protect our water sources. We have to put the health of future children ahead of the burning desire to own a monster, gas-guzzling SUV.

Most important, we have to demand reforms from our government. If the United States of America is supposed to be the beacon on the hill, a shining example for every other country to follow, then we need to get rid of the smog so other countries can see the stupid light. Our government has to commit to real change, right now

Maybe I will send President Bush a copy of the Berenstain Bears book—it might teach him a few things.

Let's Raise Children with Joy and Encouragement
"Gabrielle"
Letisha Beachy: Virginia Polytechnic and State University
Blacksburg, VA

"Social responsibility in science is of especial importance in these days of aggrandizing U.S. imperialism, backed by the jingoistic threat of nuclear warfare."

Let Us Not Be "Ordinary Intellectuals"

Josh Kearns
University of California at Berkeley, Berkeley, CA

Ammon Hennacy was an anarchist, pacifist, vegetarian, WWI draft resister, war tax refuser, non-church radical Catholic, friend of the Hopi Indians, and self-described one-person revolution in America who died in 1970 while protesting nuclear weapons. On Thanksgiving Day of 1949 he wrote these words:

"Love without courage and wisdom is sentimentality, as with the ordinary church member. Courage without love and wisdom is foolhardiness, as with the ordinary soldier. Wisdom without love and courage is cowardice, as with the ordinary intellectual. Therefore one who has love, courage and wisdom is one in a million who moves the world, as with Jesus, Buddha, and Gandhi."

To Hennacy's list of world-movers I would add Danish physicist Niels Bohr. Bohr is best known among the scientific community for his work in atomic physics and quantum mechanics, which earned him the Nobel Prize in 1922. I learned much about his scientific discoveries that have so profoundly impacted our understanding of the natural laws that govern the universe as a student of chemistry at a major science and engineering research university in the U.S. What follows is an anecdote from Bohr's life that I wasn't taught in any university science classes - I only learned of it years later in a theological school course on liberating nonviolence. I thought it timely to retell the story now at this gathering of science intellectuals in Copenhagen, Denmark, 2004.

Denmark was under Nazi occupation in the fall of 1943 when Berlin gave the order that Danish Jews would be taken to Theresienstadt and other concentration camps. What the Germans did not know is that the Danish underground had been tipped off about the Nazis' intentions. During the night, 7,200 people - virtually the entire Jewish-Danish population - escaped for Sweden on fishing vessels and just about anything else that would float. After a night on rough seas, the refugees arrived in Sweden only to find that the king was afraid to give them asylum. He did not want to incur Hitler's wrath and jeopardize Sweden's neutrality in the European conflict.

Niels Bohr, meanwhile, had been hiding out from the Nazis in Uppsala, Sweden. Bohr's mother was Jewish, and he probably felt a special sympathy for the dilemma of his Jewish country people. In a heroic act of solidarity and compassion, Bohr sent word to the king that if the refugees were not given asylum he would turn himself over to the Nazis with them. The king was proud to have this famous scientist in his country, and did not want to be held responsible for turning him over to the storm troopers. So the king relented, and despite his fear allowed the asylum seekers into Sweden.

While my well-meaning university instructors of chemistry and physics explained for me Niels Bohr's acts of scientific genius, they failed to relate his greatest accomplishment. Bohr's act of love, courage and wisdom in the face of violence and oppression saved thousands of people from torture and death in Nazi concentration camps. In this act he was confirmed as a very extraordinary intellectual, shunning the cowardice that characterizes so many "ordinary" intellectuals of his day and ours. As intellectuals and scientists we must follow the example of Niels Bohr and other humanitarian science workers, imbuing ourselves with more than languid technical acumen. We must suffuse our scientific endeavors with love and compassion, and promote justice and wholeness with our work rather than violence and division. We must be courageous, as Bohr was when he refused to hide in safety while his people were in danger. As science workers we have the supreme responsibility to be conscientious about the social, political, human health, and environmental ramifications of our research work.

Social responsibility in science is of especial importance in these days of aggrandizing U.S. imperialism, backed by the jingoistic threat of nuclear warfare. Because of the work of scientists, humanity has gained the ability to render massive portions of the Earth uninhabitable to humans, and to potentially annihilate our entire species with a 30-minute exchange of nuclear weapons of mass destruction. The design, development and production of nuclear weapons are only possible when scientists and engineers fail to recognize the ethical implications of their work. Science workers may like to believe that we are somehow immune to politics, and that science is intrinsically ethically neutral. But this is folly that holds grave consequences for all of humanity. It is time that science workers become cognizant of the world we live and work in, and muster the courage and love to refuse our support of violence and devastation. Let us no longer be cowardly "ordinary intellectuals."

I recommend the following to academicians of science and engineering to promote research in alignment with the common good of all humanity and the Earth:

1. Teach university students about the humanity of scientists such as Niels Bohr, not just about their technical accomplishments. This will provide students with a much richer education, and foster tendencies towards compassion and social responsibility in science.

2. Implement science and engineering curricula requirements with study of ethics, political science, sociology, etc. so that students may understand the context in which science workers interface with workers in other disciplines, and the consequences their work holds for humans and all of Earth's ecosystems.

3. Require that any external agency seeking to fund a research project at a university provide a complete disclosure of its interests and purposes in connection with

that project. Each professor receiving an external research grant should be required to prepare and make available for general discussion a detailed assessment of the likely applications and consequences of the research work.

4. Ensure that students are well informed about the potentially harmful (e.g. military) applications of work in their intended field of study. Provide students with information regarding the job prospects of scientists and engineers who do not want to work on weapons/military related projects.

Let us express our courage and love along with our wisdom as we work for a peaceful, just, and ecologically wholesome world.

"Now unable to openly reject or expel students with disabilities only for their 'difference,' education institutions are hiding behind 'academic standards' with very chilling consequences for the politically naïve."

Living the Revolution: College Democrats with Disabilities

Robin Orlowski
Texas Women's University, TX

In 1973, Congress passed Section 504 of the *Rehabilitation Act* which guarantees access to federally funded activities and benefits irrespective of disability. In 1975, Congress passed the *Education for All Handicapped Children Act* (later renamed the *Individuals With Disabilities Education Act*), which provides a free appropriate public education to individuals with disabilities. Affirming the personal is always political, these facts became intimate knowledge to my family by the mid-1980s only because of my own birth. In April of 1979, I was born after my mother experienced a late-pregnancy illness which had left her feeling under the weather for a short time.

My mother's happy recovery was then tempered by the high stress of my birth. Intending to deliver vaginally, my mother underwent an emergency C-section following many hours of labor. Despite her best intentions, my head was too big to pass through the vaginal canal, a medical condition called hydrocephalus. Affecting 2 out of 1,000 people born in the USA, the condition is characterized by a head this large and swelling of the brain which if left untreated can result in a vegetative state or death.

Until the 1960s, there was no operation available to treat the condition, and people were left to institutions for what passed for care before the disability rights movement of the 1970s. The condition is rare in and of itself, but overwhelmingly strikes boys. From birth, I had involuntary instruction in 'difference'. The doctors could not tell my parents why I was unlike other newborns, nor could they predict my long-term destiny in a world with rapidly changing civil rights laws. For better or worse, everyday with me brought intensive public policy instruction—and challenges.

Yet this same environment also provided an early, unintended, and strong disability rights political organizing environment for me. Growing up alongside the disability rights movement, I imbued the strength and positive internal self-perception subsequently needed to face down indifferent teachers and administrators throughout my Texas public education.

Despite federal and state regulations requiring they focus on my education, these officials instead attempted only whatever was most convenient for their own needs. Families such as my own (who both understood and openly expected their legal rights would be served) were the big exception rather than the standard rule in this 'affluent' area. I watched numerous fellow high school special education classmates react in dismay after their own parents acquiesced to our Texas district's preferred vocational educational track, instead of continuing on to the colleges which they had obviously qualified for. Even if these other students were also capable of college work, administrative prejudices and the general absence of countering information gave their own parents a very powerful incentive to avoid conflict. However expressed, all of my special education classmates also knew that external appearances did not necessarily match academic reality.

For example the special education program in my 'college prep' district itself was a large joke from the beginning levels; one elementary teacher was honestly expected to educate up to 12 different students on 3 different math courses. Consequently, the faculty only hit the middle ground, and was burned out by the end of their second year assignment. Staffing and curriculum conditions were little better in the junior high and high school classrooms, where similar experiences were the norm despite slightly smaller classroom. Ironically, some of these teachers had entered to replace others who had gotten so visibly bad they lashed out at students during class-room instruction time. As a result of the aforementioned arrangements, little official curriculum instruction happened in these rooms, but I definitely took away powerful observations about the current status of students with disabilities within the education system and my own simultaneous personal obligations to remain politically active in the hopes of eradicating those same conditions.

Never really welcome in this superficially open environment, students with dis-abilities made our school district very uncomfortable both in themselves and with previous 'success' ideas; our very existence proves more than one way to process, retain, and use information. A very sheltered world view continued to maintain all students learn the same way and 'exceptions' should be ignored as often as formally possible.

Within the 'regular' classroom a 'liberal' high school educator who took pains in a heavily Republican school district to champion Gloria Steinem, Malcom X, and Ce'sar Chavez was eager to attack special education students for our alleged academic inferiority. Although the local course material for AP government was no more (and some would argue, actually less) intense than actual college level coursework—I suppos-edly could not enroll in the intended class because my 'I's were not dotted correctly in a handwritten essay for his own class. This normally quiet teacher was adamant that 'stan-dards' (which conveniently did not affect program requirements) be maintained at all costs. At this same meeting, I easily named 10 current AP government students with far worse penmanship who did not have to beg for program admission or retention. The only difference between me and those individuals was my simultaneous enrollment in a special education program for unrelated academic instruction. During a later trip for President Clinton's 1997 inauguration, this same teacher falsely accused me of using drugs. Later he attempted to backtrack by admitting those comments were said only in order to set up my California roommates who were actually caught with the materials, but such methods would not have required my handcuffing and interrogation by D.C. police department representatives, a division rumored to be corrupt.

Bringing its own challenges, college also reinforced my disability rights organizing. Attempting to pass (or at least bypass) the state-mandated standardized testing program which supposedly proved my worthiness of a college diploma, I learned that numerous institutional vice presidents did not know how to enforce disability civil rights. At my university, the Associate Vice President for Academic Affairs did not believe students with disabilities were entitled to equal university facility access because she insisted on placing myself and other students in a degree completion track which obviously countered both the state and federal proscription while cutting operating funds for the disability support service office. For two years, I spent a better part of my time attempting to undo and then halt her most immediate and lethal policies. In addition to consciousness raising groups with other self-identified students with disabilities, I also rallied other students with disabilities to public consciousness through investigative articles and columns in our student newspaper. If the state and its representatives continued to limit our rights simply because of who we were, getting to college was not enough of an accomplishment. That vice president eventually departed and a predecessor was tellingly not named to that same position, making this self-advocacy good preparation for an even more odious task during a transient summer school session in my hometown community college.

While at that summer school, the campus's disability counselor herself informed me that - despite meeting the federal requirements - I could not use a calculator for the state standardized testing program components I was required to simultaneously enroll in until the state of Texas said I had completed program requirements to their standards. This counselor was insistent that calculator usage would either not be fair to the students without disabilities or the instructor who would perhaps not realize they were also teaching students with disabilities. We argued for a good 30 minutes about federal civil rights laws' applicability to state and local governments through the 14th Amendment before I realized this administrator also was oblivious to her job requirements. No matter what I would have said, she only defended the college's right to continue the policy.

To rectify the situation for myself and others, I filed a civil rights complaint with the United States Department of Education's regional Office for Civil Rights. Her warning that I was the first person from my hometown with a disability to oppose this college's policy did significantly more to ignite my resolve against that same practice than if I had just read about it in the school handbook. I wondered how many area students (including former special education classmates) attempted to seek justice against this same practice before their intimidation. I wondered if the same college officials would have issued a similar veiled threat against somebody challenging racial discrimination in 2000. My experience had proven that (ironically) anything was possible in the early 21st century.

Certainly, even I was periodically scared of the mammoth sociopolitical tasks awaiting me. Even though my parents had instilled self-assertion and disability pride, I never actually imagined myself filing a civil rights complaint against any entity; that was always something done by one of the leading figures in my books and movies. Now, I assumed that very same responsibility, and wasn't exactly sure of myself in the new climate. Department of Education Office for Civil Rights personnel had patiently walked me through the process, and friends from around the state (who were acutely aware of the immediate and secondary case impacts) rallied to my case, but I could not deny having reached unfamiliar territory at this point in my young life. It was one thing to talk about fighting for my rights on an abstract-romantic basis invoking an idealized version of the 1960s, but the actual process epitomized tremendous amounts of stress and precision directly resting upon my shoulders. If I did not know before how high the proverbial advocacy stakes were for people with disabilities ourselves, this incident conclusively proved it.

I felt a huge sense of relief at the end of the experience. Not only was my specific situation resolved, but that same college also knew that other students with disabilities could not be subjected to the conditions. An infamous 'local custom' was now relegated to historical footnote, with subsequent Department of Education surveillance ensuring that the college actually followed through with their complaint resolution responsibilities. Because it also impacted future/concurrent students with disabilities this victory was inherently preferable to one which only affected my own circumstances.

Continuously during my organizing, I am perpetually reminded about the role played by numerous American medical-economic access discrepancies in disability rights political organizing. Despite the hardships I faced, I had still faced them as a child of the upper middle class, whose parents had the inclination, time, and resources to ensure my health. Even when they are apprised of their federal rights, some families still lack the financial resources necessary to ensure sufficient medical health in an era of shrinking Medicaid coverage and attacks on general public welfare services. Managed care ascension does not eliminate my fears; for every child used in campaign images, many others go without access, but with display of an incredibly sobering list of ailments and conditions. Furthermore, healthcare discrepancies are broken down by race, with non-white people receiving the most substandard levels of non-profit healthcare. Most telling of their true ideologies, 'pro-life' organizations were among those not challenging these discrepancies—human life apparently stopped being sacred or innocent when the person was born with a disability. Because some 'progressive' activists do not handle disability, being a person with disabilities always forces me to choose friends carefully.

During 2003, a friend of mine made an initially good speech against militarism and imperialism - then undercut herself by arguing for a student service fee reduction because all current spending categories were allegedly too lavish. Our university only allocated one licensed disability support service counselor for students on three campuses across Texas, but those staffing conditions conveniently escaped that self-described radical - who had easily grasped and denounced other oppressions. Also aware of budget issues, I and other students with disabilities previously asked for a fee increase so enough personnel could be hired to provide accommodations to all students with disabilities in a timely matter instead of the current "rushed" conditions we were expected to endure. From our perspective, high student service fees were a much more reasonable cost compared with the university eventually facing legal fees (and potential public fall-out) because of its virtual inability to provide adequate services to students with disabilities only because of poor planning.

The activist colleague was again visibly and oddly reluctant when I petitioned our campus feminist group to reject the student government's "poster child" disability awareness approach; in addition to funding off-campus organizations at the expense of our own campus office, that proposed venture shamelessly promoted the outdated stereotype of people with disabilities as "perpetual children" who were dependent upon others for their survival and rights. Applying a noticeably lesser standard to the student government request than she did with racial/class/gender/sexuality issues, this same friend then openly wondered why student groups could not seriously support the student government in spite of the admittedly offensive imagery. She honestly could not see why I and other students with disabilities did not divide among our many (equally pressing) community loyalties, my subsequent receipt of a threatening letter from the student government (warning me not to oppose their charity work) on official school letterhead failed to raise her consciousness, and I finally concluded that some communities marginalized each other in the course of political organizing - but I personally could not endure the practice. My political organizing had to intersect disability rights with other communities and not exploit either group in the course of attempting to achieve and/or retain my goals.

During this same time span, I met a "non-traditional" college student whom I passionately disagreed with over many sociopolitical issues, certainly not including party identification. This military veteran turned student was very proud of her past, but honestly assumed that college personnel similarly would tell her what to do concerning her disabilities. Not interested in learning about the laws governing her existence and survival, she instead chose apathy. No matter how much I disagreed with her on other issues, it broke my heart when she later announced her withdrawal from college life after encountering many problems from the aforementioned approach. Ignorance about disability rights prevented this person from completing her journalism degree and then fulfilling the obvious passion flickering in her eyes during conversations about our ideal post-college careers. There was tremendous irony if students in the higher learning environment did not understand the most basic concepts governing their rights as a person with a disability, we handed the state of Texas virtual permission to discriminate against us and our communities. Ultimately responsible for our own educations, I affectionately thought of myself and other students with disabilities as a campus community sharing some very important general characteristics with each other. Like many other close-knit communities, our individual successes and failures strongly impacted the other members and we drew from each other's experiences. Including myself, most other members also readily made cross-connections between disability rights and other communities which we personally were involved with.

Because I was always trying to control my seizures, reproductive rights support was always a personal given dating back to pre-adolescence when I began noticing the abortion headlines. It was completely absurd to spend so much time and energy trying to self-control my neurological system while then allowing the state to decide the fate of my reproductive system. Additionally, eugenics restrictions had explicitly prevented people with disabilities from making their own reproductive choices---again under the guise the state should control women's bodies. Participating in the 2004 "March for Women's Lives" I thought about the connections I and other feminists with disabilities have to the issue. Our multifaceted policy analysis directly results from personal/organizing experiences inside American society. We also realized that education about and increased enforcement levels of present disability rights laws were infinitely more respectful than limiting any woman's reproductive choice - even if she would abort a fetus with a disability who could potentially grow up to be an activist colleague and/or world leader. Serious discussions about both freedom and bodily integrity demand all women have access to a full range of reproductive health care options for themselves.

In 2004, I also became the "Democrats with Disabilities" national chair of the College Democrats of America directly following my successful term as Region IV Deputy Organizer. Because the Democratic Party has a long history of prominent elected officials with disabilities and also (not coincidentally) was at the forefront of major 20th century disability rights laws, I believed our caucus should encourage party identification by concentrating on the political education of students with disabilities. My own public school and post-secondary experiences taught me that other students with disabilities actually were aware when their rights were being violated, but did not necessarily have the sociopolitical tools to challenge the treatment as I had done by attending and graduating from college in spite of both standardized testing and bigoted administrators. I knew that many more potential college students with disabilities were unfairly denied the chance for admission only by assorted standardized testing programs playing on society fears of "dumb" students.

Now unable to openly reject or expel students with disabilities only for their "differences," education institutions are hiding behind "academic standards" with very chilling consequences for the politically naïve. In addition to supporting the Kerry campaign and other campaigns, it is also important students with disabilities know their rights - including how to file a civil rights complaint when our schools do not comply with federal law. Precisely because we have things much easier than Ed Roberts (who became the first official student with disabilities when he enrolled at the University of California-Berkeley in 1962) today's college students with disabilities must know and defend their right to equal education opportunity.

At the College Democrats of America National Convention, other caucus members reiterated this theme for our national priorities. Nearly identical "war stories" from me and other students across the country reaffirmed political education's importance for growing and maintaining both the caucus and general Democratic party infrastructure - then used to save America. "Disability community" outreach campaign materials do not currently reach people honestly believing their disability is not a political issue and/or that the status quo is just fine for dealing with disability issues. Some of my classmates with disabilities who support the same conservative politicians and talk show hosts which bash special education (and other disability rights laws) only do so because they honestly do not know of an alternative addressing and then finally ending their own outsider status. Filling this information void through encouraging historic levels of community-wide political participation the College Democrats of America and general Democratic Party will reaffirm their essentiality to people with disabilities. People knowing their rights then also know which party actually fights for maintenance and expansion of those same rights.

As I am writing this, I receive word the Texas Republican party is drafting a position statement to exclude people with learning and/or mental disabilities from the Americans with Disabilities Act on the assumption these conditions are made up and ultimately abuse ADA's original intentions. Conceding that any law can be abused (the PATRIOT Act springs to mind!) I deeply resent an idea that my experiences and very existence is fraudulent. I also hope this same event facilitates a greater awareness of critical differences between the two political parties in an era when Ralph Nader continues to believe we actually are identical. Voting for a political party discounting your numerous and very real experiences and those of your, family and/or friends is ridiculous; the Democrats are the only political party with a solid disability rights public policy record.

Disability rights organizing certainly offers many challenges, but there are numerous rewards. Physical plant renovations at my University ultimately installed the exact same Braille plates and evacuation chairs I previously called for in a series of campus paper investigative articles and columns. With equal opportunity already in the books, I, other students with disabilities, and our allies must now demand enforcement for full policy benefit realization. Taking America's future seriously requires people with disabilities to apply their involuntary political educations to the public sphere in this upcoming and every subsequent election.

I and other college democrats with disabilities live the revolution every time we attend classes, graduate with our degrees and obtain jobs. We live the revolution every time we insist college students with disabilities take self-pride and are fairly represented by student government and organizations. This revolution is everywhere and we are a vital part of it!

No Man is an Island
Justin Padley
Gonzaga University, Spokane, WA

It's Tuesday. A man, silent and composed, wrestles with his own rapidly approaching end. He nervously mulls over his life and thinks of his family. The man revisits his plan, trying to remain focused. But he slips into a memory. It seems like a lifetime ago now – the day he gave himself over to the prospect… no, the *reality* of a martyr's exit. The next two hours will define him as a creation in the eyes of his Creator. And he will be remembered.

A poet he's never read famously opined that no man is an island. Everybody is connected to some degree – part of the continent, part of the main. And this man is no different.

His mother is sick. She may live out the year, Allah willing, but the pain she endures makes that prospect a wrenching, double-edged sword. "She's a good woman," he remarks pensively to himself, falling into a wash of sounds and images. At a time in his life, her smile was the first thing he'd see as he awoke and the last before drifting off to sleep. Those were simpler times; the strife, the struggle that's marked his lifetime was there, yes, but he was a child. He was free to let the concerns of a ravaged world fall to someone else. Now, it seems, the weight of so many worlds rests squarely with him.

It was also a Tuesday – the day she told him she was dying. He had a sense that something was wrong, that her recurrent illnesses were more than a persistent and nasty bug. When she told him, the word fell like a sack of flour in her quiet room. When his time was upon him, he wept until he was dizzy. Still, he didn't want her to see his tears as they parted. It would be their last goodbye and he carried that knowledge alone. He wept again as he privately entrusted her to the care of the Imam a few hours later. That day he was weak. He questioned himself and the necessity of his fight. But he's made his peace. In this moment alone, her strength gives him strength. Her lifetime of love and patience steels his resolve.

A 767 begins its final ascent. The curtain starts to fall. A bell tolls. No man is an island.

Openly (Gay)

Timothy A. O'Brien
State University of New York at Albany, Albany, NY

W hat a backwards notion,
bigotry in motion.
they'll say they aren't fit,
to raise a family quite legit,
Open your eyes.

It's claimed they are perverse,
they seem against the diverse,
it's based on an ancient text,
tell me, who's going to be next?
Open your mind.

All that's wanted is the right,
to wed your love and end this fight,
you can love and share your name,
so can they, it's just the same,
Open your soul.

We're all equal, just alike,
no more queer, fruit or dyke,
we share this world, land and nation,
let's end all degradation,
Open your heart.

"Professors are supposed to be preparing the future generation to become the policy makers and leaders of the world. However, key skills such as critical thinking and problem solving are being forsaken, due to a lack of diversity of viewpoint."

Professors' Misconduct Damaging University Credibility
Joshua Haines
Northern Arizona University, Flagstaff, AZ

The open and civil discussion of sensitive political issues is covertly and openly discouraged, throughout our system of higher education, by a faculty composed primarily of leftist professors. These professors promote a one-sided view concerned primarily with justification of their own political theories, "political correctness," and the cultivation of a student body that will helplessly regurgitate whatever propaganda is espoused from the lectern. This liberal bias threatens, in many ways, the integrity and viability of every educational institution in the nation.

First, professors are supposed to be preparing the future generation to become the policymakers and leaders of the world. However, key skills such as critical thinking and problem solving are being forsaken due to a lack of diversity of viewpoint.

Second, the professors who disseminate a mostly liberal viewpoint are producing a generation of college graduates unable to engage in a proper debate. With instructors guiding their students through history and the social sciences using only half a compass, many students leave the university prepared to view the world with only one eye. This produces a situation that commonly occurs in modern political "debate." One party makes a statement, and the second party responds to it with a personal attack. While criticizing a policy proposal, even harshly, is healthy for proper debate to occur, leaving this realm in favor of lambasting one's opponent is damaging to our system of democracy. Unfortunately this practice is encouraged in our institutions with professors making continuous personal attacks against those with whom they disagree.

Third, the political correctness pressed upon students further limits the scope of discussion and analysis of critically important issues by demonizing one side of a debate, generally the conservative side. For instance, it is politically correct, in the eyes of the liberal professor, to speak about abortion in a positive context. When one holds this view, one is considered to be "forward thinking," or "progressive," and one is considered to be looking out for the good of society. Yet, in a university setting, to hold the opposite view means that one is narrow-minded, sexist, and/or bent on pushing one's morals on the rest of the world. This conservative view of the issue is politically incorrect, at least in the eyes of leftist professors and their disciples.

Political correctness acts as a barrier to the free expression of valid political ideals, and it is not just limited to discussions of abortion. Think about how gun control is treated; or, on that note, how is the Second Amendment regarded in a discussion of the Bill of Rights? How is the notion of school vouchers treated by university faculty? Think about how theories of distribution of wealth, energy policy, taxation, gender awareness, environmental issues, or the use of military force are treated.

None of these issues is handled properly by our professors, namely because a conservative view is never given the same weight as that of a liberal one, if considered at all. In overall context the actions of the professors who choose to run their classroom in such a biased fashion, creates a campus setting in which conservative students are often ostracized by their peers. Criticism is very often directed at individuals and disrupts the cultivation of original thought.

For example, the University of Arizona College Republicans recently held an "affirmative action bake sale" on their campus to raise awareness about what they feel is a discriminatory government policy. At this event baked goods were priced according to race and gender. Customers could then either purchase food according to the price list or sign a petition calling for an end to affirmative action. While a pro-affirmative action rally on a university campus would have been embraced by faculty, the affirmative action bake sale and those who hosted it were branded as racist and sexist by many in the academic community, and they were subject to personal attacks by their peers.

Students need to realize the power wielded over their world-views by any person in a position of power. Likewise, instructors need to consider whether they wish to indoctrinate or educate their students.

The American university is teetering on the brink of failure due to mismanagement, having already lost much of its credibility in America's industrial, technological and clinical sectors, as well as much of its policy influence; thus the rise in influence of private think tanks, private labs, and private technological institutions. The university's future depends on the actions of its professors and administrators, and only when all of the foregoing issues are addressed, only when there is a renewed commitment to educating students, will our universities be able to once again claim a place of respect in our society.

This work or portions of this work have previously been published in **The Lumberjack** *(Northern Arizona University's student newspaper).*

"In 2002, 4.9% of all faculty in higher education were black and an even lesser percentage were Hispanic and Native American."

Race And Affirmative Action
Timothy Schuermer

Rutgers University, Newark, NJ

In 1977, Allan Bakke sued the University of California at Davis Medical School for "reverse discrimination." He was white, and he won. Since that defining moment, the Civil Rights Act of 1964 has become the burden of the white man and a faint glimmer of hope for oppressed minorities.

Nowadays, resentment and tension have intensified relations for all ethnic and socioeconomic factions involved. Non-minorities, such as Caucasians, feel as if less qualified, less educated, and less proven students are given priority admission into national universities and colleges. A past, yet still ever-present, problem that has gone unsolved lawfully since 1977 is once again, and even more vehemently, beginning to divide a nation. How do we correct reverse discrimination while allocating equal opportunity to those groups we seek to assist?

Affirmative action in higher education has been and is plagued by two major problems: one, the polarization of whites versus blacks, and two, the de-emphasis of class-based policies.

In 2002, 4.9% of all faculty in higher education were black and an even lesser percentage were Hispanic and Native American. Women were also minimally represented with only 36% of full time faculty identified as women. Racially speaking, the problem transcends from faculty to student as minority groups other than African Americans are still poorly represented. Because of this schism, Asian Americans, Hispanics, Native Americans, and women are lumped together and thus become marginalized. All focus is given to whites and blacks, a reflection of priority. Polarization pulls whiteness into the public and is reinterpreted as a disadvantage towards, or victimization of whites. By creating limitations and binary battles, other minorities become secondary and misrepresented. In order for affirmative action to be functional and efficient the juxtaposition of black versus white must not exist.

By incorporating all minorities and gender we have abolished any possibility of neglect or misrepresentation of a group. But in order to move beyond the problem of reverse discrimination affirmative action must abide by color- and gender-blind policies. All groups have and are represented, but affirmative action needs to become a class -or economi- based policy. During the school year of 2002-2003, 74% of students attending top-tier schools were from upper-class families while 3% were from lower class families. As a result, students with less financial and economic opportunity are innately unqualified and uncompetitive. These are the students affirmative action must seek to help. Students with limited educational resources and communal opportunities are not given the chance to showcase their potential or qualifications as worthy students. By creating class-based laws, racial and gender preference no longer cause injustices within the system. The opportunity to become educated and to attend a university or college should not be based on the luck of financial security in which you were born into, it should be based on the equal opportunity for all to become educated by implementing such laws as class-based affirmative action that gives less privileged students the chance to succeed.

Rooms

Gary Dennis
University of Southern California, Los Angeles, CA

The reality no one wants to think about is the culturally imposed system of rooms. You work in a cubicle, your little room for 9 hours everyday. When work is over, you sit in your living room, to unwind after being in a room all day. Your TV keeps you sitting and behaving in your room, it makes sure you're paying attention, and keeps you sitting still, like a prison warden. People go to school, and sit in more rooms. Parents punish you, and put you in your room. Your apartment building, is just a collection of tiny rooms. Finally, when someone gets tired of their rooms and snaps, or acts out criminally, we lock them in prison rooms. When people die, we put them in a mausoleum or crypt, another room for eternity. This is all done, until your mind is trapped inside its own room. Once this happens, no matter where in the world you are, the vasts forests of the American Northwest, or the expanse of the Sahara Desert, it won't matter, because mentally and spiritually, you will still be inside, behind four walls and under a roof, lit by artifitial sunlight, never once having the experience of getting out and exploring the wonders that are outside.

"Sally loves to teach. She loves children. She loves her students and her school and her principal. But Sally feels like she cannot teach well. Sally feels like President Bush's Act makes things very hard for her. And no one is willing to listen. No one is willing to do anything to help Sally."

See Sally Struggle
Scott D. Elingburg
Clemson University, Clemson, SC

Sally wants to be a teacher.

She wants to be a teacher because she thinks it is worth the effort.

She wants to be a teacher because she thinks that education is important.

Sally wants to teach first grade. Sally wants to teach her students things that they might not know. She wants her students to be educated so that one day they can grow up and do great things. She looks at important men and women in history and in the world today and thinks, "These men and women have all had great teachers."

Sally decides she will be a teacher.

Sally graduates from college and becomes trained, certified, and highly qualified to teach.

Soon after graduation, Sally receives a call from a local public school. They want Sally to come and teach at their school. "You are trained, certified, and highly qualified to teach," the principal of the school says.

Sally is very happy. She loves children, but more importantly she loves to teach children.

Sally cannot wait for the first day of school to arrive. She remembers being a little girl and enjoying school very much. School is where she met many of her friends, and school is where her teachers always made Sally feel welcome. She can name all of her teachers from kindergarten to high school. And even some she had in college.

Soon, the first day of school arrives. Sally is bursting with excitement. Her students begin to come into her classroom one by one. She tells her students to find their desks with their names written on their nametags. Sally spent a lot of time getting her students' nametags just right. She wants each student to feel special.

Some of Sally's students don't show up on the first day. This makes Sally worried. Also, some of her students look like they have not had enough sleep. Some of them fall asleep in class while Sally is teaching. This makes Sally concerned. A few of her students cry because they are hungry and a few of her students say mean things to her. This makes Sally very upset. She asks her students to please stop crying and please do not say mean things to her, but they do not listen.

The first day of school is over and Sally is tired. She comes home with a worried look on her face. Bob, her husband, asks Sally, "What is wrong?" Sally tells Bob that she is tired. Then she tells Bob that some of her students were mean, some cried, and some fell asleep. This makes Bob feel bad for Sally. He knows that she is working very hard to be a good teacher.

The second day of school is very busy for Sally. Some of her students are sick and should not be at school. Some of her students have trouble paying attention in class. Some have still not shown up.

Sally remembers that she needs to buy some more supplies for her classroom. So, after school is over, Sally walks into the principal's office and politely asks for some money. Sally's principal says, "We do not have any money for supplies." Sally has to have supplies, so Sally takes some of her money and buys some supplies for her classroom.

The third day of school, one of Sally's students comes in late. Sally has not met this student yet. Sally's principal wants to walk the late student down to the classroom. After bringing the student into the classroom, Sally's principal asks to see Sally in the hallway. The principal tells Sally that the reason her student was late today and has not shown up for the first two days of school is because the police arrested the student's father last night for dealing drugs. Sally does not know what to say. Sally does not know what to do. This makes Sally very sad. She wants to take the student home with her.

After the students have all gone home, Sally and the rest of the teachers have a staff meeting in the cafeteria. The principal tells all of the teachers that they are doing a great job. However, they need to do a better job.

The principal explains to the teachers that the students are not meeting the standards established in President Bush's *No Child Left Behind Act*. She says that the teachers must make sure that every child is prepared to do well on standardized tests, otherwise the school may lose federal funding.

The principal also explains that if the students do not do well on standardized tests, then the teachers may be held accountable. This means that Sally's job is at stake. Also, the principal says, there are many other things that school must do to make Adequate Yearly Progress. If the school does not meet Adequate Yearly Progress, then the school will receive a failing grade on their progress report and possibly lose funding. If the school loses funding, then some of the teachers will have to be fired. Sally is worried because she is a new teacher and could be the first to lose her job.

Sally is very concerned about meeting these standards. Some of her students do well in some subjects and some do well in other subjects. Some of her students are very practical, while some are very creative. Sally does not think that there is a standard that all of her students can meet. She tells her students, "You are all individuals. Everyone has different talents. Everyone is unique." Sally does not believe that standardized tests support this idea.

Sally decides to tell other people about how she disagrees with these standards and with President Bush' "No Child Left Behind" Act. Some people listen, some do not. Sometimes people say, "Education does not matter to me. My children are grown up and are not in school." Other people say, "Sally, do not criticize President Bush. We are at war with Iraq and he needs our support." A few people say, "We have to protect our future by finding the terrorists."

Sally wonders what war, Iraq, and terrorism have to do with education.

Sally decides that the best thing to do is to try to be a great teacher and to try very hard to help her students do well on standardized tests. But Sally discovers that it is very hard to help students do well in school when they are hungry, tired, and poorly disciplined at home. Sally thinks that some of her student's parents should be held accountable for poor standardized test scores.

Sally loves to teach. She loves children. She loves her students and her school and her principal. But Sally feels like she cannot teach well. Sally feels like President Bush's Act makes things very hard for her. And no one is willing to listen. No one is willing to do anything to help Sally.

So Sally comes home and cries.

Bob asks Sally, "What is wrong?"

Sally says, "I love to teach. But I am not allowed to focus on teaching. These standards make me feel like I must teach with my hands tied behind my back. Every day there is something new to consider. Tomorrow they may ask me to hop on one leg. Next week they may ask me to teach blindfolded. The next week they may ask me to cut off my arm. I cannot perform well at my job, and that makes me sad, because the children are the ones who suffer."

Sally still thinks education is important.

Sally still thinks teaching is worth the effort.

Sally still wants to be a teacher.

But Sally wishes someone would pass a *No Teacher Left Behind Act.*

"The censorship that has acted as a burden upon teachers and students is intended to help curtail the lack of tolerance for diversity."

September 11th in the Classroom
Gregory James Smith
Westminster College, New Wilmington, PA

The tragic events that unfolded on September 11th put a crashing hold upon America's business, educational institutions, and governmental procedures. However, these effects were only temporary and short-lived. The smoke settled, and America found itself a newly changed country, but the underlying principles upon which the country operates still remained. Business continued as it always does, America's educational institutions picked up where they had left off, and the government of the United States of America came back bigger and stronger. In spite of the "America on the rebound," critics cannot help but to question if the institutions of higher learning handled things in an appropriate manner. Many universities and colleges across the nation adjourned the classes and activities for the day, while other institutions carried on with business as normal. In this wide spread debate only one thing is certain: the classrooms of America post-September 11th have changed for both the best and worst.

Since September 11th, a new desire has been sparked in the educational process of both students and professors. As asserted by Cox:

> The attacks have markedly altered student interest in particular subjects, and in some instances have altered the subject matter itself. The attacks have also given many courses a new relevance, and the stunning scale of the tragedy has sparked a new sense of engagement in both students and professors.

The result of this new-found passion has been overflowing classrooms, new texts development, and of course, a more responsive classroom setting. Although this flatters many professors it also overwhelms them due to the sheer amount of pupils that attend the class (Clayton, "Standing Room" 13). The numbers of students causes a conflict in the quality of education that is being received, but the question is what are the professors to do?

With the rapid consumption of this new-found knowledge, campuses nation-wide have begun to accrue the devastating effects of overcrowding classrooms. Students have begun to rush classrooms on Middle Eastern and Islamic thought, professors have exhausted all possible resources for introducing "politically correct" materials, and the physical constraints of the classrooms simply cannot hold the number of students attending the sessions (Lord 56). In an attempt to alleviate the problem, universities and colleges nationwide have begun to hold symposiums and forums. Although these classes and symposiums are in high demand currently, critics wonder if this current surge of inquisition will continue. Dr. Charles Kimball of Wake Forest University seems to believe that it will. He states that

> *We've moved to a different level [. . .] This attack was on American soil, and my guess is there will be a lot more interest for years [in Middle East and Islamic studies] on campuses. People are really trying to make sense of a whole variety of images coming at them (quoted in Clayton, "Standing Room" 15).*

If Dr. Kimball's statement is true, then campuses across the nation have a relatively large problem to face and only a small amount of time to fix it.

In addition to the problems that are presented inside the classroom, campuses nationwide are battling with more complicated issues outside the confinement of classroom walls. Campuses nationwide face the problem of educating the general student population on acceptance of diversity (Leo 59). An immediate response after the attacks on September 11th strained universities and colleges to release statements calling for students not to profile groups of people by ethnicity or religion. In addition, some colleges even asked the student population to extend a helping hand to these groups of people that may undergo racial profiling (59).

Another problem that campuses face is the censorship of both students and professors. Many professors found themselves in the heat of controversy during their forums and symposiums as asserted by Dorsey:

"Working out" ideas in public about the declared "war on terrorism" has also not always been easy. At the University of North Carolina, reports about a teach-in brought calls for faculty firings. At Yale University, they spawned concerns about a renewed "culture war" on campus, pitting liberals against conservatives. Statements interpreted as anti-American or overly critical of American foreign policy, in particular, have created tensions. Consequently, at some colleges, the need to distinguish between old-fashioned "teach-ins" and other kinds of forums is now being seriously pondered.

The censorship that has acted as a burden upon teachers and students is intended to help curtail the lack of tolerance for diversity. However, many critics feel that these tactics act as an antithesis to the original intent of the colleges (Leo 59).

After examining the reactions of colleges around the nation it is only natural to analyze how Westminster College handled the horrific events that unfolded on September 11th. The college as a whole acted in a passive manner. The symbolic head of the school, President Williamson, sent a campus-wide e.mail urging students to put the victims in our prayers, resume with classes, and to try to forget the events so that the academic population could return to its daily routine. The statement releasesd by President Williamson upset first year student Alexandra Mikhaylova. She states that:

> *Westminster couldn't have prevented the natural panic that comes along with such an enormous tragedy, but there are certain methods that are an appropri ate response and this was not one of them [...] I find it absurd and almost humorous that the President of our school could be so naïve as to believe that an email could calm our nerves. Perhaps a speech or words of encourgament, but not an email.*

If the head of the school could not effectively assist the student body then how effective were the departmental components of the school in helping the academic community cope with such a difficult situation?

The religious department of Westminster College proved perhaps to be the most effective element in helping the student body move on with its daily routine and to recover from the tragedy and heartbreak. There were several different sessions of chapel that were held, which yielded over seven hundred students, about half the school's population. Thomas Sergi, a first year student, expressed his opinion that the religious section of Westminster was the "best fit [compartment] to settle the nerves of the students, and that it could only be expected that people turn to their faith in a time of [massive] despair such as September 11th."

However, the religion department was not the only department to extend a helping hand to the academic community. The political science department also tried to help the student body by holding numerous forums. The forums were all in relation to the events of September 11th, and they tried to help the student population better understand the who, what, when, where, and why. In addition to holding these series of symposiums, the political science department also renewed and encouraged students to enroll in the peace study minors.

There has been no conclusive result of how appropriately either Westminster College or colleges and campuses across the nation have acted with regards to the events of September 11th. However, it is very noticeable that America's institutions of higher learning are for at least now changed for both the good and the bad. In the following years the critical claims will subside and the truth will be told of how effectively the situation was handled, but until then, students and faculty alike will have to draw up their own conclusions.

"President Bush favored an initial small step for man in the form of his prescription drug plan for seniors. Senator Kerry, in the tradition of the party of FDR and LBJ, advocates a giant leap for mankind with his version of national health insurance."

Socialism Promotes Sexually Transmitted Disease: An Unintended Consequence of National Health Care
Eric Michael Wasserstrum
Washington University in St. Louis, St. Louis, MO

To protect them from the heat – and occasional glimmers of light – of election year debate, the empirical foundations of policy proposals are buried more deeply than usual. Fueling the flames are candidates of both major parties who have endorsed further growth in the government's role in the definition, distribution, and provision of health care for individual Americans. President Bush favored an initial small step for man in the form of his prescription drug plan for seniors. Senator Kerry, in the tradition of the party of FDR and LBJ, advocates a giant leap for mankind with his version of national health insurance. To secure health care's position in rational discourse, we must cool the quadrennial fever of election year rhetoric by surveying the empirical evidence of how government control of health care delivery has faired in other countries.

Government control may well increase the number of individuals to whom "health care" is available. However, the nature of the delivery, and of the care itself, appears to be altered by government involvement. One reliable effect is a longer "waiting period" – a longer interval between onset of symptoms, initial diagnosis, and medical intervention – for those who would otherwise have had access to private care. This may initially seem like a small inconvenience, a small price to pay for the greater good expected from "universal care." However, a mounting body of data suggests that the "small price" paid for the greater good includes an increased prevalence and incidence of sexually transmitted diseases.

The British Health Protection Agency reported a four percent rise in sexually transmitted diseases in 2003, continuing an alarming trend that has doubled STD cases over the past decade. This trend is at least partially attributable to the delayed intervention – in STD, as in most illnesses – that characterizes the British National Health Service (NHS). A survey by the Family Planning Association of 256 genitourinary medicine clinics revealed wait times of up to six weeks. Delays in diagnosis and treatment promote the spread of infection in at least two ways. First, patients remain sexually active while waiting for an appointment. Second, the inconvenience of extended wait periods acts as a disincentive for frequent sexual health screening. In the words of The Nursing Times: "As demand for sexual health services has increased so have waiting times, which causes delays in diagnosis and treatment. This in turn increases the risk of infections being passed to sexual partners" (3/8/2004). Dr. James Johnson, Chairman of the British Medical Association, similarly expressed his frustration: "[P]atients…can wait up to six weeks for an appointment. What use it that?" (ABC News, 6/27/04).

Such delays – and their deleterious effects on health – are also common in perhaps the strongest bastion of government controlled health care, Canada. Canada has experienced insufficient supply of health care since it finalized its national health insurance system, dubbed Medicare, in 1985. According to the Organization for Economic Cooperation and Development, Canada ranked 24th out of 29 developed countries in physician to patient ratio, even after spending the 9th most on health care as percent of GDP. This is largely a result of the flight of doctors - 10,000 since 1990 according to Canada News (3/5/2003). A report from the Frontiers of Freedom Institute (December 2003) notes that a primary cause of the exodus is physician compensation. Doctors' pay is based on "billing thresholds," determined only by patient volume, regardless of how comprehensive or intensive the care. If the "billing threshold" is reached, physicians must remand "overpayments" to the government. As Canadian Medicare promotes physician flight, waiting lists get even longer. The Fraser Institute published data on waiting times in 2001-2002 for: treatment after referral from a general practitioner, 16.5 weeks; initial visit to a radiation oncologist, 8.5 weeks; CT scan, 5.2 weeks; and MRI, 12.4 weeks. Hip-replacement patients must wait an average 20 weeks for surgery – that is, after the initial 13 week waiting period just to see the specialist. The Frontiers for Freedom Institute notes that this is perhaps the reason that Cleveland, Ohio is the hip-replacement capital of Canada. Hence, equality of access to care simply assures that everyone is served equally poorly.

There are those who might suggest that these problems with health care are not inherent to the structures of the Canadian or the British systems but reflect insufficient allocation of funds. This hypothesis, too, deserves the light of data. The Scotsman (8/5/2004) reports that despite Scotland's health budget increase from £6 billion a year three ago to more than £8 billion this year, the number of people on waiting lists has risen, as has the average waiting times for both outpatients and inpatients.   The executive branch of the Scottish Parliament recently came under pressure because of the lack of tangible results from this £8 billion allotment to NHS. The report by Robert Black, the Auditor General, echoes a growing body of data that suggests increases in nationalized health care expenditures yield no improvements.

Such results were predictable. In 1976, British physician Dr. Max Gammon published his Theory of Bureaucratic Displacement. The theory posits that "[in] a bureaucratic system . . . increase in expenditure will be matched by fall in production . . . Such systems will act rather like 'black holes' in the economic universe, simultaneously sucking in resources, and shrinking in terms of 'emitted' production." Of note,

Economics Nobel aureate Milton Friedman has applied the same research methodology – measuring the input and output in the bureaucratic model – to Medicare and Medicaid in the US. He attributes a large percentage of the rising health care costs in the US to Gammon's Law as applied to the progenitors of a national insurance system that have already revealed their bureaucratic core.

On the subject of output, some cite apparent statistical equivalence in the success rates of certain procedures as evidence of similar health care quality in private and nationalized systems. Cardiac surgery pioneer Dr. Michael DeBakey addressed the issue at a meeting at the Baylor College of Medicine some years ago. Dr. DeBakey remarked that the results of coronary artery bypass surgery that had been reported by British surgeons appeared comparable to those at major American centers. He then noted pointedly that the prolonged waiting times in Britain removed (by death) surgical candidates with more severe disease. Hence, in Britain, those who survived to undergo surgery were more likely to survive the surgery itself. In the United States, urgent and emergent bypass surgery has long been common, and the excellent results under these circumstances raise a higher standard. The point here is not a transatlantic comparison of cardiovascular surgical prowess. Rather, it is another – perhaps self-evident – illustration of the effects of the treatment delays characteristic of government health care.

In light of the data, a cost-benefit analysis of "a small inconvenience" versus "the greater good" deserves revision. Those arguing for that calculus, especially idealistic young adults who are at high risk for sexually transmitted diseases, may wish to reconsider. The health and life your opposition to "government care" saves may be your own.

This work or portions of this work have previously been published in **The Washington Witness** *(Washington University in St. Louis student newspaper).*

"Some people believe the answers to our problems lie in science and technology, and we have found some. However, it is both arrogant and foolish to believe that we can control the course of nature."

Sustainability
Karen E. Setty
The University of Dayton, Dayton, OH

Here's a scenario for you. A high school kid, average kid, let's call him Jimmy, decides to start doing drugs so he can fit in better with his friends. He also stops doing homework and going to classes, breaks the law periodically, argues with his mom all the time, gets into fights, steals money, etc. Basically, he's "on the wrong track." His mother is forced to sell her belongings to support his drug habit and suffers from stress that builds up to the point of a nervous breakdown, and finally a heart attack. Jimmy, with no other family to turn to, becomes depressed, homeless, and starving, and dies shortly afterward of an overdose. Let's recap what happened here. Both ended up dead because of how Jimmy chose to live his life. Pretty unhappy ending, right?

Now what if I told you that you are Jimmy… and I am Jimmy, and the majority of people alive today are Jimmy? After millions of years of evolution, the human race today is destroying the very earth that gave us life, and destroying ourselves in the process. Thinking of the earth as your mother does not make you a hippie. It's a simple fact. This planet, unlike any other planet in the solar system, sustains the biological functioning of billions of plants, animals, and human beings. Without oxygen to breath, food to nourish us, and water to drink, we would die. It's that simple. However, by some strange twist of fate, human beings have inflicted incredible injury to the earth, and are on track to continue in this pattern, all while keeping our fingers crossed that the earth will hold out. Our oceans and freshwater supplies are becoming constantly more polluted, the topsoil that supports our food production is being lost faster than it can be replaced, deforestation has already claimed the majority of land that provides us with oxygen. Even the climate is changing, the ozone layer is depleted, our coal and oil reserves are almost gone, but we're not doing much about it. And why should we, when we can just take our chances?

No, we haven't run out of anything just yet, but the fact that our resources are being used up at unprecedented rates seems to imply what's coming. When you're low on milk, you get up, go to the store, and buy more. I won't bore you with the details, but trust me, we're low on milk. Knowing this, we have several choices on how to act. We can (A) wait until a catastrophe occurs and then try to fix it, or (B) use our knowledge of what is occurring today to try and prevent future catastrophes. Both methods have their merits. With the first choice, we don't have to do anything right now (though our children may be out of luck). On the other hand, we could invest a little time and effort now to realign ourselves in the right direction. Economically, method B chooses low cost over high cost. Ethically, it chooses life over death and the continuation of our race. We know what Jimmy chose. What would you choose? What would you do if there were a ticking time bomb in the engine of your car?

Unfortunately, value systems today seldom place the earth over money or time. We don't put the planet's well-being even at the same level of worth as a person's life. I'm not bashing the value of money, time, or human life, but isn't it ironic that without this lowly planet there would be no money, no time, and no life. We often take for granted that which we should most respect.

By hurting the earth, we hurt ourselves. Rachel Carson demonstrated in the 1960s that the tons of chemicals and pollutants dumped into the environment every year do not disappear. They come back to haunt us in tiny amounts in the air we breath, the water we drink, and the food we eat. Our bodies are filled with cocktails of chemicals that did not exist 100 years ago. And it seems every other person gets cancer nowadays. Our work environments are often toxic, artificial, and depressing. The cute animals we love to see at the zoo are disappearing. Children are increasingly affected by asthma and allergies, and people are forced to make their homes next to landfills.

Some people believe the answers to our problems lie in science and technology, and we have found some. However, it is both arrogant and foolish to believe that we can control the course of nature. For a species that prides ourselves on intelligence, we must stop and ask whether we are acting out of intelligence, or greed. Science and technology ought to be directed toward working with the earth through efficient *sustainable* development rather than working against it and correcting mistakes as we go along.

The benefits of sustainable living include healthier lifestyles, a more enjoyable environment, and the promise of our children's children being able to enjoy the same opportunities that we have. On the other hand, the consequences of choosing not to live sustainably are not quite as pleasant. These include sickness, despair, disaster, and death. What would you choose?

This work or portions of this work have previously been published in **The Scientia Disciplorum.**

"To wit, though the specifics vary from country to country, the root cause of hunger is always the same: not lack of handouts, but lack of capitalism."

Teach a Man to Fish
Jonathan Rick
Hamilton College, Clinton, NY

On Monday in Beinecke, the Hamilton chapter of Amnesty International asked me for money to buy a water buffalo for a farmer in Nepal. The scene reminded me of a comparable event I wrote about last year. "So, we donated spare change in water buckets at the dining halls, we fasted, we volunteered for Utica's soup kitchen. But something was missing—an ingredient so implicit in our bounty that we overlooked its necessity. That manna is capitalism. For capitalism, in contrast to the quick fixes of Hunger and Homelessness Week, is a long-term panacea."

Indeed, world hunger is not a problem of redistribution. As psychotherapist Michael J. Hurd observes, people don't go hungry "because you throw out half a stick of butter or an unfinished Coke." In the same way, malnutrition does not develop into abundance when you donate one of those shiny new twenty-dollar bills to some charity. As they say, "give a man a fish, and feed him for the week. Teach a man to fish, and feed him for a lifetime."

To wit, though the specifics vary from country to country, the root cause of hunger is always the same: not lack of handouts, but lack of capitalism. Consider sub-Saharan Africa for instance. Echoing Julian Simon's thesis in *The Ultimate Resource 2*, philosopher Andrew Bernstein argues, "Africa has the identical natural resource fundamentally responsible for the West's rise: the human mind." Yet it lacks the social system that allows the mind to flourish, which liberates it to invent and innovate. What Africans, like other starving people, desperately need, therefore, is to marry the mind to the market.

For to the extent that it has existed, the free market has enabled abundance unmatched in human history. When was the last time a famine occurred in any capitalist nation? It is no coincidence that the hungriest countries - Somalia, Afghanistan and Haiti - are most averse to economic and political freedom.

Now, I don't doubt the sincerity of my fellow students. But if your heart bleeds for the tired, the poor, the huddled masses yearning to breathe free to whom Emma Lazarus dedicated our Statue of Liberty, then give them the gift of capitalism and watch their cups run over. We can debate the details later, but let's call a spade a spade. To paraphrase Ayn Rand, the haves have capitalism; the have-nots have not capitalism. To paraphrase President Clinton, it's capitalism, stupid. To rephrase Karl Marx, workers of the world unite for capitalism; you have nothing to lose but your hunger.

* Published in **The Spectator** *(Hamilton College),* **November 14, 2004;** *the* **Post-Standard** *(Syracuse, NY), January 22, 2004.*

"So even though you are required by law to pay the Social Security tax, you have no legal right to collect. What a ripoff!"

Thanks, But I'll Pass
Michael Inganamort
American University, Washington, DC

Social Security. It is a joke, huh? You pay into it your whole life, and then you see just some of it when you retire. It reminds me of a commercial for used cars I used to see back home. "Wow, what a deal!" the woman would exclaim. Thanks, but I'll pass. Even if you believe in the original idea of the system, you cannot deny it is now horribly broken. Do the math. Workers pay Social Security, not directly for themselves, but for the seniors retiring today. Prior to World War II, there were approximately 40 payees for every retiree. Today there are three.

It is therefore impossible to pay today's retirees what those of the past received. In fact, while retirees of the World War II generation received significantly more in benefits than they paid in taxes, baby-boomers can expect a rate of return of 2 percent. Generation X can expect a rate of return of 1 percent, and the next generation can expect a rate of return of zero.

And here's an interesting fact: did you know that Social Security benefits are not guaranteed by law? The Supreme Court decided in *Helvering v. Davis* that individuals have "no legal right to Social Security benefits." So even though you are required by law to pay the Social Security tax, you have no legal right to collect. What a ripoff!

Most Democrats and Republicans will agree that the system is not working in its current state. And, unlike some political issues that are wrapped up in partisanship, there are a number of legitimate solutions out there to fix Social Security. Some people would suggest that it is best to cut the benefits and raise the age when one would collect. (This idea would then be sheepishly retracted as soon as the aforementioned person considers a career in politics.) Others would suggest not using money in the Social Security trust fund to pay for non-Social Security projects. Who would have thought!

But there are even more ideas. Sometimes my Libertarian side kicks in and I have to wonder, why don't we just get rid of the whole thing? Pay back those who have paid into it, and let everyone else in the future actually keep their whole paycheck from now on. Imagine that, people keeping their own money in their own bank accounts.

Pardon my tangent, but have we grown callous to the fear of signing away our paychecks to the federal government? There is an assumption going around that Congress will keep a better eye on it than we will. This is why Social Security, in its worst form, is insulting.

If the rate of return is approaching zero, the system is nothing more than a holding cell. Picture this imaginary vault where the government keeps a close eye on our Social Security dollars. Its lock would be soldered through - the door bent out of shape, lying on the floor, and inside would be a pack of Congressmen plotting to spend a cool billion dollars here and there.

I'll admit Social Security reform isn't at the top of college students' priorities. We grudgingly see how much of our paycheck is taken out for Social Security and then we get on with our lives. We save the panicking for when we are 50 or so.

And as of now, Social Security reform has yet to take a prominent role in the 2004 campaign. Often referred to as the "third rail of American politics," Social Security reform was a major issue in the 2000 election. George W. Bush was the first candidate for president to seriously discuss voluntary individual accounts. As the president stated,

....because there will be an expanding number of retirees for Social Security to support in the future, we must apply the power of savings, investing, and compound interest ... by introducing personal retirement accounts. Americans would own these assets [and] they would see more retirement income." It is a good idea, but I'm still waiting.

While the relative inaction on this issue is a bit disheartening, so too is the way in which the current candidates for president have wholly ignored it. I recently visited John Kerry's presidential campaign website. I was curious to see what the Democratic frontrunner had to say about fixing Social Security. I clicked on the "Issues" button and scrolled around. The only thing that came close to the Senator's position on any kind of entitlement program, is as follows, quoted directly from the senator's website: "Many politicians have supported major cuts that cause premium increases and cutbacks in benefits. John Kerry won't."

Huzzah! Senior citizens rejoice: John Kerry is determined to fix Social Security and will... will... well, I don't know what he will do. You're going to have to take his word for it. Again, thanks, but I'll pass.

This work or portions of this work have previously been published in **The Eagle** *(American University student newspaper).*

*"Friends, we're at a pivotal time in our country. If gay marriage
is allowed, the sanctity of that Sacred Institution will take yet
another blow."*

The Sanctity of Marriage
Anthony Lemaster
Morehead State University, Morehead, KY

Marriage was created many, many years ago. It was first created in a little
place we all have come to know as "Eden." That's right, God created marriage when he
created Adam and Eve, and Adam took her as his wife. Since that time, marriage has
been under attack. For centuries upon centuries, marriage as an institution has been
plagued by divorce, spousal abuse, and other vile corruptions that violate the sanctity of
marriage. But now, we face yet another attack on marriage. Homosexual marriage.

Now, I realize that the politicians will be debating this issue on a secular level.
They have to, lest the ACLU sue them and remove them from power by buying off the
right judges (or getting lucky and finding liberal judges that were installed by Democrats
to legislate Liberalism from the bench). But I, being a simple citizen without the duty to
forget my faith at the entrance doors of a Congressional Hall, can debate the religiosity
of this issue. But I won't simply delve into the religious aspects, but the aspects of
Christianity (and yes, Christianity is a faith, not a religion, but that is another article).

In the days of Sodom and Gomorrah, it is easy to see marriage under attack
here. It's under attack, as is pretty much all of society. The men of the town, if you'll
remember, wanted to have their way with men traveling through. Now, these men happened to be angels, but nobody told these sex-hungry perverts that. For all they knew,
they were simple men passing through. Lot offered his daughters up to the perverse
wickedness of these men, but no! They wanted the men to come out and "know" them.

If the homosexual community is right, and Sodom and Gomorrah was destroyed
because the inhabitants were inhospitable, then why, pray tell, is it that Lot offering his
daughters to be basically raped would have been, apparently, okay? Why is it that it
became an issue of total destruction only after men wanted to screw other men? The
simplest answer, and the most accurate answer, is this: homosexuality is a perversion of
the natural design of men and women, which God created in His Perfect Vision. God
does not want people to engage in homosexual activity.

Now, look through the Bible a bit further. In Leviticus 20:13, the instruction is abundantly clear. "If a man also lies with mankind, as he lies with a woman, both of them have committed an abomination. They shall surely be put to death. Their blood shall be on them."

Let us take a look at the teachings of Jesus, now. See, Jesus had this annoying (to the Pharisees) habit of correcting misinterpreted laws, or even saying that certain laws simply do not apply under the New Covenant (most of these dealing with what a person eats, or must sacrifice). When Jesus corrected misinterpretations of laws, He often started with "You have heard it was said..." Now, go take about... oh, an hour or so, look through all the red words (you know, those really important words), and just tell me where Jesus says anything along the lines of the following: "You have heard it was said, 'you shall not lie with the same gender'. But I tell you, whoever is in love has a right to lie with the person they love."

Go ahead, I'll wait.

...

...

What's that? You can't find that? Oh, shame on... oh wait, never mind. I won't put a shame on you, for it's not there to be found. Why is it so important, on this issue (as well as, I am sure, some others) what Jesus didn't say?

Because the people, especially the Pharisees, had an anti-homosexuality slant! The Pharisees may have had their shortcomings, and been far too rigid for their own good, but they were rigid in the laws. If you are having trouble piecing together this ultra-hard puzzle, let me spell it out for you.

The Pharisees, and undoubtedly the people, viewed homosexuality as evil. Not once did Jesus correct this view. He did correct many other views that were based on misinterpretations (or, misspeakings) of the law. Yet, He felt no need to correct an anti-homosexuality view.

There is not one verse in all the Bible that supports homosexual activity. Now, having homosexual thoughts is not some mortal sin. Plenty of people have thoughts of a homosexual nature, but do not act on them. If one acts on homosexuality, that is where sin comes in. It is quite possible that sin is also dwelling on these thoughts; I don't know. But I'm more inclined to say that the thoughts are temptation, and the action is sin.

Friends, we're at a pivotal time in our country. If gay marriage is allowed, the sanctity of that Sacred Institution will take yet another blow. I hear liberals all the time saying things like, "well, divorce is so high, why worry about gay marriage?" Or, "how can two men getting married affect my marriage?"

Well, here's the first answer: Divorce is wrong (although sometimes acceptable if it is done to escape abuse). However, the fact that divorce is wrong and legal should not make us immediately say that homosexual marriage, though wrong, should be legal.

The pre-existence of one wrong does not automatically dictate that we should allow another one to come in and add to the mix.

The second answer: It isn't about my marriage, or yours, nor should it be. If it is, then you're selfish, at least in this regard. It doesn't have to affect you personally in order for something to be right, or for it to be wrong. It's about marriage as a whole, and how it is viewed in our country. It isn't about you, or me, or Jimmy down the street. It's about an institution that God created.

Having said all that, now let me introduce a nice little caveat. I am aware that this may be a cop-out, but I don't care. I may be ruffling even conservative feathers here, but I don't care. All I can do is offer my opinion. I don't offer up the opinion of the GOP at large, or of anyone else, unless I am simply offering their opinion so you know it and then I rebut it.

I am not sure how, why, or if, homosexual marriage should be banned from a legal perspective. Maybe in a completely secular government, there is no reason to ban gay marriage, save the people voting to ban it in a majority fashion.

As a Christian, all I can do is say what the Bible says. There's lots of negativity towards homosexual activity. There's nothing in the way of being positive, however. As a Christian, I cannot support the further degradation of society and marriage (on which society is based, as family is based on marriage and society is based on family). Now, if I were a politician, having to check my religiosity at the door... I don't really know how I'd have to vote.

Of course, there are the arguments that allowing homosexual marriage will open the door to allow bestiality, polygamy, and any other form of "marriage" imaginable by sinful minds – mine included; I make no presumptions as to say I live a sin-free life and have perfect, pure thoughts all the time – within our society. I don't know if it will or won't, as cases can be made for both sides of that, all of which are plausible to me.

For now, I'll stick to my Christian worldview, and I'll refuse to put my Christianity aside in deciding if this is right or wrong. It is true, nobody is perfect, but that imperfection doesn't mean we have to allow further imperfections that we can control, and even stop from happening.

And don't even bother telling me not to judge others, because I'm not judging them. I'm judging an action, which is indeed perfectly okay. Besides, Jesus' teaching was to hypocrites (for lack of a better example, thieves judging against thieves), not to people who did not do a certain evil, judging against that evil. Yes, Jesus' teaching was clear. But so was the context, if only one will read and pay attention.

So now, here is the question I ask to liberal Christians: Are you willing to put aside Liberalism long enough to see God's stand on an issue and go with it? Or are you going to fight Him every step of the way?

A word of caution: The Israelites wandered through a desert for 40 years for not doing things God's way.

"A picture we see of a woman may consist of five different women's body parts; one woman's nose, another's eyes, another's breasts, another's mouth, and the list goes on. This is an unrealistic portrayal of women."

The Unrealistic Portrayal of Women in Advertising
Christina Girgenti
Radford University, Radford, VA

"Over the past few decades, the so-called "norm" for a female figure has drastically changed from voluptuous and curvy to waif-like thin. Many female celebrities have been known for their figures. Historically, Marilyn Monroe and Jayne Mansfield were two women who each wore a size 12 and were glorified by men all around the world. Today, celebrities from the likes of Jennifer Aniston and Calista Flockhart are admired for their abilities to become and stay so thin, almost appearing sick" (Sedighi). Unfortunately, in this day and age the media is bigger and better. Its audience is bigger, younger, and more influenced by their surroundings. "Advertising, [is] a $180 billion a year industry […] The average American is exposed to more than 3,000 ads every day and will spend a year and a half of his or her life watching commercials" (Jean 1). Because the average woman sees these extremely thin models advertising products, she begins to think that society's standard of a beautiful woman has changed and strives to achieve those standards at any cost. As Horner quotes Wolf, the media "first erodes a woman's self-esteem, then offers to sell it back to her one product at a time" (Horner 2). Our society and our economy are ad-driven. Unfortunately, the portrayal of women in advertising is not only untrue and unrealistic, it is causing women in society to view themselves negatively.

Jean Kilbourne, a distinguished author and lecturer in advocating against advertising because it harms women's self-esteem, explains in her film that young women are often concerned with their weight and dieting because of our society's "relentless emphasis on physical perfection," yet "failure is inevitable because the ideal is based on absolute flawlessness." What the general public does not understand is the images we see of these models have been altered with airbrushing and even computer technology. A picture we see of a woman may consist of five different women's body parts; one woman's nose, another's eyes, another's breasts, another's mouth, and the list goes on. This is an unrealistic portrayal of women. The general public and most importantly young women do not understand that a fashion model's body is genetic. Only 5 percent of American women have a model-like body. Models have a genetic body type: they are very tall, genetically thin, broad-shouldered, narrow-hipped, and long-legged. This body type excludes 95 percent of American women, "yet it is the only one we ever see in the media as acceptable and desirable" (Slim 1995). In Kilbourne's book *Deadly Persuasion: Why Women and Girls Must Fight the Addictive Power of Advertising* she examines a survey conducted in Massachusetts that found that the single largest group of high-school students considering or attempting suicide are girls who feel they are overweight, "Girls made to feel so terrible about themselves that they would rather be dead than fat" (134). These girls are not told that "the average fashion model weighs 23 percent less than the average female." (Slim 1995)

The advertising industry portrays women as objects that need to fixed or helped in some way, shape, or form, yet the woman modeling the product you so badly need does not need it at all. Because we see advertisements that emphasize our weaknesses day in and day out, we first begin to believe that we are not pretty, skinny, or trendy enough, and second, we see an ideal woman modeling that product that will hopefully make us look like her, so we go buy it. The only reason we, the consumers, believe she is ideal is because this is all we have seen as acceptable and desirable in society. Girls and women of all ages are not only burdened in society as being labeled a weaker sex, now we feel that we have to achieve unrealistic body measurements in order to get ahead in life. The pretty girl gets the job, the raise, the audition, etc. Is this the goal of the industry, to make us continually feel inadequate in order to motivate us to buy their products? The advertising industry seems not to understand that they are using women to sell their products that have nothing in common with their consumers, but in another sense this is what drives our economy: the thousands of women that endlessly buy, buy, buy, in order to look like those few women. It is a never-ending, vicious cycle because the consumers do not understand that someone will always be able to find something wrong with them and be able to create a product to "fix" it.

To prove just how much the portrayal of women in advertising affects women in society, an article, "Eating Disorders and Disordered Eating" by Niva Piran of the University of Toronto, is explored. She examines the way women internalize the influences that make their self-esteem low. In her study she reviews the 1994 publication by Bloom et al. that "examined the impact of women's relational attachment to cultural images and symbols." They concluded that "the internalization by girls and women of the cultural objectification of women's bodies, desires, and appetites creates a state of disruption in women's subjective experience of their bodies and desires, which, in turn, impacts on their eating patterns and on their experience of their body" (372). Women are so influenced by society's standards that it often affects their perceptions of themselves, causing physical dangers like depression and eating disorders. Advertising is causing a generation of depressed, starving girls. Advertising is one of the most if not THE most influential things in our lives. It is unlike a group of friends that influences us for a short time and goes. It is constant, it is always there in our face. Another study explored in Piran's article was conducted by Fredrickson and Roberts in 1997 and concluded that "[...] women are acculturated to internalize an observer's perspective as a primary view of their physical selves. This leads to habitual body monitoring, which increases anxiety and shame [...]" (373). When a woman hears a primary view of herself or in other words that she is fat or overweight or that her skin is wrinkly she often takes it to heart and begins asking herself if she is fat and overweight and old. Fredrickson and Roberts have proven that women internalize another person's (the advertiser's) view of themselves and because they internalize that person's (the advertiser's) belief it affects them psychologically enough to make them withdrawal from society. Because society emphasizes a woman being a thing, a thing to be looked at, women often not only feel they are not good enough, they begin to believe it.

The media influences and affects women everywhere they go. It is all around us. The more and more women see magazines and commercials of tall, skinny, and wrinkle-less, so-called "perfect" people, the more and more they will feel fat, ugly, or not good enough; they will feel as if they are not living up to society's expectations. Women these days complain so much about their looks because it is emphasized so much in society; sadly this generation has not grown up in a society when women are considered sexy if they have a curvy, hour-glass figure. Instead we are encouraged to imitate the boyish, waif-like figure of a very tiny fraction of women. Many women think they are overweight because the mass media use and recruit the very small portion of women that are tall, slender, and most-times dangerously underweight. Unfortunately, the advertising agencies that determine who and what we see feel as if they will not sell their product unless they use these types of women. The agencies use such skinny, "flawless" models to promote products because they make the average woman in society feel negative, like something is wrong with her appearance, prompting her to go out and buy the product in order to achieve the model's appearance. By deteriorating a woman's self-esteem, the media gains the lifelong struggle of that woman trying to achieve unrealistic standards, thereby gaining an enormous profit because they sell self-esteem back to her.

The portrayal of women in advertising must change drastically and very quickly. The advertising executives and companies need to understand how much they influence and control our thoughts about ourselves and others. Women in advertising are unrealistic. They do not represent the majority of the women in the world, and until the portrayal of women in advertising starts to reflect the real women in society, advertising will continue to negatively affect women.

"By the time I got back to school, I felt deeply discouraged because I was so behind. It seemed like college was out of the question."

The Value of Education
Glen I. Hong
College of Alameda, Alameda, CA

The United States educational system is one of the best educational systems being offered in the world today; why not take advantage of this offer? Most of us can remember being enrolled in school at an early age from pre-school to kindergarten and then progressing through the school system until we became adults and enrolled in college. I never thought about the purpose of education in my elementary years, but as soon as I was attending middle school, I soon realized that my educational "career" was actually a developmental process of my future. Before middle school I had not given much thought about my future, nor did I contemplate any career options. I was too busy playing outside with the local neighborhood kids having fun every chance I would get. If anything, the sole purpose of my efforts at school was to please my parents and make them proud. I was not too fond of taking tests, working on homework, or being required to complete specific "projects," all for the sake of a letter grade on a piece of paper.

When I started attending high school I still had this perspective in mind and thought of education as a waste of time. I cut almost everyday, doing things that I should not have been doing, and was on the brink of dropping out. I simply convinced myself that I would make better use of my time other than attending school and working on time-consuming projects (which I thought to be vain at the time). I was young and arrogant and thought that I did not need "book smarts" to get where I was going. Through the progression of time, my mother finally convinced me to start going back to school consistently and continue with my academics. By the time I got back to school, I felt deeply discouraged because I was so behind. It seemed like college was out of the question.

My only goal during that time was to get out of high school with a diploma wearing a cap and gown walking off stage. When I actually sat in a classroom and started listening to the teacher, I found that learning was fascinating. There are so many useful and interesting things that a person can learn from school. As I realized that I was gaining knowledge little by little every time I attended a class, I became more open-minded about the idea of education. I realized that there were so many opportunities that are being offered in our country, and that anything was possible if I just set myself in a direction full of confidence. I think that a consideration of the educational system being offered in our country today is one of the best ways for an individual to receive motivation, confidence, and opportunity. Without going through the process myself, I would have never known my capabilities and would have never strived to meet any desired goals that I felt were necessary to accomplish. Going back to school and taking advantage of my education was one of the most unregrettable and beneficial choices that I have made in my life so far.

I think that taking advantage of our educational system consequently provides motivation for those of us who need motivation. When I was cutting in high school, I felt that going back to school would mean a heck of a lot of "catch up." I did not feel that I had accomplished much during that time, so I was not used to any accomplishment at all. I felt academically challenged at times, but I never took the time to take up that challenge head on. I simply did not want to "deal with it" because I had no passion for learning or accomplishment at the time. When I finally decided to think differently for a change, I was in a classroom intrigued and astonished at both the lecture and at my ability to listen. Little by little, the educational system seemed to be taking me for an unexpected ride. I never knew how good at math I could be because I never tried. I never knew that I would have a passion writing poems and essays because I never gave English a chance. I never thought that I would feel so pleased about getting a piece of homework done. There were so many things that I have learned about myself that I never knew. Considering and taking advantage of the educational system has provided me with motivation since I now know that all things are possible.

One aspect of education that motivated me the most was the fact that I discovered a passion for learning. As I went to school and attended several classes, I realized that learning in general was a fascinating experience for me. I soon found out that there was such a broad area to learn from. I had the power to open a book and find out whatever I want about anything I want. Taking advantage of my education helped me realize that there was nothing I could not do; I just had to put some "heart" into whatever I was doing and keep at it. Since I found out all these things that I had not known about myself, I knew that there were probably other things that probably kept me down in the same manner. From that point on, I refused to give up. Education has been a source of motivation for me even to this day.

The educational system should be taken into consideration because of the confidence and wisdom gained from the experience. One of the most simple and important pieces of wisdom that I have gained from my educational experience is to "learn from your mistakes." Having been passionate about learning at the time certainly did not mean that I had not made any mistakes. I, of course, did not receive a grade with which I was pleased all the time. However, my hard work and dedication seemed to pay off in due time. Through the wisdom provided in my experience with education, I have gained a new kind of confidence: I have convinced myself that "I will never give up," and that "I can do anything if I put my 'heart' into it." I soon found out that education was not just about "book smarts." Education has provided me with a revelation of my own self as an individual and as a student.

Not only does the educational system provide motivation and confidence, it opens up opportunities for people in the similar circumstances such as that of myself. For example, students who drop out of high school always have the choice of enrolling in community college and getting their GED. Most of these students would probably be eligible for financial aid and have their education paid for by our government. Schools provide jobs for students, counselors provide advice, and there are tutors for those who need help; basically everything an individual would need for their education would be provided for them by our government. This in my opinion is one heck of an opportunity that deserves acknowlegment and contemplation.

For me, the educational process has been an ongoing journey - a journey that has provided me with goals and objectives, certainly ones that I had not had before. I was once a potential dropout, ignorant of the opportunity and privileges that education seeks to provide. Based on my own experience, I think that education not only develops character, but it provides an opportunity to fulfill a person's need of accomplishment. I think that people should know that there is always a possibility for them to achieve what they desire to achieve. If you never try, it will never happen. Now, I know that I have only spoken in my own perspective throughout this whole piece. Looking at our society today, there are without a doubt a significant number of teens and adults who drop out of school and disregard their education. I do not know what is best for these people. I do not even know these people. However, if they consider education just once or once more, they might learn something new. After all, education is a system designed for us humans to acquire knowledge and learn. In my case, not only knowledge but also character.

The experiences of others, confidence, motivation and opportunity are three essentials that are without a doubt obtainable if the educational system is considered. Those three were reason enough for me to have continued my education up to this day. The educational system has turned me from the child I once was into the strong person that I am now.

"In other words, 'under God' was intended to remind Americans that our rights came from the Almighty, not from a government which could just as easily revoke them."

Under God

Nathaniel Nelson

University of Rhode Island, Kingston, RI

Intended to restrict government intrusion, the protection of "rights" under the First Amendment has actually been the cause for increased government imposition. Before the U.S. Supreme Court is an atheist, Michael Newdow, who claims that the words "Under God" are a violation of his "religious" rights, and therefore unconstitutional. Should his rhetoric be deemed true, the outcome would be a slippery slope from which a central tenet to our country's heritage—religion—would be erased.

Newdow argues that in having "under God", the government takes "one side in the quintessential religious question, "Does God exist?" He claims that when his daughter (who is a Christian) recites the pledge, the government is indoctrinating her and more precisely, stating that her father's beliefs are incorrect. So upset by this "slap in the face," Newdow is before the high court and wants his daughter to be there with him (quite ironic considering she would have to hear the marshal's prayer, "God save the United States and this Honorable Court").

Though Mr. Newdow makes a good argument, he is wrong. He argues his position is correct due to the Establishment Clause. But this clause aims to forbid a state-enforced denomination, not create state-enforced atheism.

"One Nation under God" was added to the Pledge to emphasize the point that our liberties came not from the government, but, as the Declaration of Independence states, from the Creator, the Lawgiver, the Supreme Judge of the world, and Divine Providence (none of which are any establishment of the Christian God). President Eisenhower added "under God" to establish the moral and religious distinction between America and Vladimir Lenin's "Godless tyranny" in the Soviet Union. As President Reagan described, "Two visions of the world remain locked in dispute. The first believes all men are created by a loving God who has blessed us with freedom. Abraham Lincoln spoke for us...The second vision believes that religion is opium for the masses. It believes that eternal principles like truth, liberty, and democracy have no meaning beyond the whim of the state. And Lenin spoke for them."

In other words, "under God" was intended to remind Americans that our rights came from the Almighty, not from a government which could just as easily revoke them.

Jan LaRue explains that the pledge is not asserting a state mandated belief. For example, imagine the pledge as, "one nation where they eat a lot of peanut butter." LaRue explains, does this suggest that when one recites the pledge, they absolutely eat, like or want anyone to eat peanut butter, or that one must "eat government-mandated quantities of peanut butter?" NO. The pledge is to the nation and not to the peanut butter. She states it is a statement not about a government-enforced diet, but about what some eat. "Under God" is a pledge acknowledging the moral and political influence of God on our society.

For those who detest such beliefs, the government upheld the notion that none is forced to recite the pledge (see *West Virginia Board of Education v. Barnette*). However, the government must never give one person the "right" to silence those who wish to express their free speech, which this current case seeks to do.

Should we remove "under God," what kind of nation will we be? Who would we be under—Bozo the Clown? We would be under our own moral scrutiny. We would become as gods, establishing our own rules. Even Nietzsche saw the danger of doing this.

Would the removal of "under God" necessarily be the end of civilization? History points to many civilizations that falter when God and religion are removed. Alexis de Tocqueville stated, "Despotism may govern without faith, but liberty cannot. Religion is more needed in democratic societies than in any other." Even Jefferson, hardly the evangelical, acknowledged the need for religion in society.

Only time will tell if society will really become endangered. But, if we remove "under God" from the Pledge, we should keep in mind that there is a difference between a merely secular government and one which is atheistic.

This work or portions of this work have previously been published in **The Good Five Cent Cigar.**

*"Sir Thomas was wrong. For when he wrote, no one took his lead
and the bohemians and the beats all ached"*

Utopian Sestina in F-Sharp
Sarah Jane Carr
The George Washington University, Washington, DC

To suppress emotion will only lead
to solitude. Closed within a box
of your own construction, your bones ache
as exhaustion takes up residence along with apathy,
filling you with an endless desire to escape reality
and enter utopia. First envisioned by More

in 1519, a society that could not achieve more
in its perfection. The walls there not lined with lead
paint, chipping for children to consume. Reality
lies within those apartments, not in box
seats at the opera or a ball game. Empathy
is all I ask of you. Understand the ache

in my heart, the pain I feel for those who ache
all over. For those who ask no more
than sustentation and are forced to play on your sympathy,
for which you judge them. Meanwhile you pump unleaded
gas into your SUV, liquid gold into your steel box,
only to drive home to your flat screen and watch reality

TV, with people who aren't people but reality
stars. Drunken porcelain dolls that have drawn aces
and are in search of Warhol's promise. Boxed
in houses like Barbie and Ken, more

plastic than flesh, choking on cellophane and leading
teens toward eating disorders. Apathetic

to their role as bellwethers. For apathy
has sunk into their bones during their "real"
lives on the small screen. Meanwhile people lead
their lives on the streets and know the ache
of a night stick and the sting of a bullet more
than the warmth of love. Residing in cardboard boxes

in alleys surrounded by co-op brownstone boxes
and dumpsters. And no one but their neighbors can empathize
with their plight. Utopia is no more
and many will wonder and theorize if it was ever reality.
Sir Thomas was wrong. For when he wrote, no one took his lead
and the bohemians and the beats all ached

as I ache now, boxed into society's expectations.
And I lead the apathetic masses toward utopia
only to be ignored. Beaten by reality.

"It is disgusting that the supposedly most developed country in the world permits such widespread and systemic violence. Allows huge numbers of its civilians to undergo sexual assault, rape, and child sexual abuse."

War on the Home Front and Some Renegade Warriors:
Lisa Bakale-Wise
University of Michigan, Ann Arbor, MI

Imagine a country in which 1 out of 3 female citizens will be sexually assaulted in her lifetime. Imagine that 83% of the victims are young women and teenagers under the age of 24. Fifty percent of all victims are children under 18, and one in six is a grade-schooler younger than 12. Sixty-eight percent of these rapes are perpetrated not by a stranger in a dark alley, but by a husband, friend, or relative of the victim. Now imagine that women in this country are so oppressed and devalued that only 16% of victims feel able to report these heinous crimes, and the federal government and justice system dismisses or acquits over half of all the cases that are even brought to court. In this country, a female citizen is raped every two minutes (Earlham, 2002).

A country like this sounds pretty bad, right? It sounds like a "stone-age" society, where men dominate their women, wives are submissive to husbands, and female children are expected to grow up and be wives and mothers confined to their homes. Like a country where rape is sanctioned by the state and a part of every day life. A country completely unlike the United States, a place that Americans have a moral obligation to save. In tune with this sentiment, our President has passionately denounced such unspeakable atrocities committed in other countries, exalting that "[e]very woman in Iraq is better off because the rape rooms and torture chambers of Saddam Hussein are forever closed. He is a barbaric person. He violated people in such a brutal way that some never thought that the spirit of Iraq could arise again. We never felt that way here in this administration. We felt that people innately love freedom and if just given a chance, if given an opportunity, they will rise to the challenge." According to him, in Afghanistan, "[t]he Taliban were incredibly barbaric. It's hard for the American mind to understand 'barbaric.' That's barbaric. Women were prohibited from holding jobs. It's impossible for young girls to get an education. That's barbaric. It's not right." (Bush, 2004). Listening to the words of the United States President, it seems obvious that ending violence against women is a major priority for Americans.

However, this mysterious country where half of the entire population must live knowing that there is a one in three chance they will be raped is not Iraq, Afghanistan, or some other similarly "un-modern," "un-liberated," or "barbaric" nation. It is, in fact, the most "developed" nation in the world - the United States. It is your home. It is your bastion of freedom, of liberty, of "compassion." It is a country in which rape shield laws and regulations barring discussion of a victim's past sexual history have been thrown by the wayside when superstars such as Kobe Bryant are the perpetrators on the stand. This is a country where the Senate approves of federal judge James Leon Holmes, a man who prohibits the availability of abortion for rape victims, claiming that the "concern for rape victims is a red herring because conceptions from rape occur with approximately the same frequency as snowfall in Miami" (Babington, 2004). It is a country where assault is so pervasive that our very own President has a lawsuit filed against him, naming him as the perpetrator of rape (Pravda, 2003).

Yet, while we readily denounce the atrocities committed against women over-seas, even the most "progressive" American citizens remain virtually silent on the epidemic of sexual assault at home. Every day on college campuses across the country, there are protests against everything imaginable. Pro-Bush, anti-Bush, pro-Kerry, anti-Kerry, against the war, in favor of medicinal marijuana, pro-choice, pro-life, anti-sweat-shop, pro-animal rights, you name it, you've got it, and people are passionate about it. Yet protests against rape are few and far between. The dialogue on rape and sexual assault has stagnated. The discussion centers on "treating" rape victims, but not on stopping the victimization on the first place. Why? Why is the question "what was she wearing" or "how did she provoke him" instead of "why did he rape" or "why did he invade and abuse that woman?" Research shows that 89% of attackers actually state that the woman they victimized was not being provocative in any way (Earlham, 2002). Yet still, we persist in victim-blaming. We spend millions of dollars on college campuses across the country on "prevention," on telling women to always walk in pairs, in providing escort services for women at night, on teaching them self defense. Dialogue about sexual assault is "progressive" when it "empowers" women, but "man-hating" and "radical" when it suggests that men can stop the epidemic by choosing not to assault. By putting the responsibility on women to avoid being raped, we are burying our heads in the sand, refusing to look at the serious societal illnesses that perpetuate such a pervasive cycle of violence.

One in four women will be sexually assaulted by the time she is in college. One in three will be assaulted in her lifetime. If you're a woman, look at your two best friends - it's going to be one of you. If you're a man, look at your mother, your sister, and your girlfriend. Which of them will it be? Even look at yourself. One in five victims of sexual assault is male, and two in five victims of child sexual abuse are male. Look at your football buddies, the guys at the gym, your frat brothers. Almost one in five men has been sexually abused in her lifetime (Advocates, 1996). Nobody is immune to sexual assault in the United States, which has the highest rate of sexual assault in the entire developed world. And the facts about assault in college are even worse. According to the Higher Education Center, in a study of attitudes toward rape at college, male students were asked if they would commit acquaintance rape if they could be assured that no one else would find out and they would not be punished. Only 40 percent said they were not at all likely to rape a woman in such a situation. A study of 24 alleged gang rapes found that in 22 of the 24 cases, the perpetrators were members of fraternities or intercollegiate athletics teams (Higher Education Center, 2002). And what are the effects? The immediate effects can include severe psychological trauma, insomnia, nightmares, fatigue, vomiting, shock, numbness, denial, low self-esteem. Later, many survivors experience depression, alcohol or drug dependence, isolation, and vivid and horrific flashbacks of the assault that are uncontrollable, come at any moment, and last for any length of time. Recovery and resolution can take decades and alter a person's life forever (George Mason University, 2004). Forty percent of rape victims contract STDs, eighty percent suffer from chronic physical or psychological conditions, and half of rape and child sexual abuse victims must receive some sort of mental health treatment as a result of the victimization. Rape victims are 13 times more likely to attempt suicide (University of Rochester, 2004). Yet we do almost nothing to prevent it.

It is disgusting that the supposedly most developed country in the world permits such widespread and systemic violence. Allows huge numbers of its civilians to undergo sexual assault, rape, and child sexual abuse. Allows people to suffer a crime that is legally defined as second only to murder, and that we have deemed severe enough to warrant the death penalty. It is sickening that we continue to blame the victim. That we must continue to tell young women not to dress provocatively, not to walk alone at night, not to talk to strange men, for fear of being raped and brutalized at the hands of their fellow human beings. Yet we still expect women to work with men, live with men, to love men, all the while knowing that there is an almost 1 in 3 chance they will be sexually assaulted by a man in their life.

For all of their justified outrage against war, sweatshop labor, racism, sexism, classism, or other progressive or socially conscious causes, activists on college campuses and throughout America are terrifyingly silent about rape. Yet sexual assault is one of the few phenomena that cut across all racial, class, gender, political, and religious lines. It can, and does, happen to anyone, and the effects are life-long and catastrophic. It is time for everyone to step up and start talking about this. It is time for everyone, including "liberals," to stop referring to it as a "women's issue" and to start recognizing that 99% of all sexual assaults are committed by men (National Organization for Women, 2001). Sexual assault is far from a "women's issue." Yes, its victims are primarily female. But women can't stop it - 89% of perpetrators admit that the women they raped was not being provocative in any way. It is only men who can really stop assault, by choosing not to rape women. So even if you're a good guy, a good boyfriend, and not one of "them," take the initiative and go further. Tell your friends, your fathers, your frat brothers, your gym buddies, your football buddies, and your drinking buddies that women are people too. That referring to women as sluts, cunts, bitches, and hoes perpetuates the dehumanization and victimization of women. That sex can be great but is not the ultimate goal to be pursued at the cost of another human's life. That the woman who said "no" last night really did not mean "yes," and he's not more of a man for forcing himself on her. That any time a man has sex with a woman without her explicit consent, even if she's drunk, it's sexual assault, it's punishable by law, and it's a traumatizing, dehumanizing experience.

        This is not liberal rhetoric or radical feminist ranting that can be dismissed because of its "extremism" or because the author is a man-hater with an axe to grind. These are real statistics from national bureaus, real experiences told to interviewers and surveyors across the country, and real people who have to live with the consequences of that unwanted kissing, fondling, or sex long after the violation has occurred. These are one in four women in your stats class, on your college campus, or at your place of work. These are women who can't walk home alone from a party at night, who always have to make plans with their girlfriends to check in and go home together, who always have to watch their drink and the guy who gave it to them, who can't even tell people that they have been assaulted because they'd be labeled a "slut" who was "asking for it." All women must live daily with the knowledge that they can try their hardest to prevent an assault but when it comes right down to it, it's the choice of someone else. So this is an appeal to men. Take some of the burden off your girlfriends, sisters, and mothers. If you're not actively doing something about rape, even just talking to people about how it's not a "women's issue" but can only be stopped by each man choosing not to perpetrate, then you're a part of the problem. The choice is yours, and the consequences are real. You have another human's life in your hands. Step up to the challenge.

"For a minute, put yourself in the shoes of a struggling single parent. If you can, picture a fallen pine tree in the middle of the road. As you single-handedly try to move this massive tree, a crowd slowly forms around you. Everyone is thinking the same thought, 'Wow, that tree sure looks heavy.'"

What I Think about Single Parenting

Leanne N. Murray
College of Alameda, Alameda, CA

I will now attempt to carry not 1, not 2, but 3 bags of groceries, a heavy backpack, a sleeping baby, and unlock the front door to my house with my keys in my teeth.. One wrong move or a fumble could set me back some time (which is something I definitely don't have), and make a casserole of raw food on the front walkway. A bead of sweat drips down my forehead. My breathing becomes heavier..........Ta Dah!

In the front door! The keys fall to the floor with a loud clink. I set the groceries on top of the paper mess on the kitchen table. Now I can finally lay my sleeping angel in her bed to rest more comfortably. After I lay her down in bed and wipe the sweat from my brow, I stand over her to adore her... So peaceful... Tears fill my tired eyes. How I long to have more time to spend with her.

Life is busy. Almost non-stop. Between work, school, errands, appointments, house chores, etc., there isn't much "family time." This is how things are when you are a young single parent. There are many times that it has seemed to be me against the world. There have been times when we were down and out, nobody would help us. It seemed like everyone was just standing around watching me struggle. It is not just me. Any single parents that I have known have similar issues. What I think it comes down to is a lack and/or availability of resources and support.

So, let's talk about resources. Some single parents might say, "What resources?" Well, there are some out there. Often they are difficult to find. Also, once you think you find a place that might have some kind of assistance, count on starting your quest at the end of a very long line. This is good though. It will give you plenty of time to humble yourself. Yes, you can take this time to prepare for the slew of embarrassing, belittling questions that you will have to answer to a perfect stranger - and let me add that it is amazing what we will do for and/or put ourselves through for our children. Absolutely amazing.

Unless you were born with a silver spoon in your mouth, if you are a young single parent, you are going to need resources and support. Why is there not more support for single parents like myself?

I would like to see a system set up specifically for single parents. By this system, I am not asking to make our lives a breeze. I just don't think that because whatever circumstances have left someone alone to take care of children, that our children should not have to pay for it with poor or no health coverage. They should not have to pay for it by eating top ramen for dinner every night.

This system should include education (college and/or parenting classes), medical coverage (at least for the children), and food assistance. It should be handled in such a way as not to degrade and belittle the already heavy-hearted. I cannot tell you how many times I have rushed out of establishments for so-called resources, to get to my car to just cry. I have cried from humiliation, denial of services, or even pending processes. It's horrible to feel so helpless and then hopeless. I would not wish for my worst enemy to feel the way I did in those times. How can we as a society treat people desperately reaching out for help like this? This is cruel and unusual punishment.

There are more than a few reasons that single parents are sent to the sharks to raise children on their own. Hypothetically, let's assume that the absent parent is not deceased and has not been in some kind of horrible accident, leaving them unable to care for their child. I am talking about the average "this is too scary, I'm too lazy, I didn't ask for this," irresponsible absent parent. Where is their punishment? There seems to be none. Oh yes, I can just see them now, humming a little tune as they go along about their day. Many absent parents don't even have to worry about paying child support unless the providing parent is receiving county or government aid. These absent parents do not have to worry who is going to watch their child while they try to get an education; they do not have to worry when their child is lying on the couch with a 103 degree temperature and there is poor health insurance or none at all; they do not have to worry if their paycheck is going to pay all the bills, buy food, diapers, and when and how the car is going to get repaired; they do not have to evaluate the places they go to be sure it is safe for their child. Why is there no punishment or consequences for not taking care of or attempting to take care of your family?

This seems to be yet another price that we as single parents pay to have a clean conscience. Worry. I guess that is what we all do as parents. Some worry a little deeper than others, all of us about different specific scenarios. But we all worry about our children. We should not have to worry about something such as healthcare or food. These things should not be considered luxury. These are necessities.

For a minute, put yourself in the shoes of a struggling single parent. If you can, picture a fallen pine tree in the middle of the road. As you single-handedly try to move this massive tree, a crowd slowly forms around you. Everyone is thinking the same thought, "Wow, that tree sure looks heavy." Now, maybe at first, you thought you could move this tree by yourself. Now it is clear that you cannot. You ask the familiar faces in the growing crowd to help you. No response. You keep trying to move the tree. You know you can't get anywhere unless this tree is moved. Your hands are getting sore from rubbing against the bark of the tree. Sap is sticking to your arm hairs. Finally, it seems as if some kind soul is stepping forward to give you some assistance. You become prematurely excited until he stops several feet away from you. He begins to ask you some questions and comments that your hands are not yet bleeding. Confused, you continue to try to lift this tree that seems to be going nowhere. Sweat is dripping down your face. Just as you are about to give up and your eyes begin to water, the stranger begins to speak. "You will be notified of my response in 7-10 business days by mail."

All obstacles, struggles, and humor aside, there is so much joy in raising a child: there is so much to learn from each other. There are so many rewards in places that you would never expect to find them. Tears of hope, joy, and thankfulness to match all the tears of defeat. Our children give us strength when we cannot stand, purpose when we feel without cause, and love even when the world seems to falling apart around us. This is our reward, and it is priceless.

Partisanship and the Election

"The greatest good we can do our country is to heal its party divisions and make them one people."
-Thomas Jefferson

"In selecting men for office, let principle be your guide. Regard not the particular sect or denomination of the candidate - look to his character..."
-Noah Webster

Animals in the House

Caroline Marie Solomon
American University, Washington, DC

The question has come to face our country...
Which animal shall come to occupy that great house on the hill?
Will it be the mighty pachyderm?
Returning for another term
Or will it be the donkey
Taking his place?
What will be the end result?
When elephants and donkeys race?
Will it be the tremendous elephant trampling
The half-bred jackass to bits
Or will it be the pack animal carrying the country through the coming storm?
Will the country favor the thick-skinned behemoth?
Or the small but strong equine
Will that house on the hill be turned into a circus
For the elephant's tricks?
Or will it be made into a tour service
For the ass to drag us along?
Or heaven forbid that house on the hill
Could be made into some domicile for the green?
But the elephant and donkey will surely devour such a party
Before it has a chance to sprout its leaves.
Perhaps that house upon the hill could be another thing
Not green house, not circus, not tour service or brothel
But a great white barn
Fit for the mudslinging pigs
Masquerading as something more noble and more useful
Than they'll ever be.

"Was there not a time when politics meant more than negative campaign ads, accusations, finger-pointing, name-calling, and demagogical arguments from both sides?"

Dear Candidate
Veronika Penciakova
The George Washington University, Washington, DC

D_{ear Candidate,}

I am an American. I hold down two part-time jobs. I am a full-time student. I pay state and federal taxes. I watch the news and read the newspaper. I care about the past, and am concerned with the future. I am 18 years old, and I do vote.

I've heard it all before. The 18-24 year-olds represent the smallest fraction of the voting block, but why?

We must not vote because we simply don't care. We are more concerned with partying, drinking, relationships, and the ever famous teenage angst. We must not vote because we don't have families of our own, and don't have to pay the same taxes as "grown-ups" do. We don't have to worry about healthcare, social security, or welfare. We simply must not care about national and international issues.

I've heard it all before, and I respectfully disagree.

My generation will repay the national debt and be burdened with the national deficit. My generation will have to support the "baby boomers" through social security. We will live the rest of our lives fighting the "War on Terror." My generation will have to continually fear losing our jobs to a faceless man in India. We will have to pay higher taxes and will be expected to invest money for our retirement because social security will be gone before we reach retirement age. My generation will be expected to work additional years because we won't have a nest egg provided by taxpayers.

My generation knows all this, and we do care. So why don't we vote?

The reason is the same for 18-24 year olds, as it is for the millions of other eligible voters who steer clear of election booths. It's the politicians who've stopped caring.

National conventions have been reduced to pep rallies, consisting of mudslinging, followed by insistence upon decency and morality. Discourse has turned from present issues, and possible future solutions, to petty kindergarten arguments about the past. The media insists on covering the most basic and superficial issues, presuming that the average American citizen can understand nothing more complex than the number of medals a candidate received over thirty years ago.

Was there not a time when politics meant more than negative campaign ads, accusations, finger-pointing, name-calling, and demagogical arguments from both sides? Was there not a time when issues were discussed and candidate selection was not reduced to who has the better hair?

I am an American. I don't care who a candidate sat behind at a peace-rally thirty years ago, or who has more medals. I care about how I am going to pay for four years of college, and whether or not I will have a job when I graduate.

So stop blaming me for my reluctance to vote. Instead, give me a reason to rush to the voting booths. Tell me how you plan to make my future brighter. Convince me that you are more mature than my ten year old neighbor.

Stop blaming me; I'm doing my job by staying informed. Now give me something to stay informed about. I'm doing my job, now you do yours.

Sincerely yours,

A concerned citizen

"I think that the reason why there is so much political contention and resentment in America today is that we are forcing ourselves to polarize our political and social ideologies to fit a certain stereotype."

Feminism and Republicanism
Melissa Warburton
Gonzaga University, Spokane, WA

Growing up in a very rural and conservative community, I always found myself immensely frustrated with the perceived role of women in American society. While my friends were learning how to cook and raise a family I was interested in learning about politics and the law. I was quickly labeled a feminist by my high school peers. I found myself comfortable in that role and embraced it as my own. I knew that I would never forgo school to get married, and I knew that I would never hide my intelligence for fear that it would make me look unattractive or intimidating. If these standards made me a feminist, then so be it. I often dreamed of the day that I could get out of the conservative culture that was choking me and finally socialize with people who had the same aspirations and ideals as my own.

I knew that college would be the perfect opportunity to expand my horizons and learn more about the feminist culture that had been my identity for the past four years. I enrolled in numerous women's studies classes and hastily declared my major as a Political Science with a concentration in Gender Studies. I anxiously anticipated my first day of class and, being the nerd that I am, sat in the front row determined to engage in discussions and grow as a women and a feminist. However, the first class left me stunned and somewhat perplexed. As the class continued and I began learning more about the feminist culture and ideology, I found myself slowly disconnecting with the radical feminist environment that I had clung to for so long.

Despite my resentment of my conservative upbringing, as well as my utter determination to break free of the conventional mindset of my social background, I am a Republican. I recognize this is a somewhat unusual political affiliation for a feminist to take, and believe me I want more then anything to be a Democrat. The idea of rebelling against my parents and teachers for social causes that seem so humanistic and youthful is very appealing. However, after a lot of reading and soul searching it cannot be denied that many of my political beliefs fall in line with those of the Republican Party. This confession induces the same reaction time and time again: "How can you be a Republican and a feminist?" My response is often, "Why not?" No one can define my political and social ideologies other than myself, but that does not stop the often incredulous and bitter comments that are thrown my way in many political discussions.

One evening I was having a conversation with a friend and she invited me to a political rally in support of Planned Parenthood. I politely declined her request and told her that I would not attend because I do not believe in Planned Parenthood's mission statement. She proceeded to gasp and ask me how I could call myself a feminist when I did not support a woman's right to choose. This question is not unjustified. For years much of the women's movement has revolved around a women's right to chose, yet I do not classify it as primarily a "woman's issue." For me, it is humanistic. I believe that life occurs at conception and should not be stopped after that fact. This does not make me a bad "feminist," this makes me a human being that values the concept of life. Yet, because of this belief I find that many women, mainly feminists, refuse to believe that I still have feminist beliefs. I am constantly amazed at how upset people get when trying to determine what political ideology I should be categorized in.

But before I am condemned as a die-hard conservative, let me just add that many in the Republican Party do not accept me either. Last semester the Young Republicans and Young Democrats had booths set up across the Gonzaga quad where students could sign petitions for or against gay marriage. My signature was expected at the Republican table. After all, I am the girl with the three Bush/Cheney campaign posters hanging in my room. But I did not sign the "Protect the Sanctity of Marriage" Petition. I did not sign it because I, the conservative religious republican, believe very strongly that gay marriage should be legal. I believe that the struggle of the rights for homosexuals mimic that of the Civil Rights Movement. I predict that twenty years from now we will look at ourselves in shame that we would ever be so narrow-minded and prejudicial towards something so basic to human rights. Gay marriage may not be legal in my parent's lifetime, but it will be legal in my lifetime. Republicans can not understand how I can call myself a conservative and take a pro-gay marriage stance. Once again I am amazed at how upset people get when trying to determine what political ideology I should be categorized in.

So what am I? I have beliefs that are conservative, but also maintain some traditional feminist ideals. I will tell you what I am. I am a feminist. I believe that women are just as smart and savvy as men, especially in the corporate world. I do not believe you have to stay home with your children to be a good mother, I believe that you have to be at home for your children to be a good mother OR father. I believe in the rights of gay, lesbian, and transgendered individuals in our society. I believe the feminist movement has been a white women's cause, and I believe that it is essential that we expand it to protect women of all colors and nationalities. I believe in my strengths and my faults, and I know that women accomplish great things in society when given an equal chance. I am also a Republican. I will vote for President Bush in the 2004 election, and I do believe he is one of the greatest presidents America has ever seen. I support the war in Iraq, and I know that the tax cuts are working. I do not support any form of abortion or the death penalty. I do not believe that we should take "Under God" out of the Pledge of

Allegiance, because it a historical belief our country was based on. I think that the *No Child Left Behind Act* is a fantastic program and needs to be implemented more efficiently by the states. My greatest fear is hearing the words "President John Kerry."

Many Republicans do not think I am a true Republican. Many feminists do not understand how I can call myself a real feminist. But that is what I am, a feminist Republican. I think that the reason why there is so much political contention and resentment in America today is that we are forcing ourselves to polarize our political and social ideologies to fit a certain stereotype. I question my beliefs every day and I know that I do not have to believe everything the Republicans believe, nor do I have to fight for every cause the feminists fight for. The only thing I can do is be respectful of other people's beliefs and work to incorporate my feminist ideals into the Republican Party. Will it work? Can I make a difference? I do not know, but I do know that I will try and that I will never say I believe in something just to be affiliated with a certain political group or social cause. I will define myself the way I chose to be defined, and not by others. I believe America could get a lot more accomplished if people took each issue separately instead of lumping them together to fit the mold of a certain group. But that is just what I think.

"While my family was taking me to the polls with them, many families were passing onto their children their own skepticism, cynicism and distrust in the government over dinner or during family car rides."

How to Make Your Vote Count and Other Things You Learned in 9th Grade Civics Class
Arianna Levitus
The George Washington University, Washington, DC

I still remember visiting the Glen Lake Activity Center with my mom and dad when I was in elementary school. That was "our" voting place. I'd grab hold of my mom's leg and squeeze into the polling booth with her as she marked up her ballot. At the time I didn't quite understand why in November we'd go to this important looking building, where my mom got a really cool red sticker in return for filling out a piece of paper. Maybe my sense of duty and responsibility as a voter is deeply rooted in these childhood memories of my parents voting. I understand that not all families place this same emphasis on voting or interest in current events.

While my family was taking me to the polls with them, many families were passing onto their children their own skepticism, cynicism, and distrust in the government over dinner or during family car rides. Because of this, and other factors, many eligible young voters refuse to have anything to do with the electoral process. Something must be done to overcome their cynicism, distrust and apathy towards politics and voting. Fortunately my parents raised me with a sense of civic responsibility. Because of this I feel obligated to help my peers understand how their votes really do count- as clichéd as it may sound. The 18-25 year old voting population holds an undeniable amount of potential in the elections of 2004. However, a movement to excite these young voters is needed to counter the trend of decreasing participation.

I am 19 years old. Yes, that does mean I've only been eligible to vote in two elections. Despite my age and brief voting history, there are a few things I've gathered in my 19 years that make the electoral process more understandable than I ever thought possible.

On a Tuesday night in November of 2000, I sat with my friend Ryan, our eyes glued to the television screen. No, we weren't watching the latest episode of Friends or Dawson's Creek like most our classmates that evening. We were tuned into CNN to watch the election results. I gave him a hard time for making a color-coded map to record the results as they were announced. But all of our friends thought our idea of "must see TV" that night was absurd. Neither of us was old enough to vote that year but we were convinced things may have turned out differently had we been able to.

The 2000 presidential election was proof that young voters are feeling removed from the electoral process. In the 2000 Election 55% of all eligible voters showed up at the polls (FOX). In the same election only 29% of eligible voters ages 18-25 – about 8.4 million people - cast a ballot for president (FOX). We have all heard of majority rule, but it is scary to consider the implications of these numbers. The opinion of the 18-25 year olds was voiced by far less than half of the actual 18-25 year old population. It is frightening to think this small fraction of the young American population has such a disproportionate representation in elections. Even scarier is this abuse of civic privilege comes three short decades after 18-20 year olds were first given the right to vote.

Has so much changed since the 26th amendment in 1971 that young Americans are no longer inclined to vote? 2004 is certainly a year of serious issues: a projected federal deficit upwards of several billion dollars, state educational institutions failing, daily threats of terrorism around the world, and our civil liberties being redefined daily. It is often a challenge to find something to look forward to. It is equally hard to believe electing a slate of representatives, senators, governors, mayors or a new president into office will change anything. I may be optimistic but I strongly believe all who are eligible must take control of their futures and head to the polls. As Plato said, "One of the penalties for refusing to participate in politics is that you end up being governed by your inferiors." Why give the inferiors a chance when you can choose for yourself who will govern?

Despite how easy voting can be, many young voters see no reason to vote. Even if young citizens are concerned or interested in the issues, a sense of political disconnect leads many to feel distanced from the electoral process. The 2000 Presidential Election was one for the record books, but it caused even more distrust and suspicion among voters across the board. 18-year-old Sarah from Philadelphia, PA said, "I don't really see the point in voting. Even if I did care about who won, the people [Electoral College members] are going to vote based on their own opinions so it doesn't matter if I vote." Even before the election, polls continually showed that young people remained suspicious of politicians (Berman). In light of recent events such as the war in Iraq, the ongoing battle against terrorism, and scandals involving elected officials, young people should theoretically be more inclined to want to invoke change in the system. What better way to show an administration, on the local, state or national level, that you don't like its policies, than exercising your right to do so? You can keep officials in office, or replace them by voting. How's that for power?

Feeling the impact of their actions is an important component of community and civic involvement for many young people. Some young voters feel that in order to sense they are making any difference in society they would prefer to engage in private volunteer activities. In a culture that increasingly emphasizes the importance of instant gratification, this makes perfect sense. Marking an 'x' on a ballot or pushing a few buttons is undoubtedly not as rewarding as watching a child learn to read, or providing a warm meal to the hungry. But can democracy survive if we only invest in our personal interests and don't act on behalf of society? According to Tony Cani, a 25-year-old student at Arizona State University and leader of Generation Dean (a campus organization that supported former Democratic presidential candidate Howard Dean) the fact that young adults don't vote is not a sign that they don't want to be involved (FOX). How do we turn desire to be involved into involvement? A quick search on the internet proves that there are numerous groups trying to answer that very question. A pop-culture must-see for everything that's hot now, MTV, has launched its "Choose or Lose" campaign (accessible at http://www.mtv.com/chooseorlose/) in an effort to mobilize over 20 million young voters in the upcoming November elections. Along with MTV, many other organizations - Smackdown! Your Vote, Project Vote Smart and Rock the Vote, to name a few - are mobilizing campus crusades across the nation in an effort to change the face of the electorate in 2004.

Because the trend for young people is to stay away from the polls, the politicians are shying away from directing any campaign energy or ideas towards the youth of this country. So as we ignore the politicians, they sit and watch as our debt piles up as we attempt to obtain a higher education. Where are their proposals to make education more affordable for families? On the other hand, if you watch any campaign commercials or read the platform of any candidate in a major race they are likely to mention healthcare costs or prescription drug plans. As active, lively young adults, these are issues we don't generally take interest in. However, older Americans care about these issues. So why do the politicians focus so much on these social issues as opposed to proposing reforms to the higher education system or other "young people's issues"? The answer is quite simple. Not enough young people turn out to vote to make the issues important enough. The candidates know that older Americans are consistent voters. If they cater to the concerns of their solid supporters, they are even more likely to vote, and vote for the candidate that speaks to them. If young people became more consistent with their voting, the face of elections could be forever altered. But for now, you name an issue and the government is creating a policy about it - without your input; all of this because we're too busy watching reality TV and trying to make it big to take the time to vote or care.

Still don't believe your vote can make a difference? Think again. No one in Minnesota ever imagined we'd have a former pro-wrestler in the Governor's Office. However, in 1998, Jesse Ventura beat the odds and became Governor of Minnesota. While he did have a non-traditional style and quirky charisma that easily won over non-traditional voters, Jesse "the Body" Ventura successfully energized and mobilized a large group of young voters that turned out to the polls and showed the career politicians what they wanted in a Governor. It is speculated that in that 1998 election, 18-25 year olds called the election. While we can't require all future candidates to don feather boas or have catchy nicknames, a lesson can be learned from this. Time and energy invested in young voters to mobilize and vote can bring excellent results for candidates.

Are hanging chads still keeping you from the polls? Pay attention to the news. Watch the progress and development of an issue you are concerned about. This should be a clear view into the way the political system can affect issues and actions to betaken.

Now, take your interest in these issues and see how the candidates for offices match up with your stance. Take all of that into consideration and head to the polls!

This American government is of the people, by the people and for the people. Each and every person. Since day one the importance of the citizen's voice has been the emphasis and foundation of this country. If young voters continue to refuse to participate in the electoral process than they are effectively throwing away all that was fought for in order to create this land of the free.

"I know I'm not alone in being a lapsed Catholic, but for me, there is something inherently disheartening about turning away from the Church; it's as if all the people I've mentioned above are floating around me whispering, 'you've betrayed us.'"

Identity
Tom McSorley
Harvard University, Cambridge, MA

To say that I "identify" myself as Catholic is an understatement. I'm the Philadelphian native son of Italian and Irish immigrant families. My Italian mother still puts pictures of the Three Wise Men above our front door to keep us safe, and carries a statue of Mother Cabrini in the car during snow storms. Her aunts still relentlessly feed me during our fish dinner every year before Christmas, and she always has a story to tell about the nuns that disciplined her throughout her school years. My Irish father's family is even more tied to the faith: his father is one of thirteen children, eight of whom entered the religious life. Among them are a slew of St. Joseph's nuns and Jesuit priests, and even a bishop. His sisters are deeply involved with the church, and his mother goes to Mass every day, religiously. To top it all off, I've spent most of my life in Catholic institutions. I went to St. Hilary's for my grade school and all-boys Holy Ghost Prep for high school. I've received all my sacraments and performed in more than a few nativity plays.

I tell you all of this because, after eighteen years, my reaction to Catholicism today is ambivalent at best and resentful at worst. I know I'm not alone in being a lapsed Catholic, but for me, there is something inherently disheartening about turning away from the Church; it's as if all the people I've mentioned above are floating around me whispering, "You've betrayed us." Yet simultaneously, every Catholic bone in my body, every Catholic value on which I was raised, makes me feel that the Church has betrayed me and all of the Catholics around me who share my beliefs.

I've seen this betrayal play out before my very eyes. A religion that once espoused social justice, praised the work of civil rights leaders, and lobbied for human rights has abruptly and maddeningly turned on these goals in the political realm. In America, they have replaced all of this with an open support of the Republican party and of its candidates. While the church does not officially take a political stance, the sermons and publications of its leaders speak for themselves.

This is not to say that the thousands of priests who are working every day for social justice, human rights, and equality do so half-heartedly or insignificantly. Rather, the church hierarchy has done an amazing job of drowning out their voices politically. Indeed, my Jesuit uncle, Father Richard McSorley, was an incredibly fierce pacifist, a close friend of Bobby Kennedy, and a passionate lobbyist. My uncle even protested with Bill Clinton while he taught him at Georgetown. Many friends of mine who are priests are quite liberal, because they recognize the work that the Democratic and left-leaning parties around the world do to promote social justice. Nevertheless, I feel tremendous frustration when talking to many Catholic family members and neighbors who like Massachusetts liberals, complain about the plight of drug addicts in our justice system, lament the poverty and hunger they see worldwide, and question how our own policies helped warp the Middle East into a bastion of terrorism, still vote Republican consistently, taking heed of their local *Catholic Standard and Times* newspaper and sermon at Mass.

The cause of this shift is fairly obvious. Democratic support for abortion has led bishops who once cherished the young JFK to now praise Rick Santorum, belittle Ted Kennedy, support George Bush, and threaten John Kerry with excommunication. Abortion is the one issue on which Catholics and Democrats fundamentally differ. Democrats view reproductive freedom as a necessarily policy. They believe that a woman must have control over her own body if she is to be considered equal and free, and they recognize the tremendous strain unchecked births place upon a resource-scarce developing nation. Catholics believe in the literal physical sanctity of the human person – they believe that God is tied to each person in the flesh, and they believe that abortion is murder and a sin. To be honest, this is an issue with which I have struggled, as have many Catholic Democrats, John Kerry among them, who are ultimately pro-choice. Being a pro-choice Catholic means recognizing the conflict in the philosophy of abortion rights and separating the constitutional arguments for choice from the theological arguments against it. Pornography, and in some states prostitution, while degrading to women and sinful, are legal because the arguments against them are not persuasive enough to choke off the rights of some for the values of others. Abortion is handled much the same by Catholic Democrats.

Likewise, the modern Democratic party's imperfect, but substantially better than its opposition's, treatment of homosexuals in society may at first appear to stand as a second incompatibility between Democrats and Catholics. This is simply not the case. Catholic dogma, though forbidding of homosexual action, is also supposedly one of dignity. Many in the Democratic party feel that granting dignity and promoting tolerance means allowing homosexual marriage or civil unions – in the state – not within religion. Others in the party do not, but still maintain a more positive approach to homosexuality than most in the Republican Party - George W. Bush among the most extreme. Catholics, therefore, can object to homosexual unions in any capacity, but would do well to support the party that promotes tolerance and inclusion. Nothing in Catholic doctrine supports the notion that anyone, even the worst sinner in our society, should be an outcast or unloved. This is not to say that I agree with Catholicism's stance on homosexuality, since the theological and canonical support for such a negative stance seems narrow, but

I am also sure that no priest, anywhere, should support national policies – such as the proposed constitutional ban on gay marriage – that threatens to break up families and deny family members important rights, like hospital visitation.

These arguments, however, are tangential to the heart of the matter, for everywhere else, Catholics and Democrats share intimately similar beliefs. The Catholic Church is founded on compassion. At the root of Christian teaching is the idea that as long as humanity suffers, God suffers. Upon paging through the *Philadelphia Catholic Standard and Times*, many of the pages reflected this: stories about the Virgin Mary's inspiration for "peace and justice," ads for courses on "nonviolence," and even an article about environmental conservation entitled "Dream of Green." The Catholic Church is a worldwide organization, primarily devoted to justice and peace. Catholics, including the priests of my high school, work around the globe to build schools, distribute medicine, and bring food to the needy. The Roman Catholic Church, following the teachings of Jesus Christ, is devoted to improving the human condition.

Similarly, the Democratic Party is the party of compassion and social justice, despite George W. Bush's lip service. It is the party that reflects both the deepest respect for all human life, and also the teachings of Christ. He who multiplied the loaves and fishes to distribute to his hungry followers would support expanded liberal social programs. He who walked amongst the outcast sects of Israel would support the party of civil rights. He who healed the sick would support the party that works for universal healthcare, independent of wealth and status. He who lived like a pauper, communally amongst his apostles, would never allow human rights to be trumped worldwide by an all encompassing focus on bottom line profits. If anything, the policies of the left are our best hope for achieving Christ's vision of humanity – one of alleviated suffering, at least partially nullified materialism, and true human equality.

This all amounts to a plea. It is not an overstatement to claim that if George W. Bush wins the election in November, if Republicans are allowed to keep power, the social programs that support our neediest will be seriously threatened, the militaristic ramifications of the Bush Doctrine will flourish, and all of our work for human rights will be incredibly strained by a radical agenda. John Kerry, a Catholic, has proved himself in his Senate record and in this campaign to be concerned, above all, with issues of justice, environmentalism, and peace. John Kerry wants to reverse the global damage of George W. Bush, who prefers a world where the United States arrogantly parades around as if it had all the answers. With a John Kerry presidency, I am sure that our foreign and domestic policies can be at least partially put back in the right direction.

I am begging those among us who are Catholic to consider what "Catholicism" really means to you, and what party truly supports the values you hold. Look beyond abortion to the other travesties of our time: the death penalty, the failures of our justice system, war, violence, poverty, hunger, and prejudice – all of the problems that Democrats definitively work to end. As Catholics, prepare for voting as you would prepare for confession – vote your conscience.

"As a student at the University of Richmond, I get my fill of pro-Bush sentiment. While at Harvard University this summer, I've gotten my fill of Democratic pride. But where do I stand?"

I'm an Open-Minded Republican

Grant Yelverton
University of Richmond, Richmond, VA

"**I**'m an open-minded Republican." When I tell my Democratic friends this, they let out a sarcastic burst of laughter in an effort to force a reaction. It's true, though. I get the best of both worlds. As a student at the University of Richmond, I get my fill of pro-Bush sentiment. While at Harvard University this summer, I've gotten my fill of Democratic pride. But where do I stand?

I want my family to hold on to the money they've worked for. I want liberal social rights for the masses. I'm a supporter turned opponent of the Iraq War. I think Kerry would make a fine President. I disagree with Democrats on their economic platform. I sometimes wonder how Bush got into office as President, but overall my allegiance lies with the party and not the man. I can understand why so many people are Democrats though, and that's part of the reward of spending the summer as a student in such a liberal town.

Case in point, I recently I went to a party at Tufts University to play "Beirut," the official favorite drinking game of the American college student. Feeling a little tired and tipsy, I decided to cab it home. The cabbie, a man in his fifties with a long, grey pony tail asked me where I was attending school that summer and immediately jumped into a conversation about politics. He first asked me about my political allegiance, to which I answered, "Well, I'm a Republican, but I consider myself very open-minded to all views regardless of the party supporting them." In response, he exclaimed that he read three newspapers a day, each covering the right, left, and moderate areas of the political spectrum. He informed me of events that were unraveling of which I was completely unaware, used names I'd never heard from committees I didn't even know existed, and described newly uncovered documents which he was confident shed light on hunches that he had bet were true. Call me ignorant, but I thought as a political science major I knew it all. I was so impressed with this man that I told him, "Walking around Harvard Square, I see people with bumper stickers, buttons and t-shirts with clever slogans aimed at announcing disdain but which instead come off as trendily anti-Bush. It's just so refreshing to hear that someone does so much research and arrives at an independent, well thought out conclusion, even if I wind up voting differently than you do in the end." He asked me if that implied that I'd definitely vote for Bush, which in reply I told him I hadn't decided yet. "Well if my argument didn't convince you, maybe this will," he told me while adding five dollars in tolls to the meter. He waited just long enough while I got upset and then turned to me and said, "Just kidding. You're lucky I'm an open minded Democrat."

Admittedly, I'm not completely sure what side I will choose, but my advice to any voter in any election is this: use every channel possible to inform yourself of the arguments on both sides to the point where you believe that you can distinguish jargon from fact. When it all comes down to it, it's the only way to prove that you're a well informed, opened minded voter.

"The large majority of signs held by the protestors were too inappropriate to show on television, so Americans watching the news only saw cute little PEACE signs. Is this what the Democratic party has become?"

Increased Polarization
Matthew Ahrens
Washburn University, Topeka, KS

The increased polarization of political parties following the infamous 2000 election has led to a continuous escalation of hostility and quick erosion of the Democratic party. I was fortunate enough to be a page at the Republican National Convention this past August, and multiple times protestors would come up to us individually or as a group and shout curse words in our face. One protestor walked up to me personally and told me to "Get the hell out of here!" As we watched the major protest march from the second level of our hotel, mobs of hateful protestors would flip us off and shout "Go home now!" The large majority of signs held by the protestors were too inappropriate to show on television, so Americans watching the news only saw cute little PEACE signs. Is this what the Democratic Party has become?

When Michael Moore showed up at the RNC the first night he did the Republicans a favor. He became the face of the opposition to President George W. Bush. He replaced Kerry as the leader of all who oppose the Republican party, and alienated many moderates in the Democratic party. This serves only to intensify the polarization of the Democratic party as a party not of the working class, but of crazy, liberal, Republican-haters. Did Republicans try to infiltrate the Democratic National Convention? No, but Code Pink worked to infiltrate the Republican National Convention so they could draw attention to radical issues.

Democrats always talk about how Republicans do not accept opposing lifestyles and should be more open. Were the protestors in New York City accepting of conservative or even moderate opinions? Why is it that liberals only love the first Amendment when they are the ones taking advantage of it? One liberal student protestor lied about being thrown in jail when she talked to me. I knew she was lying because the NYPD did not let the protestors out until later in the week. It is truly sad to see a group of grown Americans who hide behind a veil of peace to cover their inner animosity.

I think it is safe to say that most college students are thankful to be out of high school. They see the college campus as a haven away from the immature games that high school students always play. So why should they want to be involved in politics? No longer is politics reserved for the statesman, rather, today it is designed largely for those who have the "political savvy" to take a true, positive statement and twist it into a dirty rally cry for the opposition. No wonder college students have become disengaged from the political process.

"So Christians must be conservative, and by extension, the Republican party would seem to be a fit home for conservatives in our time. But parties change; ideologies do not."

Jesus is Non-Partisan
Hans Zeiger
Hillsdale College, Hillsdale, MI

Human beings like to think that God is on our side, and in Christian cultures we rather choose to believe that Jesus Christ Himself would choose our particular product, our particular cause, or our particular party. This is a convenient thought, but it is a dangerous one. God is omnipotent, so we had best think before we bear His Name, lest we bear it in vain. The Lord will not hold Him guiltless who taketh His Name in vain.

In any case, Jesus is a Republican. I know this because Republicans are right most of the time, and of course the Republican platform is right all of the time. Democrats are sissies, they're pinkos, and I occasionally call them Bolsheviks for the sorts of socialist policies they like to speak of.

Actually, I'm joking a bit, though I have been a Republican since I was born. I'm also a Christian, and I know that membership in the Republican Party is not my ticket to heaven. Jesus did not come to call Republicans to repentance; we're already good enough. Jesus came to call the Democrats to salvation from their wicked ways.

Enough of that. C.S. Lewis spoke of "Mere Christianity." Christianity cannot be hyphenated lest a man serve two masters. I can be a Republican, but I must be willing to give up my devotion to my state representative or my president for the sake of my Lord, if necessary.

Still, Christians are called to be involved in politics, and when we are, we tend to go on the further extremes of one party or the other. I like to think of it simply as the Religious Left and the Religious Right.

Republicans and Democrats alike have Christian ministers at their conventions this year. In fact, Democrats likely have a few more ministers than the Republicans; the Democrats want to speak more of faith and the Republicans want to speak less of it for the sake of their images. "Amazing Grace" graced the ebbing somberness of a September 11th memorial at the Democrat Convention, but no Falwell or Robertson will be seen on the podium of the Republican Convention this year.

Jesus is neither a Republican nor a Democrat because he is neither a conservative nor a liberal. In His time on earth, Jesus was both a conservative and a liberal. He is on one hand the most revolutionary figure ever, and on the other He is the most orderly man who sets about to conserve the eternal will of His Father.

Conservatism and liberalism are great neutralities. We attempt to dogmatize them, but we do so at our own peril. Certainly, there are doctrines to back up Christianity; this thing we call faith is rightly built on fundamental truths that can stand on their own. Christianity need not be liberal or conservative. It may be, but it may not be. In all fairness, what we most often call conservatism and liberalism have evolved into polar ideologies in our time, but we must remember that conservatism and liberalism are not new phenomena; they are as old as man. Conservatism is simply the conserving of what is proven and tried and orderly; liberalism is the breathing of change into a world of decay and rot. The necessity of one or the other is contingent on circumstances, not ideologies. Christianity itself ought to be our creed and our code, not conservatism or liberalism.

Liberal and conservative are moods, not ideologies. Well then, what mood should a Christian have?

In our age, we must conserve simple things of the spirit. The flesh abounds as quickly as the advances we make in technology and science and fashion and imagination, but a civilization cannot survive without what Russell Kirk called the "Permanent Things," those things that are timeless and unchanging, like faith and character and family.

So Christians must be conservative, and by extension, the Republican Party would seem to be a fit home for conservatives in our time. But parties change; ideologies do not. It is wrong to proclaim that a professing, church-going man is not of Christ if he is a Democrat. He may very well be doing a far more noble thing by reforming his party for Jesus than his Republican neighbor who is simply falling in line with his fellow elephants at the local precinct meeting.

So I maintain that Jesus is neither a Democrat nor a Republican, neither a conservative nor a liberal. Jesus is the Head of Christianity, not the purveyor or partisanship. So forth from Christianity may come a partisan, but only in the circumstances of his age, not the enduring things of his faith.

"As promised, President Bush has taken the fight to organized terror groups such as Al-Qaeda and Ansar Al-Islam, as well as the regimes which support these deadly actions against our country."

Kerry's International Mythology
Matthew T. Revan
Bentley College, Waltham, MA

As we commemorate the sixtieth anniversary of the D-Day Invasion, our country is remembering the sacrifices of so many of its sons and daughters, given in the hope that the world could be saved from the genocidal grasp of Nazism. Sixty years later, many of their grandsons and granddaughters are putting their own lives on the line to prevent the world from being thrust into the clutches of fundamentalist terrorists, in the hope that we will never again suffer the loss of so many innocent Americans as on September 11th, 2001.

One of our Presidential candidates, John Forbes Kerry, is perpetuating the idea that our President owes the international community some kind of apology for defending us, particularly to France. As promised, President Bush has taken the fight to organized terror groups such as Al-Qaeda and Ansar Al-Islam, as well as the regimes which support these deadly actions against our country. Whether that support is given through financial means, providing safe harbor to terrorists, or both, any government that offers it is posing a perpetual threat to the safety and security of our country.

Kerry has said repeatedly that the United States needs to "rebuild its alliances." A quick analysis of our diplomacy abroad shows that he must be thinking of our relationship with France. Personally, I can think of about nine thousand, three hundred eighty-six reasons why it is France who must rebuild its alliance with us, not vice-versa. On D-Day, 60,000 Americans attacked the German armaments on the coast of France, with the goal of establishing an Allied stronghold with which to drive the German armies out of France, and ultimately attack Berlin and defeat the Nazis. Yet at that time, our homeland was never directly attacked by Germany before the war. Those 60,000 Americans were fighting to liberate the homes and cities of people 3,000 miles away from their own native soil.

Brave young men from across this nation fought and died on that day to liberate places like Caen, Bayeux, and Normandy so that freedom could be restored to the

French people. But they also laid down their lives with the understanding that if this evil was not confronted on those beaches, it would soon be on America's shores where these battles would be fought. As a nation, we have never forgotten that important lesson, and it is that principle which is guiding us in the War on Terror.

Six thousand Americans died on D-Day alone in order to liberate France. That sacrifice is immortalized in the Normandy American Cemetery and Memorial, where our President is asking the world to remember that day when so many lives were lost in the name of restoring freedom to Europe. The current leadership of France has forgotten that sacrifice, and the important lesson that the entire world learned after World War II: that evil regimes seeking the destruction of freedom and democracy cannot be allowed to spread their influence and consolidate their power. If force is the last resort to stop that from happening, it must be used.

It was the very same mentality of Jacques Chirac and Dominique DeVillepin that afflicted the French government before World War II, an overwhelming aversion to war, which offered up the freedom of the French people as a trinket to appease Adolf Hitler. The result of this: 9,386 American gravesites at the Normandy Cemetery, and countless Frenchmen who died in the resistance against the Nazis. Those French people who remember this sacrifice and are united with us are poorly represented by these men. The government of France wanted us to appease Saddam Hussein in the same way, and used its influence on the Security Council to prevent us from having "international" credibility without a UN mandate for war, even though it was explicitly called for by Resolution 1441. To them, imperiling our own freedom and keeping the Iraqi people under the iron fist of a cold-blooded tyrant was worth it to avoid another fight. This perception of a lack of international support is continually being fed by the elite media and the Democratic party leadership, despite the fact that thirty-nine other countries have risen up to the challenge of confronting terrorism.

Many of my own generation have learned this lesson all too well, and are over in Iraq and Afghanistan fighting to prevent the need for another battle like D-Day in which thousands of troops would be killed fighting against terrorists to preserve our freedom. Hundreds of Americans have given their lives in the current war with the knowledge that their sacrifice will prevent their own families from being the casualties of future terrorist attacks. The idea that we as a country owe an apology to a leadership that tried to prevent us from defending ourselves, forgetting the enormity of the sacrifices that allowed the French Republic to exist in the first place, is anathema. It would be both dangerous and reckless for us to elect a commander-in-chief who would buy into this absurdity. The time has come for us to put aside our partisan differences and unite as a country behind our commander-in-chief, and accept nothing less than full and complete victory in the War on Terror.

This work or portions of this work have previously been published in **The Bentley Vanguard.**

"I am interested to know where you stand on the matters that we, as young African American college students,. are concerned about."

Letter To Kerry
Nikesha Williams
Bethune-Cookman College, Daytona Beach, FL

Dear Senator Kerry,

I am Nikesha Williams, a freshman business major attending Bethune Cookman College, an HBCU located in Daytona Beach, FL.

I am sending this letter because of recent interviews of five of my peers regarding issues most important to us. For the record, I am a registered Democrat who will be voting in my first presidential election on November 2, 2004. I am interested to know where you stand on the matters that we as young African American college students are concerned about.

Of course, education is among the important topics for us, we want to know how your administration would address the issues of rising tuition, and helping less fortunate students get higher education. Another important topic for us is the economy. The news tells us that unemployment is very high which makes us worry about our possibility of getting good jobs once we graduate. What are your plans to make the economy better so that we can have hope for the future?

Another important issue is the war. The war in Iraq has taken the lives of more than 1,000 Americans. We feel that we should not have gone to war, that the cost of human life is too high. As president, do you plan to call for an end to the war? How will you protect us from terrorists?

Finally, health care is a concern of ours. We watch our parents and grandparents struggle with the cost of prescription drugs, and the high cost of health insurance which some cannot afford. Is making health care affordable in your plans?

Thank you very much for your attention to this letter and I look forward to a response that I can share with my peers before the big day in November.

Sincerely,
Nikesha L. Williams

"What I'm ultimately trying to get across here is that the two-party system doesn't just suck now. It's sucked for a long time. It's sucked for most of America's history. So it blows my mind that we've sat around and let the two parties not just maintain it, but ingrain it into our culture."

Political Geek
Thom Gray
University of Tennessee, Knoxville, TN

I suppose if there's such a thing as a "political geek," I'm it. I do things like sit up all night and look at old election results. I've looked at maps, statistics, and basic historical data on every election in U.S. history in my spare time. I've picked at and analyzed every power switch, every geographical trend, every party re-alignment. And I've come to one overwhelming conclusion:

Today's two-party system sucks.

Now, this may seem like just another generic complaint from a disgruntled young voter with revolutionary tendencies. Well, it is. But dang it, it's a legitimate complaint, and one with which history agrees. You want evidence? Sit back for a brief history lesson.

To me, the strongest argument against the two-party system comes from the only U.S. election where there were no parties, in 1789. Not only were there no parties, but there was no Twelfth Amendment, which meant we got the best candidate as President and the runner-up - presumably the second-best man for the job -- as Vice-President. And who did we get in that first election? George Washington and John Adams, two of the finest Americans to ever pop a cap in a Brit. Did America suffer from a lack of clear choices that year? Heck no. Not only did we have Washington and Adams on the ballot, but another fine American named John Jay. America didn't even suffer from indecision that year: Washington is the only president to ever unanimously win the electoral vote.

In fact, Washington did it twice, the next time in 1792. This was the first election with political parties, the Federalists and the Democratic-Republicans (yes, they used to be the same party, a fun fact for those of us who think they're the same party today, too). Once again, we got now-Federalists Washington and Adams, but we had the opportunity to pick Democratic-Republicans Thomas Jefferson, George Clinton, or

Aaron Burr. Even with two parties, we had multiple candidates, and once again, they were good ones.

The first truly competitive election came in 1796. This time, we had Federalists John Adams, Thomas Pinckney, Samuel Adams (yes, like the beer), and Oliver Ellsworth, and Democratic-Republicans Thomas Jefferson, George Clinton, and Aaron Burr. And this time, we got Adams and Jefferson, a mixed ticket.

On a side note, I never have understood why we don't have that possibility today. If the "big two" really represent the basic dichotomy of American beliefs, why not have a pair working together like Adams and Jefferson? I don't seem to remember anything in U.S. history about a political meltdown at that point, folks. In fact, the nation prospered under that pair. Maybe the problem is that the "big two" DON'T represent the political beliefs of all Americans between them. Maybe the problem is that they're hungrier for power than for a better America. But I digress.

I'm sure you're waiting for the point to all this historical mumbo-jumbo, so here it is: when we had no parties, we had a far better choice among candidates. Even when we had two parties, so long as multiple people ran from each party (there were no nominating conventions back then), the choice remained, and so did the quality. This is simple economics: competition=higher quality.

Now, fast forward a few years to 1840, when the Democrats and Whigs had their ducks in a row and started giving us only two major candidates. Who did we end up with on the ticket? Martin Van Buren and William Henry Harrison. Now, I'm not disparaging either of these guys, because they were both at least decent presidents. But they're a far cry from Washington and Adams. Then came James Polk -- the only Tennessean president not to piss someone off royally -- and Henry Clay. Again, not a bad match-up, but not Andrew Jackson or James Madison, either.

And from there until the Civil War, look at the names on the ballot: James Polk, Zachary Taylor, Franklin Pierce, and James Buchanan. All good guys, and no one who let the nation fall apart (arguably). But at the same time, there's not a superstar president in the bunch. And look at their opponents: Henry Clay, Lewis Cass, Winfield Scott, and John Fremont. Again, not necessarily bad guys, but no one to write home to mother about. The disparity between these elections and the more competitive ones is quite obvious.

Now, let's look at 1860, when four major candidates duked it out: Democrat Stephen Douglass, Southern Democrat John Breckenridge, and Constitutional Unionist John Bell, and a Republican you might have heard of named Abraham Lincoln. We got one more strong president out of the ashes of the Civil War, Ulysses S. Grant. And then, back to the same old: the stolen election of Rutherford B. Hayes, followed by a string of mediocrity stretching till Teddy Roosevelt, breaking for a few years, and resuming until FDR.

What I'm ultimately trying to get across here is that the two-party system doesn't just suck now. It's sucked for a long time. It's sucked for most of America's history. So it blows my mind that we've sat around and let the two parties not just maintain it, but ingrain it into our culture. It's all over our textbooks, our media, even our legislature. We've become so blind that we now have laws on the books which appropriate taxpayer money specifically and exclusively to the Democratic and Republican parties. Primary candidates get $33 million in matching funds for primaries and are eligible for up to $67 million in the general election. And each party gets $13.57 million for nominating conventions.

$27 million for conventions alone. That's around 72,000 four-year degrees at UT Knoxville, for anyone curious.

And the money's not the only way the "big two" use the government for mutual pats on the back. They pass CIA briefings on to their big-party opponents exclusively, which should outrage the American people in this time where security is supposedly crucial. They even keep the debates exclusive, protecting each other from new ideas on both the right and left.

Our media hasn't helped the situation, throwing their "rebel vote" endorsement behind a yutz like Ralph Nader. What they're not telling you is, Nader can't mathematically win this election. He's not on the ballot in enough states to even make a dent in the electoral college. Meanwhile, the three other party candidates who can win mathematically -- Libertarian Michael Badnarik, Green David Cobb, and Constitution Party nominee Michael Peroutka -- barely even get a nod. Even when Reform Party candidate H. Ross Perot made a substantial run in 1992, he had to fund the whole thing himself. You'd better believe Teddy Roosevelt never had to put up with this crap.

But this is all a bunch of smoke if we don't do something about it. We now have the most powerful journalistic and informational tool ever devised, the Internet. We must harness its power to spread the word about these deceptions, to bring new ideas to the people, and most of all, to spur the nation to action. We need to push new ideas for election reform, like the Condorcet system, which lets people vote for their first and second choices for president like the old electoral college system. We need to end public funding of what should be the private enterprise of running a campaign. We need to demand that the government open the debates to all candidates who can mathematically win the election. But most of all, we need to start caring.

Or we could just sit back and wait for the Rs and Ds to hand us the next Millard Fillmore.

Practicality

Caroline Marie Solomon
American University, Washington, DC

A conservative shall change that which needs it
A liberal shall not change that which does not need it.
Is there any difference at all?
Fix that which is broken
Improve that which can be better
Do that which needs doing
Then take the day off
Don't fix what is not broken
Don't try to ride a broken bike
Move beyond the pendulum swing
Be more then the ends of the spectrum
There is a space between the right and left
Open and ready to be filled
It's called practicality
And it's a good idea.

Protest
Aaron Deakins
Eastern Michigan University, Ypsilaniti, MI

"Defending the American way of life should be the goal of conservatives in the future as it has been since the movement started. The elements who are trying to annihilate our way of life might have changed, but the task is the same."

The Future of Conservatism

Ryan Thompson

Hillsdale College, Hillsdale, MI

Conservatism is at a crossroads. The version of conservatism which was pioneered by William F. Buckley Jr., has two primary goals. The first, defeating communism around the world, has been highly successful, with only a few nations practicing the system of economic and political oppression. Preventing the spread of socialism across America has been successful for the most part with a few exceptions. Fewer people are reliant on the government today than were during the infancy of conservatism. So where should the conservative movement go?

In my opinion, there are three fundamental problems that American society needs to deal with these: (1) Despotism and oppression around the world in all of its forms. This includes terrorism, all forms totalitarianism including genocidal groups and the remnants of communism. (2) Defending morality from assault by the fringes of society. Elements of the fringe include the militant gays, feminists, moral relativists, and other secularists who despise the Judeo-Christian faiths. (3) Prevent the growth of roll-back socialistic elements in American society. Privatizing elements of Social Security and Medicare are leading elements of this philosophy, along with preventing the development of a nationalized healthcare system and increased taxation. These three principles should be the basis of our political philosophy for the upcoming decades. The first two fundamental problems are the prevailing issues for me.

Despotism is the greatest threat to civilization, because it's fundamentally against every tenet of ours. If the threat of despotism is not dealt with, our civilization will be destroyed. Gone will be the days when we can openly debate the issues and practice our faith without fearing for our lives. Defeating despotism and tyranny should be the goal of our government and society. It should be defeated by every tool in the arsenal of our nation including military force if necessary. No other issue should be as important to the government. Conservatives should lead the charge in promoting democracy around the world by stressing an agenda that undermines all forms of tyranny.

Defending the moral fabric of America is the second most important goal for conservatives. Why should we defend America if the nation we love has been degraded morally and socially to an irretrievable point? The institution that we should defend the most should be the family. No new versions of the definition of the average family should be allowed. There should be a mother and a father with kids and nothing else. The government should promote no other arrangement, and should give tax breaks to families and mothers who stay home to take care of the children. Any attempt at destroying the family and morality in general should be shunned by society as a threat to our culture and heritage. Conservatives must press this issue to defend our society from corruption. This is our biggest strength electorally because our society statistically is getting more conservative and moral.

The third goal of conservatism in the future should be to prevent the growth of socialism in America and to begin the privatization of socialist-like elements of our government. The average citizen is the best at determining what he or she wants and needs, not the government. Further, forcing a person to spend his or her wealth as the government sees fit undermines economic innovation and hurts the society. People will not have the incentive to take a risk if there is not a payoff possibly at the end. Taxes should be low and government involvement in the economic process should be suppressed as much as possible.

Defending the American way of life should be the goal of conservatives in the future as it has been since the movement started. The elements who are trying to annihilate our way of life might have changed, but the task is the same. Maintain freedom while having civil order with a foundation of morality. The best way to defend the American heritage is to expand the gift of freedom to every corner of the world without exception. Most importantly, our heritage rooted in the Judeo-Christian faith should be our guiding light in the struggle. That, in my mind, is the future of conservatism.

WHY
Jason Kauffman
University of Dayton, Dayton, OH

W hy do we simplify our lives into two sides?
Without noticing what our dichotomy hides?

Our day to day lives are not just black and white
We live far in between the dark and the light

Yet somehow we have agreed to let our future be
Nothing more than two choices we see

Shoved down our throats, drilled into our minds
Nothing but two choices is all we can find

We are the people, the people of choices
Yet we choose to speak with only two voices?

It's time for a change, and change we all must start
To vote not from two parties, but to vote from one's heart

"I feel that the two major parties that have ruled this country for the past 200 years have exponentially gotten worse at serving the people that put them in office and that government has become more of a machine for business than a machine for citizens' needs and rights."

Why I Support Ralph Nader
Ben Marcus
National Campus Coordinator:
Nader for President 2004

I have always, since I was a little kid, felt some sort of responsibility for this country. Maybe it's because my dad started taking me to a soup kitchen when I was 7 to help serve food to those who were less fortunate than I was, or maybe it's just my fascination with world events and international relationships that I've had since I was a little kid.

For whatever reason, I've always felt that the government needs to take an active role in meeting and going beyond the needs of the people it serves. I feel that up until this point in history, the government of this country has not done that, and I feel that it's time for a change in this country. I feel that the two major parties that have ruled this country for the past 200 years have exponentially gotten worse at serving the people that put them in office and that government has become more of a machine for business than a machine for citizens' needs and rights. Don't get me wrong, there have been many points in American history when individuals in the government stood up for what was right and were able to get things done, but the main word is INDIVIDUAL. Parties have never gotten anything done except for dividing up the different ethnic and religious groups in this country and pitting them against each other in a battle for control.

Because of this belief, I think that the only answer is to have more voices and choices in this could-be-great democracy of ours. I'm not against the idea of parties, just how it's set up right now, where two parties are completely in control and there's no breathing room for other ideas and where the law is actually designed to keep it that way.

Ok. On to Ralph. I feel that Ralph is my man because he does, and he always has spoken my language. I admire what he's done for this country and I feel that he is the candidate that fits my brand of idealism and morals. He stands up for the little guy and for a government that responds to the needs of its people, not its business interests. He stands up for the idea that this country could be a beacon for a "perfect society" in the world, but we need to work at it. He refuses to back down when there are people in this world that think that he's running purely to satisfy his ego, or to spoil the election. I think that he is one of the country's greatest heroes, and I think that anyone has the right to a fair shot at the presidency.

"Republicans and Democrats at the state level pass laws restricting third-party access to the ballot, even for established parties such as the Libertarian Party, which is the largest third party in the country and has consistently grown since it was founded in the early 1970s."

Young Voters Should Look to Libertarians in the Next Election

Tony Torres

Virginia Polytechnic Institute and State University, Blacksburg, VA

The causes of so-called voter apathy among those between the ages of 18 and 24 are not what most experts believe. The fact is the two major parties offer young voters almost nothing.

Except for promising every election year to bribe students with more financial aid giveaways, most social programs are aimed at the poor of all age groups or the elderly. Both major political parties take youthful voters for granted because they know not many of them vote. They also push laws at the national, state, and local levels that punish college-aged people for relatively harmless youthful indiscretions.

Most young people want to be able to experience and enjoy their youth, to be left alone to do so in peace and to be able to keep more of the money they earn. This last part is especially true when one considers young people generally make a lot less than most older voters.

Young voters know the two parties offer nothing but a cynical choice, and so they tune out the political process and don't vote. The media, the establishment, elected officials, and bureaucrats all work together at all levels to ensure voters of all ages are unaware they have other, better alternatives available to vote for.

The mainstream media only covers high-profile independent or third-party candidates who are either famous, rich, or known for some other pursuit first. Ralph Nader, Jesse Ventura, and Ross Perot come to mind.

Republicans and Democrats at the state level pass laws restricting third-party access to the ballot, even for established parties such as the Libertarian Party, which is the largest third party in the country and has consistently grown since it was founded in the early 1970s.

Campaign finance laws are passed with the excuse of cleaning up corruption in politics, but in reality they protect incumbents and limit the ability of third-party candidates to raise money and the awareness of their stances on the issues.

Finally, third-party candidates are excluded from presidential debates, unless they are shown in polls to have the support of 15 percent of the electorate. It doesn't matter if a candidate is on the ballot in all 50 states or if he is on the ballot in enough states to win the Electoral College, he still cannot debate. Despite the broad appeal of Libertarian ideas — Libertarians are outnumbered as a percentage of the electorate only by moderates or centrists — most voters are either unaware of the party or believe it can't win because of this combination of restrictions on the electoral process.

The solution is simple. Young voters should reject the Republicans and the Democrats. Throw the bums out! They never tell the truth, they take the voter for granted, and they couldn't define the word "principled" if they had a dictionary sitting in front of them.

The Libertarian party will not prosecute young voters or anyone else for victimless crimes. It will work to repeal all ballot access laws, lower your taxes and allow you to live your life as you choose. It will allow you to actually save the money you earn rather than going deeply into debt just to start your life and get an education.

A Libertarian officeholder will allow you to live in freedom, without the government regulating every aspect of your life. The only thing a Libertarian asks of his fellow citizens is to use that freedom responsibly and not to harm anyone else. Libertarians will never ignore an entire age group, race, gender, or any other group in the way that the other parties take people for granted.

If youthful voters were to stand up and vote as one group for the Libertarian Party, they would change the country forever. Republicans and Democrats could never take them for granted again. Other Americans would finally have a viable third choice besides the stale old status-quo parties.

So when you walk into the voting booth in November or mail your absentee ballot, think about what throwing your vote away really means.

This work or portions of this work have previously been published in **The Collegiate Times** (Virginia Polytechnic Institute and State University Student Newspaper)

Our Generation

"The dogmas of the quiet past are inadequate to the stormy present. The occasion is piled high with difficulty, and we must rise with the occasion. As our case is new, so we must think anew, and act anew. We must disenthral ourselves, and then we shall save our country."
    -Abraham Lincoln

"Our country is in danger, but not to be despaired of. Our enemies are numerous and powerful; but we have many friends, determining to be free, and heaven and earth will aid the resolution. On you depend the fortunes of America. You are to decide the important question, on which rest the happiness and liberty of millions yet unborn. Act worthy of yourselves."

    -Joseph Warren, commander of the forces at the Battle of Bunker Hill

A Shrine to the Unbelievable

Amanda M. Glover
Virginia Commonwealth University, Richmond, VA

Lighting fires
in iconoclad shrines,
such a small price
to save a life.

A different place,
the same old game.
Roman law
fighting
to rule today.

Takes me back
to private school.
Bitter, British...sisters.

Nuns.
Smacking your hand
with a ruler.

The word of God,
a damned ruler.

America

Amy Kline

Virginia Polytechnic Institute and State University, Blacksburg, VA

The exploitation of exoneration in this nation is the cement of its detriment
Blocks crumble as we continue to fumble and forget to be humble
Frames remain the same because it's the image we tame
Vacant insides corrode or implode to fit the status quo
We no longer feel, heal, or know what's real.

Excite the senses! Rewrite the sentences. Recite the sins again. Fight to win!
We're paying for the sayings that are enslaving to keep our minds raving
We're shallow like it's a skill to thrill those who still have goodwill.
More fake smiles are pasted and true beauty is wasted.
We will continue the show because we don't know where else to go.

An African-American Step Show
Alexandra Pajak
Georgia Institute of Technology, Atlanta, GA

T he Voice of the Next Generation

Thirteen approach the stage dressed as fat policemen.
Teeth of plastic, some incisors "knocked" out,
Afro wigs like black galaxies spinning
Into the gym's rusting bleachers and five hundred faces.
Sauntering on stage then into single file.

Militaristic. Bold. Right.

[Stomp] Alpha! [Stomp] Phi! [Stomp] Alpha! [Cheers] [Stomp]
Strip their stuffed costumes, swing those plastic smiles
Behind them. The wigs slide slowly off, peel
As—[Stomp] [Stomp] Ladies . . . ! [Stomp] Ladies . . . ! [Stomp]
Air swallows sweat, dimness a dirge [Stomp].
The wooden platform is a shadow, shoes
Step on South African soil [Stomp] [Stomp] [Stomp]

Gumboot miners of the darkened heart
Dance tonight, today's shells, ancient souls.
Straight line proclaiming a swelling pride.
The heavy bass of the speakers blare
The King's heartbeat:
We here. We now. We step.

"The lack of imagination and kindness that leads to war is saddening. All these movies and video games that have come out that glorify war have added to the debasing of humanity, where the object is just to kill the enemy, the person who is different, and not to actually try and understand the differences."

Arms Are for Hugging
Maia Sheesley Banks
James Madison University, Harrisburg, VA

Arms are for hugging. "Extinction is forever." "Make the scary Republican go away." These three statements have become the three mottos of my life, currently resting as flashing billboards of my ideals, on a bag I carry with me everywhere. They are pins. Pins that I have picked up over the years, and pins that have come to define what I really care about. The daughter of the first generation of hippies who protested the Vietnam War, I find it my duty to carry on the tradition, and stand up for what I believe in. And what is it that I so strongly believe in? First and foremost, as a budding vegetarian, I believe in the rights of all living things to inhabit their equal shares of this world. To all those gung-ho Bush supporting fundementalist Christians, proselytizing the beauty of the Lord Our Gods' beautiful and bountiful creation I want to say, "How can you support a man who is everyday ruining the environment in which we live?" It is a horrible hypocrisy that they are living. If I could get them all together I would shout, "Get out there, protect the beautiful creations you are so proud of! Stop driving your damn gas guzzling SUVs!" I suppose they should count their blessings; I never will be able to gather them all together to give them such a lesson.

My second belief as stated by my pin is one of nonviolence. In my opinion, there is never a just reason for war. There are always ways of working things out without it. The lack of imagination and kindness that leads to war is saddening. All these movies and video games that have come out that glorify war have added to the debasing of humanity, where the object is just to kill the enemy, the person who is different, and not to actually try and understand the differences. I have to say that one of the saddest things to me is that after the September 11th attacks, we were simply angry and vengeful, but not in the least concerned with why the attacks happened. We did not question why those who were in charge so hated Americans. I would think this would be the first question asked after such an event, not "How can we get even?" My third and last pin is simply a statement of my leanings. I am a Democrat, and certainly the things that George W. Bush and his Republican cronies have done do scare me.

I am the girl who cried at the beach when my friends threw fire crackers into the sand one night, out of sadness for the hermit crabs they had probably just scared or blown to pieces. I am the girl who became a vegetarian after seeing a truckload of skimpy and lifeless-looking chickens being hauled off to the slaughterhouse. I am the girl who is searching hard in her college career to find a major that can help me to actually make a difference in this world. I am that little girl who once founded a Protect the Animals club, and I am the teenager who was part of an anti-war march. I am a girl, a woman, a person who has begun the infinite search of my being, in a world that is so full of hate, confusion, but above all else, hope.

"While Columbine *pretended to tackle the problem of America's 'culture of fear,' Moore used every opportunistic trust-twist and turn to stick another jab at George W. Bush and the political right for whatever he chose to lambaste them for at that particular moment."*

Bowling For Fahrenheit
Eric Kohn
Millikin University, Decatur, IL

I haven't seen *Fahrenheit 9/11*. Do I really need to?

Is there any reason to believe that the overarching point of Michael Moore's newest "my large inner child isn't getting enough attention" temper tantrum is going to be any different from his last diatribe, *Bowling for Columbine*? If Moore was able to turn a mock-umentary about the state of gun violence and fear in American culture into a Bush-bashing festival, I can only imagine what he has been able to accomplish in dedicating an entire film to maligning the President.

While Columbine pretended to tackle the problem of America's "culture of fear," Moore used every opportunistic trust-twist and turn to stick another jab at George W. Bush and the political right for whatever he chose to lambaste them for at that particular moment. Moore's assaults are comparable to the reaction of Rick Moranis' Dark Helmet character in Mel Brooks' *Spaceballs*, who after inadvertently slashing down a cameraman in a pseudo-lightsaber duel defensively points to his opponent and utters, "Umm, he did it."

Feeling the need to defend their new demigod, leftists tout the improvements that Moore has made from his *Columbine* film. They say he's even gone so far as to have himself make fewer appearances in the film, so that the audience is more free to focus on points raised by the movie. Well, certainly with Moore in the film less, the audience's view is going to be less obscured. But, in reality, all this step taken by Moore has proved is that some time between *Columbine* and now, he discovered a mirror.

After his critics at the Wall Street Journal and watch-dog websites (such as MooreWatch.com and MooreLies.com) nailed his hide to the wall – certainly is a big job, isn't it? – exposing how Moore had played fast and loose with the facts in *Columbine*, Moore vowed that he would burn the midnight oil to make sure that he was accurate in *Fahrenheit*. As is to be expected, shortly after the movie hit the screens, Moore's critics took it to him for once again changing to truth to suit his vision.

It's not very surprising that pundits, not at all unlike myself, took to noble task of even further discrediting Michael Moore. It's to be expected that his opponents would dig up even the most miniscule piece of data that was misrepresented in *Fahrenheit*. But, it's the degree of the errors – or should I say lies? – Moore commits in the film that is what would be funny if it weren't so ridiculous.

Within days of the release of the movie, Slate.com – which is about as much of a right-wing institution as the Democratic National Committee – published a lengthy piece pointing out the grievous errors in *Fahrenheit*. Christopher Hitchens, a former columnist for *The Nation* and one of the few people that can be found who has actually admitted to being on Air-Franken America, meticulously and effortless cut Moore into ten million pieces, each of which weighed roughly half a pound.

And yet, while people who agree in ideology with Michael Moore are chiming in to take him down, we are expected to believe that this film is set to change the political landscape in the months leading up to the election. But in the end, Moore isn't going to win over any more potential voters than the Democrats expect will be won over by Ann Coulter. While Ann actually does take an interest in the truth, her hyperbolic style makes her a great voice of the conservative movement to conservatives. For Moore, it's very much the same. He knows how to preach to the choir and get them all riled up. Just as we don't see too many curious individuals picking up Coulter's *Treason* with out knowing exactly what is contained in those pages, there aren't too many people wondering into a theater thinking, "I wonder what this flick is all about."

The American people are smart enough to see through Moore's guise as an avenger of the common man to the propagandist that lies buried very, very deep within him. But still, I'll make my way to the theater and donate my ten dollars to the film's total grosses. After all, I haven't seen a good comedy yet this summer.

"It is not difficult for us to laugh at someone we hate. After typing in "Saddam Hussein Celebrity" on Google, I can pay to find his 'celebrity address.'"

Celebrity Worship: A Shameful Joy
Stephan Schwartz
Columbia University, New York, NY

America's celebrities are its gods. They are followed obsessively in newspapers and on television. Magazines are devoted to them.

California Governor Arnold Schwarzenegger's gubernatorial race was covered by every major form of media for months, and it was difficult then to find anything to read on, say, poverty in Latin America or the AIDS crisis in Africa. It seems that these topics are featured only during the brief periods when celebrities aren't doing anything interesting.

If "celebrity" is colloquially defined as "a famous person," then to me, Osama Bin Laden and Saddam Hussein fit the definition of celebrity. How many people would recognize the faces of these men, but not those of Thomas Jefferson, Rosa Parks, or Mohandas Gandhi? After his capture, Hussein bathed in complete media attention. Is that a problem?

This mingling of politics and entertainment has blurred the line between the two, leading to the birth of "infotainment." While Schwarzenegger moved from the realm of entertainment to politics, Bin Laden and Hussein have moved in the opposite direction.

The American public refuses to turn off the television when news about Hussein is playing. Everything is "Breaking News." Yes, toppling Hussein's statue was a memorable moment, symbolizing the fall of a regime, but does America need to see that image replayed on every news station and featured on every front page, for weeks at a time? Why does the media obsess over these images and over celebrities in general?

The answer is simple: as a culture, we love to see people rise and fall. Just as emperors and nations rise and fall, so do celebrities in today's entertainment industry. Movie stars and musicians rise from nobodies to somebodies, if only for a fleeting moment. Their fame is short-lived. Whether their crimes are dishonesty, drugs, or a sex scandal, it makes no difference. We simply love to hate.

America loved seeing Richard Nixon's name destroyed during Watergate, and the story was covered for months, even years. A similar thing happened to former President Bill Clinton, with regard to the Monica Lewinsky scandal. While we love to watch the rise and fall of celebrities, it is their fall that is particularly sweet.

The "52 Most Wanted Iraqis" cards sold like wildfire. T-shirts, posters and bumper stickers declaring Bin Laden to be a "Wanted" fugitive were everywhere, as if anyone in America were not already conscious of this.

Hitler went from being named *Time Magazine's* Person of the Year in 1938 to being decried as the world's villain. Today, we even regard Hitler as an object of entertainment. The movie and recent Broadway musical *The Producers* allows us to mock a man previously feared. Luckily, Saddam is not yet dead, and we can begin mocking him immediately.

It is not difficult for us to laugh at someone we hate. After typing in "Saddam Hussein Celebrity" on Google, I can pay to find his "celebrity address." I doubt that anyone other than the U.S. military knows where he is these days, and before his capture, it was unlikely that any celebrity-finder Web site could ensure that Hussein received its customers' messages. Additionally, an October 2002 article posted on Wired.com revealed that Hussein received hundreds of e-mails from both fans and critics around the world.

The emergence of satirical television shows devoted to covering politics exemplifies the way that politics has become a form of entertainment. Saturday Night Live has mocked political candidates and officials since its inception. A more recent example of televised political satire is Comedy Central's sitcom "That's My Bush."

People Magazine is devoted to following the lives of celebrities and watching them descend into oblivion. We saw that Hussein didn't look so great following his capture. Why wasn't he on the cover of *People*? If he learned English, he might make a great host for a talk show - the Saddam Hussein Show! If he traded in his military regalia for some tan slacks, a shirt and tie, he'd be a hit. He'd have more viewers than The Simple Life.

Criminals who would normally be prosecuted for crimes go free when they have celebrity status. We recognize their talent and would prefer to see them continue making movies or records than rotting in prison or being put to death. Hussein is clearly an example of such talent. One doesn't rise to the position of president of Iraq without being resourceful. The wheeling and dealing required to launch a successful coup and retain power for so many years can not go to waste. He managed to survive the Persian Gulf War against the U.S. and quell the opposition of his populace.

As Andy Warhol said, "In the future everybody in the world will be famous for 15 minutes;" in Hussein's case, celebrity may last much longer.

"Instead of aspiring to greater levels of prosperity and enlightenment, we are embracing cultures that our ancestors fled. We are moving backward toward barbarism and thuggishness."

Don't Save the Whales, Save Yourself!
Judson Cox
Lees McRae College, Banner Elk, NC

An unholy combination of liberal social engineering and a mistaken interpretation of Christian charity is the second greatest threat to humanity. The greatest threat is Islamic fascism, whether it is advanced by terrorists or governments. The second is more subtle: well meaning, misguided idealists are using the powers of government to subvert natural selection. This column will not address the origin of life or species, which evolution cannot adequately explain.

Natural selection is the process through which species adapt to changes in environment. Superior species survive and reproduce, passing on genetic traits best suited to their environment. Inferior species lack adaptability and eventually become extinct. It is the survival of the fittest. Our environment is in constant flux: it produces ice ages, warm periods and changes in weather patterns. Our ability to thrive in various climates and even our skin pigmentation and body types are due to natural selection. Bacteria and viruses adapt and mutate as well, producing new diseases that can devastate populations; our immunities to diseases are the result of natural selection. Man is not excluded from the laws of nature; superior species must adapt even to the influence of man.

Interconnectivity is exaggerated. Dinosaurs were once the dominant species; their mass extinction did not threaten all life on earth; to the contrary, it enabled the prosperity of mammals. To measure the impact of an extinction, one must ask what other species eat the endangered animal with exclusivity. For instance, few species fed exclusively upon woolly mammoths or saber toothed tigers; their extinction had little impact. Similarly, the extinction of whales, manatees, spotted owls, eagles and alligators may be a loss from an aesthetic view but would have little negative effect on other species. Likewise, more common animals are not indispensable. If dogs, cats, horses, etc. became extinct, it would not imperil life on earth. Even if cows were to suddenly disappear, humans who rely on cows for food might switch to venison or chicken for meat and goats for milk, we would not starve — we would adapt.

The giant panda cannot adapt; its diet consists mainly (99%) of 9 varieties of bamboo. The panda requires a minimum of 26 - 33 lbs. of bamboo per day. Bamboo is becoming less available and pandas are nearing extinction.

Fortunes are being spent to save the panda — why? No species requires panda meat for survival. The panda is an inferior species. In his folly, man is resorting to cloning to defy the laws of nature under the banner of protecting nature.

As the science of cloning progresses it will be increasingly employed to preserve not only rare animals, but particularly admirable specimens (such as show dogs) and even humans. A clone is an exact genetic copy of an existing organism. Cloning halts evolution and subverts natural selection. Absent gradual adaptation, species cannot survive environmental changes. Clones would perish when faced with an ice age or a new disease. Such mass extinction would have catastrophic consequences, as non-cloned species would not have the opportunity to adapt to the absence. Well meaning do-gooders could endanger all life on earth.

Similarly, social programs that minimize the negative consequences of human actions imperil our society. One learns what not to do through discomfort: for instance learning not to touch a hot stove by burning one's hand. An 800 pound. woman was reported last week to have been unable to fit through the doorways of her public housing in Cleveland. A dozen firemen were required to remove her from her bedroom and transport her to the hospital. Taxpayers will now be required to build her new housing with doorways adequate for her girth, in addition to continuing to pay for her food, medical care, safety and all other needs. Such sloth is a flaw inherent to human nature, but a few generations ago it would not have been tolerated. She would have had to adapt to become a productive citizen or perish. She has become a giant panda.

Governmental social programs that protect the stupid, subsidize the lazy and coddle criminals are producing a society of giant pandas. If we continue to embrace this subversion of natural law, our nation will soon suffer the same fate as the panda. Don't save the whales, save yourself!

There has always been inequality among cultures; one culture discovers a new skill that allows it to dominate its neighbors militarily and achieve greater productivity, the other is conquered. Over time, inferior cultures adopt the ways of superior cultures and the superior cultures incorporate the redeeming qualities of others. This merging of cultures results in ever advancing societies greater than the sum of their parts. The history of human advancement has been a bloody affair.

It has become fashionable to claim that all cultures are equal. It is a romantic notion of noble savages, much like the desire to preserve endangered species. Cultures fall due to inferiority — to preserve them is to undo societal progress. When you realize how far humanity has come, and how much to the better, you quickly abandon such romanticism. When Muhammad Ali returned from his first boxing match in Africa, a reporter asked him what he thought of his ancestral homeland. Ali replied, "Thank God my grand-daddy got on that boat!" Ali had seen Africa's dehumanizing poverty, internecine war, brutal dictatorships, rampant disease, and vital slave trade.

My heritage is predominately Irish. Before Saint Patrick civilized Ireland, it was a land of warring tribes, who practiced human sacrifice and slavery. It was devoid of literacy, mathematics, and science. I play Celtic music and know hundreds of folk tales by memory; however, I would not wish to live in ancient Ireland. Even Saint Patrick went there for the first time only because he was captured as a slave! Ireland's is a sad tale of conquest by more advanced cultures, but no reasonable person would wish to undo the progress conquest brought. The same is true of my other ancestors: English, French, German, and Cherokee — all have benefited from conquest by superior societies.

Western civilization found its apex in America due to our Constitutional rights. Chief among these were property rights. The individual owned himself, his land, his possessions, his means of production and the fruits of his labor; he had the right to bear arms to protect his property, and with this self determination, he had religious freedom, freedom of association and a representative government. The American was not a peasant, slave or serf, ultimately owned by a king — he owned himself and could do with himself as he pleased. This unique code of law brought the ambitious, from all over the world. In America, they could realize their dreams, they could make use of the knowledge their ancestors had sacrificed to gain. Within a few generations, America had advanced the arts and sciences further than any other culture on earth.

Due to multiculturalism, Americans are taught to embrace their ancestral heritage and identify with it more than with America. Americanism is portrayed as a negative force. Americans are breaking into tribes of peoples, each vying for dominance. We are forced to become multilingual, and our arts and sciences, the culmination of thousands of years of knowledge, are derided as the worthless writings of "dead white males." This has resulted in social promotion for students who don't know the material, remedial classes in college, and illiteracy rates approaching pre-Civil War levels!

Instead of aspiring to greater levels of prosperity and enlightenment, we are embracing cultures that our ancestors fled. We are moving backward toward barbarism and thuggishness. Even Bill Cosby, Spike Lee and Sista Souljah (individuals who hate white/European culture) have given speeches warning of the negative values promulgated through hip hop/gangsta culture. These values encourage criminal behavior and denigrate women; the popularity of such music shows the direction we are heading as a nation. How long will it be before America follows Canada's lead in incorporating Islamic law into its legal system? How long before Americans are squatting in the dirt and practicing slavery like the Taliban?

There is no master race, no genetically superior people; there are superior cultures. There are those who practice slavery and squat in the dirt, and those who build space shuttles and computers. Right now, there is a great debate over manufacturing jobs going overseas and the resulting unemployment. Companies are finding better-educated people in the third world whose wages are not increased by regulations, unions, and taxes levied to pay for myriad social programs. The dirt squatters and the computer makers are changing places, and we have no one to blame but ourselves.

"In a nation rife with conflicting viewpoints, it's hard not to blame people for tuning out. But it's also understandable, because the causes for indifference are twofold, and include both external and internal culprits."

Generation Care Less: Why Apathy Can Destroy Us
Shabina S. Khatri
University of Michigan Graduate

It's not easy being the future leaders of America. We've got the last generation's problems – race relations, the environment, and gender discrimination – plus new dilemmas like national security and globalization to deal with.

But talking problems is dangerous, because it gets out of hand and overwhelms us.

And to save ourselves in this oh-so-crazy Information Age, we've learned to shut down when overwhelmed.

Frustration and helplessness are not new feelings, but I fear the long-term consequences of these sentiments because of their prevalence.

I'm an optimistic person that holds a lot of hope for our collective futures. Broadly speaking, our generation loves more and shares more – but doesn't seem to care more. That's where the trouble starts, that most of the time we couldn't care less. That's where it could all end, with indifference becoming our dominant defense mechanism.

In a nation rife with conflicting viewpoints, it's hard not to blame people for tuning out. But it's also understandable, because the causes for indifference are twofold, and include both external and internal culprits.

Externally, it starts with our culture.

It started when the extended family shrunk to the nuclear unit, shifting the focus off the community and onto the individual and his immediate family members.

Capitalism took it a step further and glorified the struggling individual as the hero pursuing the American dream. Class-consciousness sprang up, and with it came that smug secure successful feeling that wholly affirms that the system works (I got here on my own merit and those bums are only homeless because they're too lazy to get jobs). God was removed a degree and acknowledged as Creator, so man assumed the now-vacant position as sustainer, proven through and through by technological advances that give people instant gratification, what we want when we want it. Never a dull moment on the World Wide Web, because there's always something new popping up. Plus, the convenience of machines is fast becoming a substitute for human interaction, and we all know how mind-numbing that can be.

Which brings us to today, why the average student's attention span is 20 minutes and why ongoing news like the war in Iraq and the flailing economy don't kick up as much interest anymore. Gone are the fiery days of anti- and pro-war rallies, as is the anticipation over lower interest rates. Reality becomes sterilized, war reduced to strategies and unemployment to statistics. It's gotten to be that if it doesn't affect us directly, we aren't expected to care – we aren't conditioned to care. The nation's AIDS epidemic is bigger than us, we're told. One person cannot save the world from global warming, so why try?

That's where the internal element comes in. It takes a lot of energy to muster up compassion or dismay or grief. It's so much easier to remain in one constant, safe state: apathy. That apathy stems from disinterest (we get bored easily because we've come to expect a constant flow of information) and disenchantment (our idealism has been tainted and replaced by a growing sense of powerlessness). The advent of the Internet also makes it easier for us to look at global issues with a certain sense of detachment – it's all happening way over there on the other side of the plasma screen, to them (not us).

Thus far I've used only my own analysis to identify the root causes of a problem I contend to be the largest facing our generation today. But countless psychologists and sociologists have used the same disturbing trend to explain historical tragedies like the Holocaust as well as dilemmas in today's political arena (e.g. "voter apathy").

The late behavioral scientist B.F. Skinner points outs that Western cultural practices promote the "pleasing effects of behavioral consequences at the expense of strengthening effects." He elaborates by saying we spend too much time alienating workers from the consequences of their work, guiding behavior with rules instead of supplying consequences, and reinforcing pleasures that are not contingent to our survival. In other words, we work like programmed robots and use sex and love to reassure us of our humanity. I'm not being melodramatic.

Think about your favorite book or movie, or the escapist entertainment that followed September 11th's tragedy. Those diversions evoked feelings within us, sentiments that may have lingered a few hours or days after the fact, but no longer. That's called canned emotion, and it's fooling us into believing we're not losing ourselves to indifference. Oftentimes, we mistakenly believe that television and movies reflect reality – so we try to concern ourselves with the latest American Idol's identity crisis instead of the nation's rising suicide rate.

In his essay, Skinner carries the effects of apathy to their logical conclusion: cultural stagnation.

But that's only hakuna matata - no worries, no progress – for the masses, not the movers and shakers of this nation. To a certain extent, the status quo needs the public's indifference in order to hold on to those privileged positions. And to push those agendas.

Why else has the PATRIOT ACT II – a complete violation of our constitutional rights – gotten so far? The newspapers are writing about it, and city council resolutions are condemning it. But the masses haven't gotten behind it, and the question is why?

Section 201 of the Act's text states: "The government need not disclose information about individuals detained in investigations of terrorism until disclosure occurs routinely upon the initiation of criminal charges." Goodbye, Bill of Rights.

Or affirmative action. Take my own alma mater, the University of Michigan, the hotbed for a national debate. A poll taken right around decision time showed that nearly one in five University students surveyed simply didn't hold an opinion on the issue. We just don't care, one way or the other, the consensus was.

Scary stuff. But I'm getting into problems again, and I don't want to lose you. So let's jump to solutions.

Basically, if it's going to be we who will inherit this planet, we're going to have to step up and do a few things to ensure its survival. The first thing, of course, would be to show a sign of life. Educated expression, and not ignorant indifference. The second thing relates to the first: education. Hey, knowledge is power.

But be careful. It's easy to sit back and watch CNN and "objectively" observe and then talk to your friends and sound all edumacated, now that you have the "facts" and have drawn your own conclusions off of them. It's the whole taking it a step further and trying to look at things from a multidimensional viewpoint that tends to be our problem. We're comfortable with what we've got, what we know. It's unsettling to hear different things, to reject the tide of the crowd and to figure out the truth.

It's human nature to want to simplify information into easily-processed bite-sized morsels. But truth is often never so simple as black and white, especially in times of crisis and suffering. It's multifaceted and it deserves to be scrutinized as such. And man, that takes so much work!

But exerting that effort is critical, I promise you.

How many of you have traveled overseas? How else would you understand that people are not happy with our foreign policy? That certainly doesn't bode well for us and our future endeavors at international relations, as globalization further intertwines our economy with other countries'.

There are also many domestic issues we don't seem to see, like the stratification of wealth in this nation. It's just mind-boggling that 10 percent of American families hold two-thirds of the wealth. And that divide between rich and poor is growing because we're still pushing tax cuts and school vouchers and trying to convince ourselves that everyone's competing on equal footing.

These are difficult concepts to grasp, I understand. Education is vital, but it's wasted without critical thinking skills. That's another arena we need to work on, analyzing the stuff that's being shoved down our throats, war and abortion and homosexuality and religion and politics and terrorism. Analyzing rather than swallowing politely, turning our heads, and throwing it all up.

Please, take everything I said here and mull it over – and then tell me I'm a complete idiot. I'll thank you for it, because you'll have proved me wrong by showing that we're still picky about the information we consume. The memory of your criticism will help me feel better when I see students shudder at reading assignments and forego the *Guardian* for the *Enquirer*. Or worse, watch the local news instead of reading a credible newspaper.

Perhaps you agree that we have a problem here, but that this problem does not affect you. "To think that we can escape control is a delusion that prevents us from attending to the task of making a better world," our man Skinner said. So to those of you that think they are exceptions to the rule: you're deluding yourselves. You're as much caught in this mess as the rest of us, myself included.

Ok, so processing information and sorting the wheat from the chaff (the gems from the crap) is the first step. But there's still enough important information out there to fry our synapses and send us into overload. That's where priorities come in. Choose your battles carefully. Perhaps championing for campaign finance reform is your true calling, or maybe it's finding the cure for cancer. Remember that you don't have to solve all of the world's problems by yourself, or in just one night. If enough of us start to care and wield our fortes to fill the gaps in the system, then our futures really will have a fighting chance.

"'I'd say we shouldn't have cared, but that is extremely insensitive and Hitler was an outrageously cruel man, plus we wouldn't have the only thing that the French were good for - chocolate mousse.'"

How Many Frenchmen Does It Take?
Max Buccini
Boston College, Chestnut Hill, MA

How many French men does it take to defend Paris? This and countless other jokes about our French "friends" have permeated American culture for years. But why has there been such an inundation in the media, pop culture, comedy routines, and even on Main Street of anti-French jokes, boycotts, and general frustration with France? What is still more interesting is the arrival of anti-French sentiments to the college campus. Here at Boston College, there have been many displays of a general frustration with our fellow Western democracy. On the first floor of Kostka dorm, there was a less than flattering "Military History of France" on the wall. On the doors of various dorm rooms, there appear slogans like "F*ck France." Even in the dining halls, there was the all too famous serving of "freedom fries." But the French are just as French as they have always been. Ever since Julius Caesar invaded Gaul and Vercingetorix revolted in 54 B.C., the French have been putting a bad taste in the mouths of other nations. So why now are all these demonstrations of our distaste for the French coming out in a deluge? Shouldn't Americans and Boston College students have expected as much?

Some Americans believe that the anti-French sentiments are a bit over the top: "freedom fries" really? But some venting, purging, or catharsis is considered harmless and even right on target by many. It is much better that Americans do not demonstrate our displeasure by, say, initiating a tactical strike on Jacques Chirac's personal residence; so most would say, let them munch their "freedom fries." But other Americans have taken it further. The Associated Press reported that a WWII veteran, "has returned a certificate of thanks he received from France two years ago, saying he is upset the country he helped liberate isn't supporting America's efforts to disarm Iraq." The brave WWII veteran, Angelo Pizzuti, 80, felt betrayed. This position is considered justifiable. Exercising a veto in the United Nations Security Council, voicing one's opposition to a certain policy, and offering critical advice is one thing; lobbying other governments against the United States, conducting deliberately obstructionist policies, and distorting and hiding the facts is quite another. Just like Angelo, Boston College Arts and Sciences' freshman Michael Parker ('06) feels the same way, "France - they need us but we definitely don't need them. Seriously, when is the last war they won? The only reason they aren't Germany is because of the United States. I'd say we shouldn't have cared, but that is extremely insensitive and Hitler was an outrageously cruel man, plus we wouldn't have the only thing that the French were good for - chocolate mousse."

Boycotts of France have become extremely popular, whether they are organized boycotts like NewsMax.com or individual boycotts of French products. Even Capitol Hill is getting involved. Some ideas flouted in our nation's capital have been meant to apply pressure on French imports to the United States. Speaker of the House Dennis Hastert suggested that the US put warning labels on French wine warning the American people that the French use bovine blood (which is high risk for mad cow disease, mind you) to clarify the wine. Sorry to all those vegetarians on campus who thought French wine was drinkable. Another Boston College student, Derek Scott ('06) believes the boycotts are health: "I think that a boycott is really the only way to make a statement about another country's foreign policy without hindering public life, sacrificing safety, or making inflammatory gestures towards the people and government officials comprising the opposition."

But there is opposition to these recent anti-French sentiments at Boston College. Professor Rebecca Valette of the French Department of Boston College opines, "According to the New York Times – of several weeks ago – much of the impetus for the anti-French sentiment was provided by conservative elements of the US Government and pushed by Murdoch and his news outlets. It was picked by the conservative talk shows." Professor Valette goes on to say how in "more conservative" parts of America this anti-Frenchism is prevalent but not in areas like "Boston and San Francisco." Valette does not agree with the assertion that France is in some way no longer a friend of the United States. Instead, France and the United States have different meanings of friendship. The French feel that, "If your friend is making a critical decision, or if you feel he/she is going down the wrong path, it is up to you to criticize and explain the pitfalls." Professor Valette finds the jokes about the French military to be the most offensive and ultimately grounded in malicious intent.

Getting reaction to Professor Valette's statements I again asked Derek Scott ('06) his opinion: "Clearly, Boston and San Francisco are more enlightened and civilized than the fly-over parts of this country…if France is a good friend for obstructing and delaying every move we made, shouldn't they at least remove the knife they stabbed in our back?" This reporter attempted to get further reactions, this time from the French Consulate in Boston about anti-French sentiments. Regretfully, the French Consulate in what appears to be proper French fashion avoided conflict and did not respond. Perhaps France is still upset over America's transforming their beloved croissant into the McDonald's "croissandwich." So, when buying French wine, make-up products, or clothes take into account both views on the issue; decide whether you are in the "Vive la France!" camp or the "Vive la Liberte!"

Impassioned by a Famous Photograph, Profundity of Past, and Aftermath...

Tyrone Collier
University of Cincinnati, Cincinnati, OH

Influenced by a sentiment of pride
and honor rather than superior-
ity, I tuck my fingertips inside
my palm - my heartline - brazen but unsure
and lay my thumb atop my knuckles. Un-
ashamed I bow my head and close my eyes
and with my fist I touch my heart undone
then thrust my tightened fist into the sky
(a fist that's fitted with a titan glove),
expel a breath for sprinter Tommie Smith,
oppression, and the protestants thereof.
And, just as dandelion tufts, my wish
disperses through this atmosphere of smoke
so thick my lungs contract and make me choke.

"I've been called faithless because I'm a liberal, a cynic, and basically an atheist. But I believe in Jacques Brel and Bobby Dylan, organized labor, and the old maxim that pitching wins championships..."

In One Epiphany
Mischa B. Sogut
The George Washington University, Washington, DC

In one epiphany, I realized I was out of touch. I go to my computer and sign onto the AOL Instant Messenger. So the AIM News pops up, and the 2nd headline is "Carter Tells of Break With Paris." So I'm thinking, "Oh nice, this article must be about Jimmy Carter and Franco-American relations." So I click on it hoping with only a twinge of doubt that I'm going to get the aforementioned discussion on foreign policy. Of course it was actually about Nick Carter's and Paris Hilton's breakup. I hate the media. Fuck the media.

Look, I'm a New Deal McGovernik and I'll stand on a soapbox for hours about the war and the economy and the PATRIOT Act and Pentagon waste, but there's one thing that I can't stand about The Movement. I see a lot of people around on the college left (and college dropout left) who have this righteous coolness to them, a terminal case of self-aggrandizement. It's these paragons of alt-rock and Indymedia who consider themselves to be so nonconformist that their mere continued existance is sticking it to The Man. I have no problem with these people's politics, and if they're really fighting GE/NewsCorp/Bush's Manichean dualism, that's all well and good and my hat's off to them. I just can't comprehend their attitude that they're sublimely free from the hive-mind of the rest of us, that their radical politics constitute a genuine freedom of the spirit and an exemption from social pressure and conformity. This thought came front and center to me when I realized one day that all anarchists dress the same.

I've been called faithless because I'm a liberal, a cynic, and basically an atheist. But I believe in Jacques Brel and Bobby Dylan, organized labor, and the old maxim that pitching wins championships; I believe in listening to Sinatra before a date and that any meal tastes 25% better if you're out with a girl; I believe it when Dubcek tells me that "hope dies last" and when the Beatles tell me that "love is all you need," and I believe in sheer dumb unexplainable luck; I believe that life is too short to be planned, that music can save your soul, and I believe in old-fashioned tax-and-spend liberalism; I believe in the *Sunday Times Magazine* with bagels and the afternoon Giants game, that all progress is subjective, and that health care is a right; I believe in jazz, especially jazz, vodka, especially vodka, and I believe in quoting dead white men while sitting in cafes; I believe in the Czech irony of Kundera and the Irish soul of Van Morrison, and I believe in that sublime hymn from the 4th movement of Holst's "Planets" suite; I believe in Victor Frankl, in repealing the Rockefeller Drug Laws, and in picking the 12-5 upset in the NCAAs; I believe in the value of education and the absurdity of teaching to the test, the value of living wage and the absurdity of the "growth" statistic, the value of affirmitive action and the absurdity of white guilt. I believe in Lawrence Ferlinghetti and George McGovern, Graham Greene and Bernie Sanders, the *American Prospect magazine* and the Michigan-Ohio State game. I believe in walking the monuments at night, in playing in the snow in shorts, in Bergmann's "Seventh Seal," in Bertrand Russell, and in more than one scene from "Casablanca.

I'm a New York blue-state nonbelieving Jewish liberal on a massive scholarship to a private urban East Coast university who reads the papers every day, who could never give up eating meat, who thinks McCain is overrated, who went to public school, who carries an ACLU card; who drinks chai, who has a Federal Work-Study job, who cried watching "Glory" and "On the Beach," who donates to MoveOn, who was Drum Line Captain in high school, who people-watches, who speaks mediocre French, who always stands up on the subway, who puts bumper stickers on his car, who overspends his means at the bookstore, who loved "old" Europe, who illegally downloads music, who thinks Hollywood for the most part sucks, who overtips waitresses, whose mother went bankrupt, whose grandparents were union members, and whose great-grandparents were Communists.

Next time someone tells you that liberals and agnostics and city folks and college kids don't believe in anything, don't stand for anything, aren't representative of the mythical "real" America, tell them your own story.

"A further look at Michael Moore and Co.'s ideological identification and the logic, or lack thereof, of his work and their stances, exposes the true faces behind the mask of propaganda and puffery."

Michael Moore: The Freedom Fighter?
Erich Mattei
University of Georgia, Athens, GA

W hen in history has there been a single piece of art, theater, or literature that has had such a profound impact on society as what liberal icon Michael Moore's latest cut of motion picture propaganda, *Fahrenheit 9/11*, has? Released at a pivotal time in both international affairs, in the wake of a much-debated military action in the ever-uneasy Middle East, and domestic politics, on the eve of the United States presidential election for perhaps the most powerful office in the world, the film has no doubt caused quite a ruckus. The reason for this much anticipated response is simple, for Moore's film strikes a universal chord within the consciousnes of people from all cultures, classes, and ideologies: liberty. How, then, has this common interest in freedom that is exclusively shared among all of mankind come to serve as the seed for such a jungle of disagreement?

Interestingly enough, both support and opposition to Moore, and likewise the Bush administration's decision to incite a military conflict, are rooted solely in freedom. Most conservatives and other supporters of the military operation cite liberty as the motive for such action, while most liberals and other opponents cite liberty as the foundation of such objection, both sides all the while sharing two common characteristics: inconsistency and contradiction. An analysis of what purpose the film serves in the struggle for liberty and what the underlying ideological threads of Moore's work are comprehensively, lends itself to determining what credit Moore deserves, if any, for undertaking this project.

The single greatest asset, and indeed only legitimate premise, of Moore's *Fahrenheit 9/11,* is that it publicizes the coercive, grim face of the inevitable impoverishment that is the result of warfare. It investigates the rapid growth of the United States government and its trend of trampling the rights of individuals, and the corporatism that is spawned out of the close ties between big government and big business, especially in wartime. However, these undeniable strengths of the film are also its greatest weaknesses, for the liberal Moore focuses his efforts on the conservative Bush administration instead of addressing the crux of the matter: the institution of government. Also, given the passionate disgust that the filmmaker has for the current authority at the helm of the United States government, and the equally passionate fondness he has for an alternative dictator, one may rightly question whether Moore's motives are sincerely rooted in liberty or merely in detraction. In light of this, and the positive and negative publicity the film has received, it is clear that indeed all sides of the mainstream political spectrum are horribly mistaken in their attacks against each other, because the true enemy is statism, a system that each side wishes to instill such that it may benefit at the expense of the other. A further look at Michael Moore and Co.'s ideological identification and the logic, or lack thereof, of his works and their stances exposes the true faces behind the mask of propaganda and puffery.

Referencing Ray Bradbury's dystopian sci-fi novel *Fahrenheit 451, Fahrenheit 9/11*, according to producer Moore, was titled as such for being the "temperature at which freedom burns." One need not see Moore's latest work to conclude, based on any viewing of his past work (specifically *Roger and Me*) or his website (www.michael-moore.com), that he is certainly not the freedom fighter he espouses to be, but is actually the exact opposite. Given that Moore has recently been given feature interviews on many major networks, and landed headlines and cover stories in newspapers and magazines around the world, including the cover of *Time Magazine*, it is time for the truth about Michael Moore and Co. to be revealed and the logic of their agenda and proposals unveiled. The task at hand, therefore, is not to question whether or not Moore's findings surrounding the United States' military occupation in Iraq are valid (if such a study were even remotely possible), but rather to expose the face of his oppressive political intentions and the fallacies of his reasoning.

Given the staunch opposition that Moore and his sympathizers have toward free enterprise, one is pressured to question, first and foremost, which "freedom" Moore is referencing in the title to his latest blockbuster. Is it the "freedom" to tax, or steal, or manipulate that only government, and certainly the socialist welfare-state government that Moore endorses, has? Free market capitalism is positively the only manifestation of the natural right that each individual has to the ownership of oneself. It is also the system that Moore, a self-proclaimed civil rights activist, undeniably rejects with much conviction. For capitalism is the only system wherein consensual acts between consenting individuals are permitted, be they civil or economic. Further, capitalism is the only system in which unprovoked, pre-emptive aggressions and rights violations committed by individuals or bands of individuals are prohibited. In his opposition to capitalism, Moore is explicitly opposing the only solution to the war-mongering imperialism he purports to counter. Government, a zero-sum game at best, is often a negative sum game, notably during war or conflict, which necessitates orchestrating actions and policies such that those who benefit do so at the expense of others. Free market capitalism, the only system of positive sums and liberty, for that matter, does not earn the approval of Moore or his followers because of the very fact that it offers individuals the right to voluntarily interact with whomever they please, utilize and trade the fruits of their natural, diverse abilities, and profit from these exchanges. Should the liberal ideology that Moore purports, and its conservative counterpart for that matter, ever accept free market capitalism as a principal component of its philosophy, then it would cease to have any foundation on which to justify the violations of freedom it commits to maintain itself, and would therefore necessarily have to forego such actions to save face. Indeed every piece of legislation or public policy initiative that redistributes wealth in any way, or pumps more money into an ever-failing public works or government program, most of which Moore openly supports, subjugates the fundamental freedom of self-ownership from which all other legitimate freedoms stem. While a critic of the free market such as Moore may attack these assertions about capitalism as ideal or utopian in comparison to current social and governmental trends, one cannot deny the truth of these declarations any more than they could those of mathematics, for they are founded in pure logic.

What, then, does Michael Moore stand for? It is not difficult to infer from his works that Moore favors welfare-statism, which equates to a big government priding itself on redistributive economics. Surely, he and his cohorts would valiantly argue to the contrary by drawing attention to the bigness of the imperialistic warfare-state that is currently being bred, but what both the modern left and right wings of mainstream political thought fail to realize is that the welfare-and-warfare state, empirically speaking, are one and the same. Thumbing through the pages of any history textbook, let alone a focused work such as Robert Higgs' *Crisis & Leviathan*, one will notice the radical growth of government regulations, programs, and public policy that occurs in conjunction with wartime. In these periods of national unrest, the time preferences of authorities shift and decisions are made to satisfy some short-run interest with little, if any, regard for individuals, their natural rights, or the long-run repercussions of such decisions. Moore undoubtedly realizes this assertion, and indeed sets out to prove it in his new film, but what he fails to understand is that this same formula also applies to the socialist government apparatus that he backs. Certainly, in the market, interests and plans change to accommodate unforeseen alterations, but individuals, being held accountable for their actions in such a setting, have a tendency to react with a greater concern for the well-being of others, even if such a concern stems purely from their own self-interest. The fact of the matter is that government, be it welfare or warfare, holds a monopoly of power in the territory it administers while private individuals and corporations are vulnerable to shifts in the market, namely the competitive market environment resulting from changing preferences of their fellow market participants, and are therefore encouraged to satisfy these changes in order to survive.

Finally, a logical depiction of Michael Moore's ideal system, a socialist welfare state, marks out how misguided such aims are, what such a system would hold, and Moore's contradiction of supporting such a system in light of his supposed support of freedom and peace. State socialism, the epitome of modern left liberalism and the logical end of its philosophy, is the antithesis of free market capitalism and, hence, all of the freedoms afforded the individual in the natural order setting of capitalism. Socialism encompasses the absence of private property rights and the concomitant trade and markets that evolve from this propertied capitalist system. Certainly, voluntary socialism is feasible and indeed exists in a free market setting whenever individuals choose to pool their resources or share in the use of some property, but this is far from the coercive redistributive sort that Moore and Co. endorse. National socialism, the state-coordinated socialist system of Moore's sort, is the culmination of the state, a system wherein the individual has little if any choice but is rather regarded as a mere component of the state and granted rights and privileges to the state's property and resources. While the utopian communist philosophers throughout history, which the modern left liberal sentiment resembles and often emulates, envision great prosperity and peace, such ends are only achievable in a free market environment, and basic logic, concludes otherwise. Ludwig von Mises' *Omnipotent Government* does just this, mapping out the logical path of the rise of the total state and total war and the historical examples of such a system. The blueprint is quite concise: socialism, being the absence of markets and trade, and hence the inability to utilize any resources beyond the states' borders, necessitates conflict, in place of trade, to acquire those previously unattainable resources. This is the implicit contradiction that Moore makes of attacking the current warfare state and yet supporting the welfare state. For a consistent application of Moore's stances on economic issues would, in time, necessitate war if the total state wishes not to perish.

Liberal propagandist and guru Michael Moore's *Fahrenheit 9/11* certainly divulges some of the repercussions of the current United States imperialistic war jugger-naut, but credit should be bestowed all but generously to Moore, given his true ideology and motives. As expected, one may indeed leave the theater disturbed, not so much by the premise of the film - it is merely a visual depiction of the terrors of not only war but big government that philosophers, economists, and commentators since the time of the early classical liberals (Thomas Jefferson and Co.) have written of - but because of the message: BIGger government. Moore no doubt insinuates that government action and aid is (1) too slow, and (2) not enough! As far as the facts of the business ties and PATRIOT Act are concerned, the film does a good job of depicting it in a way that is understandable, but still it has totally missed the mark on the crux of the matter: big gov-ernment. Therefore, one must ask: is any credit due, and if so how much? It would've been like a German Neo-Marxist in the 1930s-40s doing a film on the terrors of the Nazi rise to power - he would speak of the obvious to classical liberals, but his motives, his ends, are almost just as bad. Until Moore reconsiders his stance on the many forms of welfare statism he supports, he will continue to be everything but the advocate of free-dom he would like the public to think he is, and the philosophical framework of his ban-tering will remain little more than unreasonable and simply illogical.

*This work or portions of this work have been previously published through the Ludwig von Mises Institute

"Every night after rehearsals I gorged books and balanced equations and composed essays, determined to one day prove that the world held something much more for me."

On Being Different in the South
Alexandra Pajak
Georgia Institute of Technology, Atlanta, GA

St. Joseph wasn't meant for the county jail, but that's where the town landed him.

He traveled to our sleepy Georgia town one early August when the Southern sun hangs the brightest in the sky like a white ball reaching with six arms in all directions. His round body and plain face clashed with the athleticism and good looks inherent in the town's cultural identity. I don't know much about his past, his family or what the world holds for him today. I do know he ended up in jail when he deserved it, though. And that's the truth.

Early in the year I learned his real name was Steven Coddler, and we were both sixteen at the time. Auditions for the school's annual one-act play arrived with him that autumn. The same one or two students always seemed to get the lead roles, and the rest of us with lesser roles, myself included, would get to listen about their movie star aspirations in between gathering props in their dad's pickup trucks and painting homemade sets on reject plywood donated from the local Home Depot. The play that fall was entitled *The Butterfingers Angel* and detailed the story of Mary's and Joseph's journey to Bethlehem with the help of a clumsy, yet kind-hearted angel. According to its script, the angel drops things and stumbles, but somehow in the end everyone gets to Bethlehem just fine.

A public school performing a nativity play seemed to me at the time to contradict the separation of church and state law, but for some reason the school board approved it anyway. Steven snagged the lead part of Joseph. Without any formal voice or acting training, without the background of theater courses about which the usual leads boasted, "the new kid" simply gathered the courage to show up and do his best and scored big.

Too bad he'd later pull a knife on half the cast.

I played a part in *The Butterfingers Angel* along with Steven. The director, who must have had quite a sense of humor, cast me as one of the barn animals in the nativity scene - the cow. Possible implications about my weight upset me initially, but I soon thought little of it as I weighed only 110 pounds and felt just fine about my appearance. The costume consisted of a brown sweat suit with painted spots and black Sketchers running shoes on my hands and feet. I stuck my tongue into my cheek during scenes in which I didn't have any lines, pretending to chew cud and making the most of a small part. I managed to get a few laughs here and there from the audience, which always felt great.

Steven and I also had chemistry class together, bright and early at 8:13 a.m. each morning that autumn. He didn't talk much, but did answer questions when called upon. We were placed in a lab group together, along with a girl from Trinidad named Alana. The three of us always completed our assignments on time and sometimes chatted together after class. Steven once asked me about a necklace I often wore around my neck. I made it myself out of a piece of string and four beads with printed letters.

"What does that mean, 'WWDD?'" Steven asked, pointing at my neck.

"What would Darwin do," I answered.

He scrunched his face up, smiled a little and walked away. During the "What Would Jesus Do" fad, that necklace provoked a good handful of folks to tell me I was going straight to hell. (At least with the necklace I had more control over when it occurred.) I was glad at least one other person found it humorous, too.

Steven and I continued to get along pretty well, but in between learning about chemical bonds and the ways of the universe I noticed Steven's unpredictable temper. While always justified, his fiery nature disconcerted me enough to distance myself from him. I began completing my portion of the lab reports with the usual precision necessary, but if he asked me a question outside of our chemistry topic, I would apologize, say I was busy and pull a strand of my brown hair behind one ear.

The habits of our chemistry teacher didn't help. Mr. Grimme would playfully tease us with such test questions like, "How many fingers and toes are in this classroom? Estimate to one significant figure." Mr. Grimme smiled from his desk as we all turned around in our seats and counted each other, and multiplied by 10 - no wait, 20! - trying to determine the number of appendages. I still view the man as a teaching genius, but the class proved demanding. Each Friday promised a quiz with complex questions about fingers and toes or moles and forces. And each Friday, Steven cursed under his breath as he entered class, and sometimes flew wildly from cordial greetings to sputtering anger as he anticipated, took, and recovered from the quizzes.

After earning the lead role in *The Butterfingers Angel*, though, his outbursts nearly ceased, and he started walking more upright, his spine supporting his legs and head on a straight beam of perfectly-stacked bone. He waved cheerfully to people in the hall. If he saw any cast members on his way to class, he'd shout "Hi," which really came out like "Hah!" from his thick accent. Steven always wore imitation Birkenstocks, even during wintertime, and now his sandals and hairy legs made him seem more and more like a Franciscan monk wandering the halls.

The usual lead - Nick Dubell who, ironically, was cast as King Herod - used his dramatic antics to create enough scandal to turn a large portion of the cast against our school's St. Joseph. Nick - the Liam Neeson of our tiny town plus about ten inches around the waist - criticized everything he could about Steven. The way Steven delivered lines, the way he dressed, the manner in which he spoke. Soon a rumor began that Steven had a crush on the girl who played the Virgin Mary. Although Steven, in spite of his occasional outrages, always held doors open for female students and never told dirty jokes, the Virgin Mary blatantly avoided him in between dress rehearsals. I often worried she'd get whiplash from swooshing her blue veil so hard each time she turned away from his attempts at conversation after rehearsals. As the semester continued, Eric's smile relaxed and his eyes turned downcast. The cradling of the plastic baby-doll Jesus onstage continued with a tension between the cast and Steven strong enough to split a curtain in half.

As I walked to chemistry one morning, I overheard Nick complaining to two of his theater buddies about Steven. "And he sounds goddamn awful with that Southern accent of his."

"At least he can act!" I shouted sarcastically from behind him. He didn't know I'd overheard. He turned around to face me, and I met his eyes in a fierce gaze.

He paused and literally stopped in his steps for an instant, seeming to falter. He began to say something quietly, then waved his hand defensively. "Aw, go to hell, Pajak."

To this day, I'm glad I defended Steven. After my brief confrontation with him, Nick started taunting me, too, particularly in front of any young men who expressed any hint of romantic interest in me. For some reason, one of his friends, the girl who played a donkey in the nativity scene, punched me in the stomach backstage when the lights were out and so I didn't have any witnesses.

Every night after rehearsals I gorged books and balanced equations and composed essays, determined to one day prove that the world held something much more for me. The wide spaces between needles on pine, the washboard of blackness behind the open night's low horizons, the way the humid Southern air lifts and squeezes your lungs before a summer storm - I hid my feelings well, and I spent my spare time with just a few close friends and my family. Sometimes I longed to run away and leap onto a railway car to Buffalo where my parents grew up and eat fish fries and assemble airplane parts in a gigantic factory like my grandma did during the war. Busy streets and fast-talking strangers churned in my blood hot and alive like freshly transubstantiated Communion wine.

For the time, though, I aimed for contentment playing my role, as both a student and, temporarily, as a cow. In a technical sense, the final rehearsals went smoothly. Steven had about 10 million lines, all of which he committed to memory skillfully. Unfortunately, about the same number of rumors also spread during the final week of practice. On opening night, my mother used her blue collar street smarts to caution me. After the play, leave right away for home, she suggested, after I described the mounting tensions to her. That kind of backstabbing atmosphere between high school boys could lead to a fight.

She was right. Frustrations peaked as Nick continued to criticize Steven and as the Virgin Mary lost her voice and sounded more like a tortured frog with his behind on fire than a mother of a deity. As the story goes, during intermission Steven flew into a rage, pulled out a pocket knife and carved "shit" into the wall of the men's dressing room. Actually, it was more like, "Shi—" because Nick and his drones yanked Steven away before he could slash out the final cross of the "t." Then Nick yelled, "If you make it so the school doesn't let us have plays anymore, we're coming after you!"

Now, I wouldn't have found that particularly threatening myself, because Nick Dubell's entire being was composed of about 25% water and 75% talk and the worst he could have done to a person was sing a showtune off-key. As the second act continued, though, word of what happened spread backstage like an STD from person to person, spoken of in whispers and magnified each time. After the play concluded, the girls, including me, rushed into the boy's dressing room to see the vandalism.

Steven had disappeared almost immediately after curtain call and could not be found, but "Shi—" remained on the wall. I began thinking to myself how the wall would look vastly improved with a little paint, when the girl who played a talking Christmas tree decided she wasn't satisfied with the current level of horror.

She pointed at the crooked letters and shouted, "I don't think it says 'shit!' I think he was carving . . . [dramatic pause] . . . 'Satan'!" A collective gasp sucked out all the logically-bonding oxygen atoms in the room and I nearly choked. The town's preacher's daughter who played a barnyard animal along with me (she was a sheep) opened her eyes and mouth so wide, I swear the cotton balls glued to her face almost peeled off.

I don't know what happened after that incident in regard to detention or any sort of formal punishment, but Steven never got another part, and his new nickname in the school was "Psycho," coined by our very own King Herod. The next time I heard about Steven was ten months later in the county newspaper, which my mom showed me with sad eyes. According to police blotter, he'd been working part-time at the local Taco Bell—one of two franchised restaurants in the town. He came to work his usual time at 10:00 a.m. on a Saturday and, without any clear reason, cursed and yelled with increasing severity as the morning wore on. By 11:30 a.m., he pulled a knife from his back pocket and waved it in the air, shouting profanities and threatening his coworkers.

No one was hurt, but two of the employees called the police, and rightfully so. The police arrived to Taco Bell, arrested Steven, and that's how St. Joseph ended up in jail.

Since I left town to pursue my own paths, I never found out whether he left prison or even graduated from high school. That particular jail stood erect next to the post office and library where letters traveled around the world almost unnoticed and where minds could expand for only two bucks and a piece of plastic, if you felt like it. The jail was a beige color that looked oddly soothing, at least from the outside somehow. The color matched many of the houses and churches in the town, a smooth plaster whose lower edges wore a dusting of red clay.

I never saw him again, that new boy in chemistry, that nomad who arrived to our tiny society that was once to all of us an entire universe. One of the things I remember most about Mr. Grimme's class was a lecture about how, at subatomic levels, particles "jump" from one energy level to another, simply disappearing for an instant and then reappearing the next, like a spirit moving on an invisible train track in space. Mr. Grimme also once said that he believed in God and that he believed there are rules in the universe but that God sometimes breaks them, at least when it comes to physics.

I spoke last with Steven just before I found out about the carving in the wall and before he left the theater to avoid the dramatic co-ed scene in the men's dressing area.

"Hey, you did a great job," I told him. My cow costume wasn't the most flattering or feminine of garbs, and I was still wearing four sneakers on my hands and feet. I expected him to laugh or offer a casual "thanks" or a "you, too." Instead Steven looked up at me, picking worriedly at his costume with his fingers. His eyes shone a glassy red, and the tight convex curve of his lips widened into a smile.

He cried out, "Really?" He yanked me close into him in a firm hug, his brown robe crushing into my spotted sweat-suit fur.

Our Voice
Kyla Schoessler
Gonzaga University, Spokane, WA

Our World
Jake Olzen
Saint Mary's University of Minnesota, MN

The world does not belong to any one country, corporation, or individual. It belongs to all of us. Each and every person of the six billion in this world has a voice. We breathe the same air, drink the same water, eat the same food. Each person in this world has a responsibility to pass his or her share of the world on to someone else. We were all given the gift of life by older generations...they gave us their world to pass on. It is not ours to destroy, to desecrate, or to defile. It is ours to rebuild, renew, and restore. It is ours to give to the future.

Requiem
Christopher Continanza
Villanova University, Villanova, PA

Etched in flesh
and in the name of all that is,
bordering on oblivion,
I sing.
Before I knew I couldn't know a thing
The muses sang a song
For me.
Before the logic
But after the thought,
Etched in stone
These tired hands wrought,
The ephemeral gestures
Of angels caught
Singing, of the freedom
from the ticking by
Which I've measured my deeds,
Before time became
temporality, sickening,
I sing.
And the song I wrote
Before song was lost,
Spoke no thing
Of meaning
But found some rhymes to accost
With feeling.
And when I tell you
Of this holy pleasure
Before rhythm and rhyme

Were metered by measure,
Now as the towers stand
Glistening tall,
In your fear, you fools,
You've lost it all.

Satisfaction
Sarah Timm
Washington State University, Pullman, WA

When Gloria Steinem or Eve Ensler are more well known than Jessica Simpson or Paris Hilton... When girls can be in a band or hold an office without it being a gender statement... When more than 13% of Congress have vaginas... When girls can be tough without being called "the Man," or can be brave with ovaries instead of balls... When boys can wear pink without being gay and stop being judged upon height... When "girlie" and "gay" are not insults... When girls go to college for an education as opposed to a "Mrs. Degree"... When boys can follow a degree for more than money... When date rape on college campuses is not expected... When there is a "Pecs" next to "Hooters" and a Playgirl mansion... When boys can suck at mechanics and girls can suck at sewing... When we stop assuming and judging based on gender and start seeing individuals, maybe I'll be satisfied.

"I was given time to contemplate as I stood alone at the rear of the chapel, and I realized how much I have been given and how much has been given up for me. I knew at that moment that the fallen men that lay before me lay not in vain."

Small White Crosses
Alison Marie Amyx
Mercer University, Macon, GA

"Homeland, Homeland. Renew your youth. Restore your soul." These words of Randall Stroop's "Homeland" flew from my soul as our choir's voice danced upon the small white crosses. A bronze sculpture symbolizing American Youth towered beside us, echoing our words. The mist in the air clung to my heart and I sang with a passion I have never known. Our audience: the graves in the American Cemetery at Omaha Beach in Normandy, France.

This past summer, Chorale, an auditioned voice ensemble at my school, was invited to tour France in an American Salute to Liberation. We were able to travel throughout the country and experience the rich culture, but most importantly, we learned the true meaning of sacrifice. I have heard about the Normandy Invasion in school for many years. I have heard of how our brave troops were killed. I knew these things, yet I did not know. The lessons meant nothing to me until I visited France. Then, they came alive. I was able to see this important event in history in a way that would not have been possible otherwise.

One elderly couple in a small community we visited expressed their appreciation for the American soldiers' sacrifice; they were there that day. Over fifty years later, I was there, too. Troops stormed the beaches as I walked down a winding path leading to the waters. Tears filled my eyes as I saw each man that gave his life as row after row of small white crosses stretched before me across the horizon. The grief of their families touched me as I entered the small chapel overlooking the graves. I was given time to contemplate as I stood alone at the rear of the chapel, and I realized how much I have been given and how much has been given up for me. I knew at that moment that the fallen men that lay before me lay not in vain.

Our country and so many countries in the world survive because of the bravery of our troops, and I have come to appreciate that. I have been filled with a pride for our country and a gratefulness to each man who fights in wars and sacrifices his family and time for us each day. I did not know and appreciate the true meaning of sacrifice until I walked onto the American Cemetery in Normandy, France. I know now; sacrifice is defined by those small white crosses.

So You Wanna Be Japanese
Takeo Rivera
Stanford University, Stanford, CA

You have the nerve after
Consuming some animanga
You say you wanna be Japanese
Not Nikkei but Nihon
Unknown and enigmatic
Exotic among Zen gardens
Katanas and bowing pardons
Yeah you like the culture
So you sip it like green tea
To escape that boring suburban reality
Maybe get some t-shirts with "serenity" in Kanji
Wear 'em to your anime party
They'll say you're "deep"
As if you actually know
What it's like to be Japanese
Like when WE didn't want to be Japanese
Looking at those Chinese wear those buttons
"I am a loyal Chinese American citizen"
Rightfully afraid of the FBI and lynching mobs
Who beat up no good Jap sobs
But we were stripped from our home, from land
To the arid sand of Manzanar and Topaz
Women and children behind barbed wire
As we tire of our damning slanty eyes
That white guys say we have trouble seeing out of
Like to see you imprisoned
detained
humiliated

caned for nothing
but your eyes and yellowness
Or you can see what it's like to be bombed
    melted
    burned alive
    or survive
As American hawks leave behind the carcasses of your family
Or hell, even coming here
Raising a farm doing no wrong
But denied citizenship 'cause they say you don't belong
What the hell do you know
About being this color, having these eyes
We're more than geishas and cyber-schoolgirls
And samurai with slashing sword whirls
You can't buy us in a store like Pocky Sticks
Or try us on like some clothing mix
You objectify to deify
But I defy
So get your hands off me

Steady Rain
Erica Sanchez
University of Illinois Chicago, Chicago, IL

it was the day of steady
rain, water heavy
with nostalgia,
staining everything,
my aching heels
wailing
beneath me.
at the train station
i saw a large heap of shit
hidden in a corner,
the rain washing it
towards us,
making the timid shit visible.
    i saw jesus
on the 60 bus today,
bearing a wooden cross,
drinking a coke
and quietly dying
for our sins.
    it was the day
my nails hurt and my body
decided to gush.
appropriate for today,
an homage.
i'll lose blood too,
only painlessly, almost.
on the tv screen -
the man on the throne

speaks words that sound
like salt and taste like steel,
a necklace of limbs
on his skinny neck.
    i look outside.
to my backyard-
a naked desert
       full of flies.

"I dream of a day when we will not be judged by what we wear but by who we are. I was always taught that with time our country has gotten better, but with time I have seen our country become more materialistic and less family-oriented."

Sunday, October 26, 2003 (Journal Entry)
Brook Elizabeth Thompson
James Madison University, Harrisonburg, VA

There is a constant battle that goes on in my head. A battle that is being fought to control my actions and my ideology. The opposing forces are what I have been brought up to think and do as an American and what my conscience tells me is the right thing to think and do. The former tells me to be selfish, to strive for wealth, that the more money you have the happier you are, that our society and our government is the best, so we should encourage other countires to be like us. My country tells me that it is important to look good, so important that you should starve yourself, go into debt for designer clothes, and let someone mutilate your body so that you never look your age because being older doesn't mean you're wiser it just means you don't look as good as you once did.

My conscience tells me it is important to BE good. Martin Luther King Jr. said that he dreamed of a day when his children would be judged not by the color of their skin but by the content of their character. I dream of a day when we will not be judged by what we wear but by who we are. I was always taught that with time our country has gotten better, but with time I have seen our country become more materialistic and less family-oriented. I have seen guilty people not punished for their crimes because they were wealthy or famous. I have seen people work hard for a little money and seen people work little for a lot of money. My conscience tells me that these things are wrong. My conscience tells me that the amount of clothes in my closet and the amount of money I spend to look good is unethical when so many people are barely able to feed themselves and their families. At the end of the day I am not sure who will win this battle. The influence my culture has on me is strong. But I know that if my conscience doesn't win then I will never be at peace, I will never be free, and knowing this empowers me to resist the urge to cater to my American side. It is not my wish to move out of my country but it is my wish that one day my Americanism and my conscious will work together to make me who I am. More than anything else I believe in the power of change. If enough people come together to rewrite the social and cultural norms of this country then it will change. My country will change.

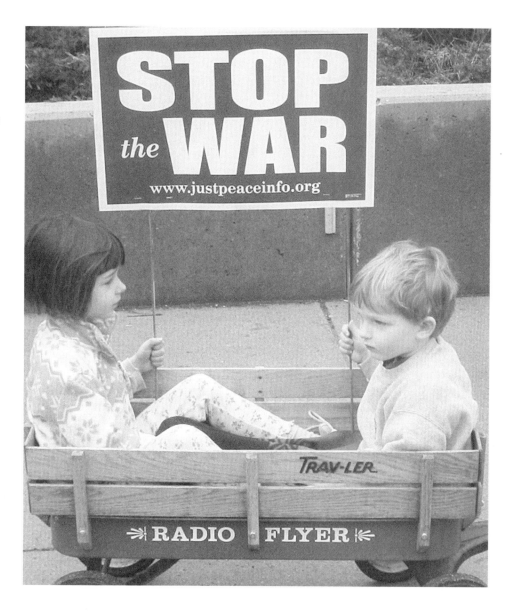

The Future
Aaron Deakins
Eastern Michigan University, Ypsilanti, MI

"She dropped to her knees yelling that her son had passed away. She said the words with her face towards me but eyes towards the skies. The words pierced my heart, not so much the words as her cry, my knees bent, and I kneeled down to hold my aunt."

The Loss
Mohammad Akbar Sharifi
College of Alameda, Alameda, CA

I was so beat up returning home from work that night. I stayed a couple hours overtime and was ready to go to bed. I pulled into the driveway and heard numerous wails from what sounded like my mother and many other women crying from inside the house. My mood changed abruptly, I was no longer exhausted from work but dazed and scared. I heard the front door of the house swing open with force and I was in no way prepared for the events that would come. My aunt ran out the door with tears flooding down her beloved face. As she got closer, I noticed her eyes were blood shot red, so red that it seemed like she was tearing out blood. Her face looked weary and terrified. Her appearance was so disturbing that multiple chills ran down my back and my heart rate increased significantly. She dropped to her knees yelling that her son had passed away. She said the words with her face towards me but eyes towards the skies. The words pierced my heart, not so much the words as her cry, my knees bent, and I kneeled down to hold my aunt. My aunt stared into my eyes as if trying to recognize who I was, her distress caused tears to slowly drip down my cheeks. She caught some breath and said, "He's gone, dear God, my baby's gone, he's gone…" I sat on my lawn grasping my aunt for 30 minutes before she passed out...

Wars are fought at the cost of innocent lives. Battles are fought on the backs of the common man. We as a society are aware of all war's ills, but they are ultimately inevitable. Ironically, the more powerful democratic nations are usually the ones who are at war more often than peace. Both failure in power structures and lack of intelligence in the common citizen strive to be the main factor behind wars. Wars are supposedly fought for the benefit of the people, but they very often don't turn out that way. Modern wars are mostly fought over land disputes, internal dissension, or the biggest cause of war, money. With any war, casualties are often numerous depending on the size and intensity of battles. Along with the casualties, the greater picture is the so many mothers who have lost their sons and every one else who lost their loved ones.

War in no form is an honorable situation. Whether you're protecting your nation from radical Islamic fundamentalists or you believe that the Western world is aiding your enemy in stealing your land, war is not a viable solution. There are countries in the third world that are always engaged in tribal warfare. Those people have grown up with the idea that fighting over land and political disputes is the only way to go about things. Many of the countrymen are uneducated and illiterate. The case with Western countries is quite different. With highly educated citizens and a very intelligent and powerful government structure, they still tend to engage in just as many battles as those in the third world. The difference is that the people in third-world countries fight over land and tribal disputes, while Western countries almost always starts wars for financial purposes.

One similarity between western and third world countries is the lack of sense the general citizens posses towards wars. Presidents, ministers, and warlords rally citizens by the dozens; after stating who the enemy is, the purpose follows and finally, the promise of victory concludes the gathering, and everyone departs repeating what had just been said to their families at home. That's all it takes to get thousands of people in support of war. In western countries, the same occurs, only here we watch it on television, in the comfort of our homes.

Hundreds of young men in their teens are sent to war. Fresh out of high school, instead of going off to college to further their educations, they are sent out to fight for causes that lack much relation to themselves. Most of the soldiers, young, and still maturing aren't prepared for war and its effects. War is a plague, victory is unattainable on both sides. For even if statistically one side loses, the victor loses just as much. Soldiers are sent back home traumatized and distraught. War is psychologically more painful than death. The young men now home have nightmares and are challenged by all they've witnessed.

I can never personally understand a mother's perspective of losing a son, but I can describe what I have witnessed. My aunt lost her son nearly a year ago, and I still can't shut out that day and its events from my memory, as much as I'd like to. My aunt lost her only son, he was a casualty of war. She never fully recovered from her loss. To this day, I don't see the radiant smiles she used to give off so much before it all happened. Such is the way so many mothers feel who have lost their sons and daughters in war. No one can relate to their troubles but them. Mothers are to be buried by their children, it isn't supposed to be the other way around.

Society has grown incredibly since the first days of civilization recorded thousands of years ago. Even though we've come so far, we still fail to reach agreements on certain issues and fail to avoid war and bloodshed. When one country is struck, retaliation occurs swiftly. As we know, death will comes to us all, and there is nothing we can do but let life take its place. Only when death comes unnaturally and takes away young sons, brothers, cousins, and friends from people who love them dearly, we must work together to stop it.

"It seems as though it is unacceptable for a student to voice his opinion on controversial matters if it happens to go against the popular movements of the time. A student who is against gay marriage is seen as homophobic and discriminative."

The Plight of the College Catholic
John Raymond Muir Ferrigan
Gonzaga University, Spokane, WA

Traditionally, America views its university students as bra-burning, war-protesting, politically correct liberals. Today it is apparent this is not always the case. There are a growing number of conservative minded students who are being ignored or quieted. It seems as though it is unacceptable for a student to voice his opinion on controversial matters if it happens to go against the popular movements of the time. A student who is against gay marriage is seen as homophobic and discriminatory. One who is pro-life is viewed as anti-woman and insensitive. An individual who would like to see prayer allowed in a classroom is imposing his beliefs on others. It does not matter how cordial, understanding, or charitable these individuals are, they are discriminated against and silenced.

The problem seems to be an overwhelmingly progressive, politically correct, relativistic culture which is nurtured on university campuses. Equality and understanding have now become movements to keep feelings from being hurt. In turn, disagreement and confrontation are frowned upon even if they are done in a setting of open dialogue and compassion.

For the Catholic students in our schools of higher education, this is all very disheartening. Catholics are against abortion, view homosexuality as a disorder, and are prayerful people. Due to the reaction this type of behavior attracts on campus, Catholics are limited to a few, very unfortunate choices. In order to be welcomed as one who is willing to open his mind to new ideas and be accepting, the student must either renounce his faith or ignore his faith. There is always the other option of remaining true to the faith and being seen as an unsympathetic, discriminatory, domineering bigot, a view which has become synonymous with Catholicism in this nation.

The question this situation poses is simple. What should be done? The Catholic student must remain at all times charitable and compassionate. The student, professor, or administration opposed to the Catholic point of view must remain true to the tenets ascribed to the liberalism of today. The Catholic student must be accepted for who he is and not brushed aside. The Catholic student should not be made to feel ostracized. The opinions of the Catholic student should be heard and fairly critiqued just as those of anyone else. When this occurs, the polarization which is growing on so many of the campuses in this nation will dissipate. True Catholics are not looking to create problems, because just as their well meaning opposition, they are hoping to solve them.

"The hard days are over, but I will never be able to forget the experience of being a little girl anxious to go to school because her jeans are ripped and there are no other clothes to wear instead."

Why Am I Involved in Politics?
Jessica Eastman
Auburn University, Auburn, AL

Why am I involved in politics? Why have I chosen to align myself with the Democratic party? Well, I'll tell you why. When I was seven years old, my parents were divorced and my father moved onto the military base on which he worked to live in the Bachelor's Office Quarters (BOQ). During the following year, my mother, brother, and I continued living in Charleston, South Carolina so that my brother and I could be near our father. When he was deployed to Bahrain, we moved to Huntsville, Alabama to be near the rest of my mother's family. Our life was hard and much different from the one we had enjoyed when my parents were married. My mother had a difficult time finding a steady job and at points was working three temporary jobs at the same time to try to pay the bills to cover our small apartment and needs. New clothing for school and extra snacks for the pantry were things I coveted of my friends. My brother and I ate school lunches at a reduced rate for a year before qualifying for totally free meals. I remember saving my lunch money for two weeks once instead of eating in order to save money for a class field trip that I knew my mother could not afford to pay for. After a few years, my mother secured a good job, and we moved into a nice house in a suburb of Huntsville, and have had most everything we needed since then. The hard days are over, but I will never be able to forget the experience of being a little girl anxious about going to school because her jeans are ripped and there are no other clothes to wear instead. I couldn't have known at the time how that difficult portion of my childhood would affect my career goals and aspirations until I began my interest in government and politics. I have heard how others describe those people in similar situations to mine, both in positive and negative lights. My direct and personal experience with that lifestyle has given me an understanding and passion for those who are in dire situations. I am very aware of how hard-working and caring humans generally are, and how sometimes a helping hand can mean everything to a family. I experienced how easy it was for people to cast judgment upon a struggling family, and I will strive to never be guilty of the same. In contrast, I will dedicate my life to fighting for the least among us.

"Despite the media's daily deliveries of doom and despair, the next generation of American kids isn't the reckless, valueless band that the networks' marketing moguls would have us fear."

Y
Max Buccini
Boston College, Chestnut Hill, MA

Generation Y, Generation Net, the Echo Boomers, the Dot-Coms, the Millennial Generation, or the Ritalin Generation. Take your pick of labels for this post-1982 generation. We are the new kids on the block and the underdogs with something to prove. But is this generation any different from all the other up-and-coming generations throughout history? All generations have the pressure to meet the expectations and the accomplishments of their predecessors; furthermore, the older generation underestimates them from the day they are born. This cycle of skepticism and cynicism toward the new generation is nothing new, but in this War on Terror era, the criticism increases more as the latest generation is called to duty. Unfortunately, many believe this call to have fallen on the deaf ears of Generation Y, my generation. We are considered materialistic, self-absorbed, capricious, success-oriented, and vain. Our commitment to world events, politics, local issues, current affairs, and economic developments is thought to be a distant second to our commitment to pop culture, what's in and what's out, entertainment, celebrities, reality TV, and the constant and unyielding pursuit of "cool" that ceases only in death. But is there truth to this broad generalization? Or is it just the natural condition of those in their teens/early-twenties to be individualistic and perhaps slightly disengaged? I will endeavor to prove that this is in fact the case, and that it is universal in nature, as all teenagers and twenty somethings have shown throughout history. All generations experience this phenomenon of self-absorption and draw the consequential criticism; however, when a generation is called to upon to fulfill a duty to their nation and themselves, they are more than fit for the task.

Since the founding of this nation, Americans have been concerned for the future of their country as the reins of power are handed over to the next generation. Just as children inherit the family from their parents, the next generation inherits the nation. After James Monroe, the fifth President of the United States, did not seek reelection to a third term, it was clear that the next president would not be one of the nation's founding generation. Although party politics had been in full and divisive swing ever since the Washington administration, domestic issues of public credit, the national debt, and states' rights, in addition to complicated foreign disputes, threatened to rip apart the country. Nevertheless, everyone had faith that the nascent United States would survive because the founding fathers who had established the nation itself were at the helm. As long as names like Washington, Adams, Hamilton, Jefferson, and Madison were still on the ballot or in the administration, the nation knew they were in good hands.

As always, eras come to an end, and the founding generation was on its way out of public life. The Era of Good Feelings under the Monroe presidency was ending, and concern over the next generation was looming. There was particular concern over the new generation's inexperience with the War of Independence and first hand knowledge of the founder's intent; some quietly doubted whether the nation would even survive the transition. When John Quincy Adams was voted president in the election of 1824, the new generation had its chance to prove itself in deeds as well as words. This generation, dubbed by some historians as the "second founding generation," faced some of the most crucial issues of American history, and they did it with all the majesty of their predecessors.

Even though the colossal statures of the founding fathers would cast shadows over subsequent generations for years to come, those generations performed admirably under tremendous pressures - most notably, that of the Civil War. This comparison of the founding fathers to the generations that followed is quite similar to today's comparison of the "Greatest Generation" to all subsequent generations. They have become the new yardstick by which all current and future generations are measured. They are larger-than-life figures whom we now read about in history books. As a historian, I can understand the comparison of eras, but all generations must have their own calling. History does not exactly repeat itself. How can any generation ever have the chance to top the already proclaimed "Greatest Generation?" You can't beat the greatest. But at some point, even the "Greatest Generation" was not considered to be at all great.

In Brad Warthen's article for the *Ventura County Star*, he attempted to provide hope for the next generation just a day after September 11th, 2001. The title of his article, "Greatest Generation's Grandchildren Will Prevail" articulates the strength and resilience of Generation Y in the face of perhaps the most terrifying event in American history. Warthen draws a comparison between the Greatest Generation and Generation Y by creating the link between Pearl Harbor and September 11th. Warthen maintains that September 11th was more of a shock because it hit so close to home. It hit us in the economic center of our nation, not on some far removed military base. This just does not happen to us; these conflicts are never supposed to reach United States soil. But they did. In his comparison, Warthen states, "We marvel at how a previous generation responded to an unprecedented crisis—a sudden attack by a ruthless, remorseless enemy. We think of those people as the 'greatest generation,' and they deserve that appellation because of the way they came together to settle their own crisis and secure our future. And we all wonder: Are we like them? Do we have it in us? We're about to find out." (Warthen)

Is Generation Y proving that we do have what it takes? The nation did unite behind a common goal and purpose after September 11th and proved that we will not be paralyzed by fear. Instead, we showed our spirit and our undying love for the United States and the freedom for which it stands. Warthen goes on to say that, "We may not be the greatest generation, but we are their grandchildren. We are Americans. We are shocked, and we will mourn. But then we'll dust ourselves off, and find a way." (Warthen) We in Generation Y are not forever relegated to fear; it simply would not be in keeping with our character as the grandchildren of the generation that saved the world from tyranny. Warthen makes a compelling case that Generation Y can be counted on in the long run.

Charlton Heston takes a similar view, but he also realizes that the commitment of Generation Y is still a toss up. Heston believes that the media and society have been portraying Generation Y all wrong. Even though Heston is confident in this generation's ability to become the "new greatest generation," he also feels that there are some areas where Generation Y could throw away all their potential. Heston begins to make his case by stating that:

> *Despite the media's daily deliveries of doom and despair, the next generation of American kids isn't the reckless, valueless band that the networks' marketing moguls would have us fear. On the contrary, for the first time in a long time, the next generation appears to be the next great generation, who like those who won World War II, could spell the salvation of freedom around the globe. The key question is whether we give them the passion and the vision to do so. Because if we fail, with freedom facing such grave new threats in the interna tional arena, the Millennial Generation could be the generation that throws it all away. (Heston)*

Heston refutes popular claims by the media and others that we are simply a hyper version of Generation X, self-absorbed and shallow. Heston uses data to direct his argument against the stereotypical Generation Y when he cites the book Millennials Rising by authors Neil Howe and William Strauss. The facts he uses are that Generation Y is unusually optimistic where nine in ten think they are "happy and confident about the world they are inheriting," and nine in ten also say they are close to their parents with over half saying that they can trust their government to do the right thing. Heston also cites government statistics demonstrating that Generation Y during the past 6 years has seen a dramatic and unprecedented reduction in the number of homicides, violent crimes, abortion, and teen pregnancy. We are the first truly global generation who embrace multiculturalism and cosmopolitan society. But Heston does see a potential dilemma:

> *So we have a double-edged sword: The Millennial Generation is active, engaged and expects to play a leading role in the history of America and the world. But their worldliness and sophistication could blind them to the genuine miracles of human freedom that constitute America's signature and singular, unsurpassed blessing. (Heston)*

Heston continues his appeal to Generation Y's predecessors to prepare this generation well. A sleeping giant has yet again awakened and the annals of history rarely deviate, so make certain Generation Y is as well equipped as others have been because their grandchildren will thank you.

George W. Bush has been on the vanguard of calling Generation Y to duty. His two inspiring speeches, first on the Normandy memorial day and second to the West Point grads, proved that the President of the United States is confident in our abilities and courage. Like many others, President Bush draws the comparison between Pearl Harbor and September 11th. This uncanny connection between the two events is forever emblazoned upon the minds of the American people. Somehow, these two events are so effortlessly linked by members of the press to the President of the United States. At Normandy, the President issued his appeal for the new generation to begin its fight against terrorism, and that each generation will confront the face of evil itself, and Generation Y is no different. The worst in human nature was displayed that day on the 11th of September, and it is our responsibility to take the field of battle and meet it head on. When speaking at West Point, President Bush articulated a similar message by summoning this class of new officers to take up the mantle of freedom and democracy by dispatching the evil that reached America's shores. It is chilling to know that your generation has this much confidence from the most powerful man in the world. A man who is respected immensely at home and across the world. The President of the United States has formally called upon this generation to fight for the innate human right to freedom.

Ong Soh Chin's article, "Gen X, Y or Z...Kids Are Still Kids" takes a unique look at this issue from the perspective of a Generation X-er. As a member of Generation X, Chin takes a very sympathetic view of Generation Y. Feeling slighted by the media and society in general during his teens and mid-twenties, Chin sees that Generation Y now has it ten times worse. Chin bemoans the creation of such unimaginative names for the generations:

> *Once upon a time, letters were found only in addresses, bra sizes or Campbell's alphabet soup. Now that we're at an age where demographics have been reduced to playschool babble of ABC's, perhaps it is time the world grew up. Blame it on the market hype that ruined the party for Generation X a decade ago...X-er's like myself, defined as those born in the 1960's and early 1970's...Ta-dah! Enter the unimaginatively named Generation Y. (Chin)*

Chin's observation of the lack of creativity and the negative influence of marketing shows how the generations can be exploited and modeled by these types in order to create a solid demographic marketing figure. Chin does not see much difference in the alleged attitudes and behaviors of Generation X and Y. The reason Chin makes this statement is that he thinks, "All young people are basically the same." (Chin) This puts an interesting twist on generational conflict and stereotyping. Instead of having this conflict be a generational condition, Chin proposes that it is a young people's condition. A universal condition that permeates all society and eras where young people are defined in this way,

> *After all, at the risk of being frank, a 20something who isn't into trendy clothes, instant gratification and the latest technologies is little more than a freak sure ly...And this has always been the case. The 20s have always been the age for discovery, experimentation and heady pleasures. Through these hits and miss es, bumps and scrapes, emerges - one hopes - the confident and wiser 30some thing."* (Chin)

The spirit of young people remains the same today as it did hundreds of years ago as Chin cautions us not to let ourselves be defined by the letter of our generation.

There are similarities in the observations of the already cited commentators and the local people who I have interviewed. These people represent three generations and have no apparent agenda or biases. I will endeavor to demonstrate these similarities and derive the conclusion that Generation Y is no different than any other generation; it is just the human condition of the ages being discussed, the teen and twenty-something years. I begin with Susan Buccini, born in 1951 and therefore considered part of the post-World War II "Baby Boom" generation. She presents a unique perspective of Vietnam and the Cold War. Susan, a native of Quincy, MA, watched as her family worked frantically to save her older brother from serving in Vietnam:

> *I really didn't feel that I was in the war, but two events stand out. One, my older brother was being drafted and everyone was trying to pull strings to get him in the National Guard so he wouldn't have to serve in Vietnam. Luckily, he was dating a girl who lived across the street from a commander in the National Guard and he got in. I remember that Dan Quayle was accused of avoiding service because his father got him into the guard."* (Buccini)

Susan expressed a common sentiment of her "Baby Boom" generation: a Baby Boom sense of disconnect, skepticism of the government, and lack of clear intent about the goals and purposes of the Vietnam War. Susan even received criticism of the war from her Greatest Generation father, "I remember my father saying that it didn't make sense to him. He was a WWII vet who had seen combat and served in Europe. In WWII, you knew what you were fighting about and the whole world was at war, but the issues were not clear in the Vietnam conflict and the country itself seemed far removed." (Buccini) The Baby Boom generation seemed to have a similar sense of lack of purpose and focus so this lack of purpose cannot be consigned only to Generation Y or any other genera- tion. Susan also comments how her generation was called to serve:

> *I understood the conflict to be about preserving democracy in the world and was taught about the domino effect that communism could have. I believed communism to be bad and could believe the threat that the USSR was to us see ing Kruschev banging his shoe on the table at the United Nations and saying, '*

> *'We will bury you!' over and over, made a great impression on me and a few million others, no doubt. But the baby boomer generation served their country in the end.*

In the end, even though dissenting opinions were heard, they accepted their call to duty.

The MTV generation took the stage during the presidency of Ronald Reagan and George Herbert Walker Bush, and coincidentally, their conflict also involved Saddam Hussein. Commenting for Generation X is 34 year old Matt Smith who recalls his memory of Operation Desert Storm: "Slight fear of unforeseeable events cascading into major global crisis of some kind, but at the same time I know that we MUST do this." (Smith) We MUST do this. It is clear that Generation Y was called to duty, and they responded even though they had been pigeonholed as Gen X-ers. Matt also observes that:

> *I think the 'gen-x' thing isn't talked/thought about very much, at least not like it was. It's certainly not a part of the popular lexicon anymore. Though I do dis like the "slacker" label, I think it is kind of apt. I know a lot of people in my generation who got bogged down somewhere in the transition from school to adulthood and did not move on. I think too many gen-xers took comfort in the stereotype of the hippie to yuppie myth about baby-boomer's progression to adult hood. It is indeed a myth... I think we, as unidentifiable group with sup posed monolithic views and sensibilities, have been forgotten about. Now we are just the current crop of 30-40 year-olds. (Smith)*

Matt makes a key observation as he was part of that Generation X and now had become just one of the run-of-the mill 30-40 year olds. This brings more evidence to prove that the teens/twenty-somethings are naturally how they are categorized, and that their behavior is not a symptom of a decadent Generation Y or X. As an alternative, I would proffer that teens/twenty somethings stay in their own superficial world until catastrophic events rip them out of that world to give them a purpose and clarity of mind.

Samantha Lawyer, age 10 and a member of Generation Y, now reflects upon the events of September 11th, and the current war in Iraq. Her responses illustrate a similarity among the two previous interviews:

> *My first reaction was just initial shock, everything seems fine and then hun dreds of people die in the World Trade Center and we're having a war. Everything seems to be happening so fast. I first realized that I was in this war when I would turn on the television and there would be a live update on Iraq, people began asking my opinions on what I thought. That's when I realized that the war wasn't going on, on a different planet, and realized that I was part of the war whether I liked it or not....As time goes by I want to go to war and stop waiting for Iraq's army to disarm, I am tired of waiting. I feel like we shouldn't do nothing. (Lawyer)*

"We shouldn't do nothing." This sentiment reflects the opposite view of the media and some of our elders who expected nothing of Generation Y. Despite the carping and discouragement by some, we pulled through and decided to come out of our shell and be a part of this world community. Samantha was shocked out of her isolated world on September 11th and now she is able to see that events around the world directly affect us, and it is her duty to take part in those events by being informed, voicing opinions, and uniting behind America.

However, there are still some who disagree. In Kerry-Anne Walsh's <u>Self-Image is King For Generation Y</u>, she articulates the usual position that Generation Y is self-absorbed, materialistic, and self-interested. She directly links these traits to only Generation Y, and not as being a part of a common rite of passage for teens/ twenty-somethings:

> *Whatever you want to call them, these leaders of the future born after 1982*
> *have been raised in such vastly different circumstances from preceding genera*
> *tions, that educators and marketers are devising new approaches to reach them.*
> *(Walsh)*

Her comments sound eerily similar to the old line given by our elders, "When I was your age..." She cites no facts to back up her assertion, and her overall claim that marketers had to change their tactics for Gen Y is absurd. Every generation is marketed to differently, as we are not uniform beings and trends never stay the same; that is why they are called "trends." Pop-culture is not a static phenomenon. Walsh audaciously goes on to state that "Generation Y people are the only [generation] never to have known war, deprivation, depression or uncertainty. They have not witnessed any large scale economic or social disasters." (Walsh) How does Walsh not recognize her error? Our generation has been scarcely in existence for 20 years. It appears throughout history that once the new generation comes into adulthood, they quickly learn how to prepare for the challenges. Was the generation of the roaring '20s ready for the Great Depression? Were the baby-boomers set to face the horrors of Vietnam? Did Gen X-ers demonstrate their courage during Desert Storm? Was Generation Y prepared for the War on Terror? No, but they all learned quickly. Citing statistics about dropping classes after seven minutes and portraying us as pop-culture and image fiends presupposes the fact that we are teens. If there is anytime in one's life when that kind of behavior is acceptable, it is during this time. But as generations before, we have awakened and are ready to prove people like Kerry-Anne Walsh and John LeBoutillier wrong.

Kerry-Anne Walsh was influenced by John LeBoutillier's article attacking our generation entitled, "The Most Selfish Generation." LeBoutiller claims that, "The United States of America is now suffering for the social and personal excesses of that Selfish Generation. Virtually all our national problems stem directly from this Cult of Self that has permeated virtually every aspect of our society." (LeBoutiller) LeBoutiller asserts that education, parent involvement, school violence, teen relation ships, and lack of a cause are all the problems that have shaped Generation Y into the scourge of America. LeBoutiller accuses us of taking the Greatest Generation for granted:

The Greatest Generation survived the Depression and won World War II. They also rebuilt Europe and began a successful Cold War versus the Soviet Union. All of this was possible because these brave American men and women thought of themselves 'last.' Too many people today are rude, arrogant, anti-religious and greedy for what they don't have. (LeBoutiller)

These sweeping generalizations are unfair. He does not consider people as individuals; instead, he almost compares them to a well-oiled machine that completes its tasks. Perhaps, he should have made this a cultural analysis as opposed to a blatantly ill-spirited attack on a maligned generation that is finally getting the chance to prove itself.

The march of freedom and democracy will leave terrorism on the ash heap of history just like the fate of other tyrannies that stifled freedom and attacked the very existence of a people. Although slavery, fascism, communism, and tyranny have been at different times consigned to history, they are forever remembered as failed ideologies. Generation Y has now taken up the sword of freedom in Operation Iraqi Freedom. Statistics from the military show that the mean age of all enlisted men and women is 18 which makes it a war fought by Generation Y. We prove our valor while our brave service men and women carry on defending the freedom and liberty we have come to treasure and expect. Generation Y is now responsible; the torch has been passed. We are the keepers of freedom until the next underestimated generation finds their mission or their mission finds them.

BIOGRAPHIES

"Let the American youth never forget, that they possess a noble inheritance, bought by the toils, and sufferings, and blood of their ancestors; and capactiy, if wisely improved, and faithfully guarded, of transmitting to their latest posterity all the substantial blessings of life, the peaceful enjoyment of liberty, property , religion, and independence."
    -Joseph Story

Name: A. Katherine
Age: 18
School: University of Michigan Ann Arbor
Major or Area of interest: English/Anthropology
Hometown: Ann Arbor, MI
Inspiration for "Hey Everybody:" I faced when trying to convince my parents that it was o.k. to fall in love with a person without giving regard to their gender. I was inspired by the strength, warmth, and love I felt when I was with her...

Name: Aaron Joseph Deakins
Age: 27
School: Eastern Michigan University
Major or Area of interest: Anthropology Major with a concentration on Cultural Anthropology, and a Political Science Minor with a concentration on International Relations. My personal interest is in Middle Eastern politics, mega-media conglomerates, and 9/11.
Hometown: Ypsilanti, MI
Inspiration for "It's Selective Service, Not a Draft, People:" I got inspired to write this article after I took the pictures that were included at a pro-peace rally. I was sick of listening to the two major candidates running for President, and their inability to have a concrete policy when it came to our international conflicts, and what role we will be playing in the future conflicts in other areas of the world.

Name: Alexandra Pajak
Age: 22
School: Georgia Tech University
Major or Area of interest: History of Technology and Society
Hometown: Watkinsville, GA
Inspiration for "An African American Step Show" and "On Being Different in the South:" Nearly all my creative works are inspired by how 'big ideas' can emerge in daily events. I am a firm believer that it is still very possible--and indeed, more necessary than ever--to gaze at the world from the eyes of one who wonders, who appreciates, who struggles to understand and who constructively fights for positive change.

Name: Alison Marie Amyx
Age: 18
School: Mercer University
Major or Area of interest: Political Science
Hometown: Calhoun, GA
Inspiration for "Small White Crosses:" I was deeply moved by a visit to the American Cemetery in Normandy, France, and inspired to write this piece. I also hope that it may serve as a reminder for Americans dealing with a new war. Whether or not we agree with the War in Iraq, our troops need our support and gratefulness for the sacrifices they are making overseas.

Name: Allison Richardson

Biographies

Name: Amanda M. Glover
Age: 19
School: Virginia Commonwealth University
Major or Area of interest: Anthropology
Hometown: Norfolk, VA
Inspiration for "A Shrine to the Unbelievable:" I first had the idea for this poem in a small Eastern Orthodox church in Skala-Skamia on Lesvos, when I went there this past summer. I was lighting a candle for my godmother, and felt odd about doing such a thing when I'm not at all spiritual or religious. The poem in its original form was a short piece to her and later came to include a more political statement.

Name: Amy Kline

Name: Anthony M. Lemaster
Age: 22
School: Morehead State University
Major or Area of interest: Music Education
Hometown: Ironton, OH
Inspiration for "Marriage was Created:" The idea for this piece came to me just out of nowhere, and I decided to write the piece.

Name: Arianna Levitus
Age: 20
School: The George Washington University
Major or Area of interest: International Affairs (Middle East Concentration) and Communication
Hometown: Minnetonka, MN
Inspiration for "How to Make Your Vote Count:" I was assigned to write a persuasive essay on any subject of my choice. I felt that the issue of young-adult voter turnout was a natural choice for me and was extremely timely. I have personally experienced several elections- not just for local, state or national government, but within other organizations where if voter turnout had been greater, election results would have been very different. I strongly believe, as my submission demonstrates, that turning out to vote is the first, easiest and most important way to effect change in our political system.

Name: Ben Marcus
Age: 20
School: Plans of attending the University of Florida. He is working as National Campus Coordinator for the Nader for President 2004 campaign.

Name: Brian Fanelli

Name: Brittny Nielsen
Age: 22
School: Seattle University
Major or Area of interest: Political Science and Women's Studies
Hometown: Renton, WA

Inspiration for "A-Day" and "Waiting": The inspiration for my poems came from the war on Iraq. When it officially began in the spring of 2003, I was completing a course on international relations in which we had delved into the perceptions of America throughout the world. I felt very strongly that the war was wrong and spilled my frustrations and fears into the poems I submitted.

Name: Brook Thompson

Name: Bryan M. Steele
Age: 22
School: San Diego State University
Major or Area of interest: Journalism
Hometown: Shoreline, Wash.
Inspiration for "Choking the Red, White, and You:" This piece stemmed from a total disenchantment with the current state of the world. These outbursts of emotion and angst are one of few things that keep me sane these days, especially in a country that has lost its identity and its mind.

Name: Caroline Marie Solomon
Age: 17 years old
School: American University
Major or area of interest: My major is Anthropology but I also have interests in Biology.
Hometown: Hohenfels Germany (American military base in Germany)
Inspiration for "Animals in the House" and "Practicality:" All of my work is inspired by what I observe around me. I like to take a skeptical view of life and really examine what goes on in my environment and when I find thing that I think need reform I express it through my writing, most often through satire. Being in Washington DC has inspired a lot of my work as I observe the aspects of our policy making and one of my biggest inspirations for satire is our political parties.

Name: Christina Girgenti
Age: 20
School: Radford University
Major or Area of interest: Major: Media Studies with concentration in Advertising/Minor: Psychology
Hometown: Chesapeake, Virginia
Inspiration for "The Unrealistic Portrayal of Women in Advertising:" I am a woman bombarded daily with ads of seemingly flawless women who are essentially unrealistic. I believe women of all ages should be made aware that these women are a small percentage of our population and that it is ok not to look like them.

Name: Christopher Ross Continanza
Age: 20
School: Villanova University
Major or Area of interest: Interdisciplinary Studies and Continental Philosophy

Hometown: Wayne, NJ

Inspiration for "Requiem:" Essentially, it came from an area of my consciousness I am granted only temporal access to. If the timing is right and paper is handy, I can catch the thoughts before I lose them.

Inspiration for "Before I Sleep I Lie Down:" I was inspired to write this essay for a school publication after reading Vincent Miller's Consuming Religion.

Name: Daniel Falkner
Age: 22
School: Canisius College (Buffalo, NY)
Major or Area of interest: English, Secondary Education
Hometown: Spokane, WA
Inspiration for "The Modern Parable:" Ultimately, the inspiration for the piece was in the hope that my thoughts might, in some way, affect the views or opinions of another student in our generation. In writing The Modern Parable my hope is that others will look at the current administration and consider its actions more thoroughly. I was further inspired through my professors, friends, and various social/political commentaries.

Name: Dheeraj Jagadev
Age: 23
School: College of William and Mary
Major or Area of interest: Public Policy (Graduate Student)
Hometown: Manassas, VA
Inspiration for "The Bombing:" It was a response to the Kosovo air campaign in 1999.

Name: Eamon Aloyo

Name: Eric Kohn
Age: 22
School: Millikin University
Hometown: Decatur, IL
Major or Area of interest: Music Business
Hometown: Belleville, IL
Inspiration for "This is World War III" and "Bowling for Fahrenheit:" I'm inspired to write by all those who have ever come to me for my opinion.

Name: Eric Michael Wasserstrum
Age: 19
School: Washington University in St. Louis
Major or Area of interest: Economics
Hometown: Houston, TX

Name: Erich H. Mattei
Age: 22
School: University of Georgia
Major or Area of interest: Graduate Student, Department of Economics

Hometown: Metairie, LA
Inspiration for "Michael Moore: The Freedom Fighter:" The Truth; free market capitalism is the only system that necessitates peace.

Name: Erika L. Sanchez
Age: 20
School: University of Illinois at Chicago
Major or Area of interest: Latin American literature, creative writing
Hometown: Cicero, IL
Inspiration for "Steady Rain:" This was written during the height of the war in Iraq. I was feeling alienated and disillusioned with the state of our world. I wanted to ground the setting in an urban environment to emphasize the sense of solitude and desperation. The Jesus character is an actual man that lives near me. He dresses like Jesus and carries a cross. I found it amusing that he was wearing sneakers and drinking a coke. I had seen him the day I wrote this poem and decided to include him to reveal the hypocrisy behind war and religion not to mention the pervasiveness of globalization (the coke).

Name: Galena Mosovich
Age: 21
School: Temple University
Major or Area of interest: Broadcast Journalism, Political Science minor
Hometown: Coral Springs, Florida
Inspiration for "America is Under Attack:" I wrote this editorial in the wake of September 11, 2001. The current administration began to limit freedom of speech immediately following the attacks when the American public was too distracted. My example of ABC yanking "Politically Incorrect with Bill Maher" off the air portrays the current administration's infiltration of the media and how it influences the information that is disseminated to the public. With new legislation, media conglomeration, FCC crackdowns, and the pure fear of losing their livelihood, journalists are playing politically correct... Too bad this form of journalism has no place in a democracy.

Name: Gary Dennis
Age: 23
School: University of Southern California

Name: Glen I. Hong

Name: Graham Cawthon
Age: 23
School: Radford University
Major or Area of interest: Journalism
Hometown: Woodbridge, VA
Inspiration for "A War of Uncertainty:" The editorial was born out of frustration that I was having with both the media and fellow students, many of whom perceived the war as a wrong decision done for the wrong reasons. I wanted to offer a different perspective explaining why it was necessary while at the same time mentioning that U.S. military intervention has been very beneficial for us all, from gaining our independence from England to ridding the world of Hitler's forces.

Name: Grant Yelverton
Age: 20
School: University of Richmond
Major or Area of interest: Political Science
Hometown: New Orleans, LA
Inspiration for "I'm an Open-Minded Republican:" It seems as though many people arrive at conclusions after surrounding themselves with others who hold one dominant viewpoint. Talking with the cab driver whose opinion was so impressively calculated and so articulately defended gave me a few moments to question my own stance on politics and gain insight which I would have been otherwise lacking.

Name: Gregory LaVoy
Age: 20
School: Kalamazoo College
Hometown: Kalamazoo, Michigan
Major or Area of interest: Political Science, minor in Sociology
Hometown: Howell, Michigan
Inspiration for "Unilateralism, Multilateralism and the War on Terror:" Two people: John Kerry and Ted Kennedy. After listening to their attacks of the President on the campaign trail and at the Democratic National Convention, I thought it necessary to examine the illogic behind such arguments and how they should or should not factor into the emerging political policies of our government.

Name: Gregory Smith
Age: 21
School: Westminster College
Major or Area of interest: Political Science and minor Speech Communications and German
Hometown: Allison Park
Inspiration for "The Tragic Events:" Inspiration for this piece came from an assignment in a writing class that I took my freshman year of college. It was an interesting way to examine and try to understand the events that occurred on September 11th and how they would affect the higher educational systems of America.

Name: Hailey Witt
Age: 20
School: Lehigh University
Major or Area of interest: Political Science
Hometown: Duluth, MN
Inspiration for "Bush, Religion, and Iraq:" The work that I submitted is a reflection of issues I feel are very socially important yet misunderstood. I was glad to be given the opportunity to research these topics because I feel that in our constantly changing culture it is important to have a firm understanding of the social climate of our society.

Name: Hans Zeiger

Name: Jake Olzen

Name: Jason Kauffman
Age: 21
School: University of Dayton
Major or Area of interest: Mechanical Engineering
Hometown: Centerville, Ohio
Inspiration for "Why?:" The fact that in the most free country in the world every recent major election has come down to two choices. Also they way people categorized them selves into one of two political parties. In what truly is the land of the free, there is no way two choices or parties can accurately represent democracy.

Name: Jason Miller
Age: 21
School: Michigan State University
Major or Area of interest: Political Science
Hometown: Grand Rapids, MI
Inspiration for "Good and Evil:" I was inspired to write about the use of the word evil in American foreign policy and the inability of Old Europe and the ability of New Europe to recognize the use of that word based on a lecture given by Dr. William Allen of Michigan State University.

Name: Jason Walter
Age: 21
School: Clemson University
Major or Area of interest: English major and Playwrighting minor
Hometown: Summerville, SC
Inspiration for "America is Fighting the Invisible Man:" The main inspiration for my piece was Micheal Moore's "Fahrenheit 9/11". Also, I had been reading a lot of Allen Ginsberg poetry and wanted to toy with fixed line repetition. I had also been listening to a lot of Rage Against the Machine and wanted to pay homage to Zack de la Rocha. Part of the piece, comes from a poem that I wrote called "Decadence and a Manifesto". The first part is "decadent" because the style is like that of Gertrude Stein. It's also decadence because it's a digression about a girl that rejected my love. The second part is a manifesto and it came from me compensating for the rejection by getting political and revolutionary.

Name: Jeannine Lindley Sikora
Age: 21
School: State University of New York at Albany
Major or Area of interest: Urban Studies and Planning
Hometown: Warwick, N.Y.
Inspiration for "Peace:" Symbolizes the urgency of peace in these troubled times.

Name: Jenica Mariani

Name: Jessica Eastman
Age: 21
School: Auburn University
Major or Area of interest: Political Science

Hometown: Meridianville, AL
Inspiration for "Why Am I Involved in Politics:" The inspiration for this piece is my life. Growing up in a poor family and outside of the United States as a military kid gave me a unique worldview. My motivation in passion in life is to help those who lived like I once did.

Name: John Raymond Muir Ferrigan
Age: 21
School: Gonzaga University
Major: Philosophy & History
Hometown: Santa Cruz, California
Inspiration for "The Plight of the Catholic Church:" Too often on college campuses I have seen the Catholic point of view shunned and mocked. Sadly this happens even at Catholic institutions. The desire to be all inclusive and politically correct has made honest and open dialogue something very hard to achieve. No one tries to prevent Brigham Young from being Mormon, so why is it that outside forces and sometimes even the Catholic universities themselves feel it is not their place to embrace and defend their faith?

Name: John Teresi
Age: 21
School: Southern Illinois University
Major or Area of interest: Political Science
Hometown: Lemont, IL
Inspiration for "An American Bond:" September 11th has impacted the lives of all Americans. Through this shocking time I saw how Americans come together when we hear others in need. This is what September 11th means to me.

Name: Jonathan Rick
Age: 21
School: Hamilton College
Major or Area of interest: Political Science
Hometown: Short Hills, NJ
Inspiration for "Teach a Man to Fish:" On Monday in Beinecke, the Hamilton chapter of Amnesty International asked me for money to buy a water buffalo for a farmer in Nepal...
Inspiration for "The Immorality of Conscription:" Congressional calls to reinstitute the draft in light of the forthcoming war in Iraq.

Name: Josh Kearns

Name: Joshua Haines
Age: 23
School: Northern Arizona University in Flagstaff, Arizona
Major or Area of interest: Psychology and Political Science
Hometown: Williams, Arizona

Inspiration for "Professor's Misconduct:" I have been inspired by the countless numbers of professors and faculty members who have gone out of their way to obstruct the learning process by intimidating their students, and by presenting only one point of view.

Name: Judson Cox
Age: 27
School: Lees McRae College
Major or Area of interest: Politics
Hometown: Linville, North Carolina
Inspiration for "Don't Save the Whales, Save Yourself:" Probably a bottle of Old Crow and El Rey Del Mundo Rectangulare. Or, it could have been a theological argument that took an odd turn. Or, maybe I was annoyed by PBS hitting me up for money again - GET A REAL JOB YOU FREAKIN' HIPPY SOCIALISTS!

Name: Justin A. Padley
Age: 22
School: Gonzaga University
Major or Area of interest: History, Classical Civilizations
Hometown: Pasadena, California
Inspiration for "No Man is an Island:" I was incensed to see Bill Maher lose his job over a description of terrorists that was not in line with the understandably reactionary mentality of the time. As time passes, I feel that we are better equipped to discuss enemies as humans with real grievance, no matter how right or wrong their actions. Sadly, that dialogue has not yet opened.

Name: Karen E. Setty
Age: 21
School: The University of Dayton
Major or Area of interest: Environmental Biology
Hometown: Youngstown, OH
Inspiration for "Sustainability:" I was first introduced to the concept of sustainability as a freshman at the University of Dayton, where some great people a few years older have been working for awhile to get recycling on our campus and improve energy efficiency. They formed a club based mostly on the ideas of Bill McDonough. I've been involved in the club ever since, and have had plenty of experience working for sustainability on our campus.

Name: Kyla Schoessler
Age: 22
School: Gonzaga University
Major or Area of interest: Art and Education
Hometown: Kirkland, WA
Inspiration for "Our Voice:" I was sitting in a field, contemplating the absence of our voice in politics. I found myself staring at a tree, the lone tree in the middle of this field, and realized it wasn't that our voice is absent, it simply isn't listened to. Our voice *is* that tree in the middle of the field, until now.

Name: Lance David Collins
Age: 24
School: University of Hawai'i at Manoa
Major or Area of interest: BA, Political Science, 1999 MA, Indigenous Poliitcs, 2001 JD, 2004 Ph.D. student (Political Science)
Hometown: Kahului, Maui
Inspiration for "Delusions of Sovereignty": Tools of so-called liberation have merely become the newest technologies of oppression. The question before me is: What is possible? Where does negotiation begin?

Name: Lanni Alecia Lantto
Age: 24
School: University of Michigan (Ann Arbor)
Major or Area of interest: Major in Women's Studies, Minor in French
Hometown: Marquette, MI (the U.P.!!)
Inspiration for "Is God on Bush's Side?:" I kept hearing our leader and commander of all patriots, GW Bush, using God's name in his speeches on war. Not only could I see it's effectiveness in subduing or coercing the masses but I knew in my gut that the grassroots teachings of Jesus could not possibly support his stances. We see Jesus in the faces of the poor & suffering around us, not on a podium creating even more.

Name: Leanne Murray

Name: Letisha Michelle Beachy
Age: 20
School: Virginia Polytechnic Institute and State University
Major or area of interest: English Major with a concentration in Creative Writing
Hometown: Roanoke, Virginia
Inspiration for "Operation Stand-by:" I first learned the details of the Rwandan Genocide from my Nations and Nationalities class during my freshman year, in which we read the book "We Wish to Inform You That Tomorrow We Will be Killed With Our Families" by Philip Gourevitch. Then I saw the movie "Tears of the Sun" and ever since then, my heart has been with Rwanda.
Inspiration for the photograph entitled "Let's Raise and Educate Cildren with Joy and Encouragement:" I was inspired by conversations with friends and family members who are teachers. They were mentioning how hard it is to educate children these days because many parents fail to teach their children to respect others. Education has also been made difficult by government limitations, such as a decrease in funds among other mandates.

Name: Lianna Carrera

Name: Lisa Bakale-Wise
Age: 20
School: University of Michigan
Major or Area of interest: Political Science and Sociology
Hometown: Troy, MI

Inspiration for "War on the Home Front and Some Renegade Warriors:" I wrote this piece because I see daily the way in which sexism and sexual assault are marginalized as "women's issues" by men, and are generally ignored, belittled, or tokenized even in progressive circles. I want to wake women and men up to the reality that sexism and sexual assault are far from "women's issues" and can ultimately only be stopped by each man making a personal choice not to assault and actively renouncing sexism and sexual assault when among other men.

Name: Maia Sheesley Banks

Name: Matthew Ahrens
Age: 20
School: Washburn University
Major or Area of interest: Accounting
Hometown: Pratt, KS
Inspiration for "Increased Polarization:" This past August I was fortunate enough to be a page at the Republican National Convention. While there I saw the hatred of those on the left, and realized that decent American citizens are not doing enough to expose the blatant contradictions in core liberal beliefs. Their hostility has inspired me to stand strong for the beliefs that have made our country strong, and will keep our nation strong for generations to come.

Name: Matthew T. Revan
Age: 21
School: Bentley College, McCallum Graduate School of Business
Major or Area of interest: Master of Science, Finance
Hometown: Stoughton, MA
Inspiration for "Kerry's International Mythology:" My inspiration for this piece came from watching the ceremony at the Normandy American Cemetery to commemorate the sixtieth anniversary of the D-Day Invasion. Watching the camera pan across those thousands of white crosses got me thinking about the ultimate sacrifice all of those men made to liberate millions of people that they themselves never knew. The men and women wearing the uniform today are making the very same sacrifice in the Middle East, and that is the key to understanding the current foreign policy debate.

Name: Max Buccini
Age: 20
School: Boston College
Major or Area of interest: History and Communications Double Major
Hometown: Weymouth, MA

Name: Melissa Warburton
Age: 20
School: Gonzaga University
Major or Area of interest: Political Science and Criminal Justice, (Pre-Law)
Hometown: Idaho Falls, ID

Inspiration for "Feminism and Republicanism:" I was inspired to write this piece because I know that a lot of young republican women have the same frustrations that I do. We believe strongly in women's rights and the republican ideology, yet find it difficult to defend those beliefs because they are perceived as contradictory.

Name: Michael Inganamort
Age: 20
School: American University
Major or Area of interest: Political Science
Hometown: Sparta, New Jersey
Inspiration for "Thanks, but I'll pass:" As a conservative editorialist for The Eagle (school newspaper), I was always interested in getting beyond the rhetoric of modern politics and looking at the core of the issues. Whether it is Social Security or campaign finance reform, the approaches from both parties can slip into stale redundancy. Once an individual can clearly identify his or her central beliefs, that person can judge policy based on its merits, not the latest party talking points.

Name: Mischa Sogut

Name: Mohammad Akbar Sharifi
Age: 18
School: College of Alameda
Major or area of interest: Graphic Design
Hometown: Alameda, California
Inspiration for "The Loss:" The inspiration for the piece arrived through my personal attachment to war and it's numerous ills. My parents fled Afghanistan during the Soviet war for the safety of their children. Shortly after, my uncle fled Kuwait before it was attacked by Iraq. Many of my relatives underwent the harsh restrictions of the Taliban regime. And finally, my neighbor lost her only son during the Operation Enduring Freedom campaign in Afghanistan in 2002.

Name: Nathaniel Nelson
Age: 21
School: University of Rhode Island
Major or Area of interest: Political Science
Hometown: Coventry, Rhode Island
Inspiration for "Under God:" In today's relativist society, absolutes are no longer accepted. Therefore, to the average college student who has been brainwashed by the Left, a traditional conservative who believes in, for example, political and ethical absolutes, is seen as a hindrance to the advancement of society. Every piece that I write is geared to remedy this false notion that the Left has introduced. My goal is to show my peers that there is room for absolutes in society and that Conservative issues, such as religion, the traditional family, individual responsibility, a strong military, limited government and low taxation, are what helped to make America the sought after, "city upon the hill."

Name: Nikesha Williams

Name: Patrick Sciacchitano
Age: 19
School: George Mason University
Major or Area of interest: Doubled Majored Government/Philosophy
Hometown: Vienna, Virginia
Inspiration for "Citizenship Project:" To serve, to Love, and to spread the Glory of God.

Name: Rebeca Bell
Age: 22
School: Denison University
Major or Area of interest: political science, especially domestic policy formulation
Hometown: Toledo, Ohio
Inspiration for "How To Save the Earth:" One random day, a friend of mine had an idea. He wanted to write a book that would speak to our generation. It would be political and hopeful and intelligent. So, we went to work. We picked our subjects and began to research and write. Our chapters were good, but the book never materialized. My essay in What We Think is the final product that was inspired by my friend's awesome idea.

Name: Robin Orlowski
Age: 25
School: Texas Woman's University
Major or Area of interest: Women's Studies (Concentration: Government)
Hometown: Katy
Inspiration for "Living the Revolution:" Seeing the political ignorance which public school classmates with disabilities repeatedly had about their own rights.

Name: Ryan Thompson
Age: 18
School: Hillsdale College
Major or Area of interest: Political Science
Hometown: Carmichaels, PA
Inspiration for "Future of Conservatism:" All of my columns are based on my personal beliefs.

Name: Samantha Vinograd
Age: 21
School: University of Pennsylvania
Major or Area of interest: Middle Eastern Studies
Hometown: Fairfield, CT
Inspiration for "Issues of Palentinian Identity:" My inspiration for this piece came from my experience at the School of Oriental and African Studies. While taking a class on Israeli history, I was fortunate enough to be learning alongside Palestinian students. As a Jewish-American, it was fascinating to be presented with the viewpoints of Palestinian Muslim and Christian peers.

Name: Sarah Carr
School: George Washington University
Age: 18
Major or Area of interest: English and Art History
Hometown: Cranston, RI
Inspiration for "Utopian Sestina in F Sharp:" I can't say there is any single event that inspired this poem. However, I have been heavily influenced by the writing style of Bob Dylan.

Name: Sarah Timm
Age: 21
School: Washington State University, Pullman
Major or Area of interest: Environmental Science
Hometown: Okanogan
Inspiration for "Satisfaction:" My piece was inspired by a combination of sources including the book "Young Women, Feminism and the Future" by Freedman. My class on Gender in Society, Soc 385 has also been a source of my questioning gender stereotypes that we hold in our culture.

Name: Scott Elingburg
Age: 24
School: Clemson University
Major or area of interest: English/ Contemporary American Literature
Hometown: Simpsonville, SC
Inspiration for "See Sally Stuggle:" This piece was born out of my primary and secondary observations of the South Carolina public education system. Both my wife and my mother are public school teachers and I have always been fascinated with the problems they encounter in their careers and how the public, namely politicians and parents, respond to the problems of education.

Name: Scott Tarazevits

Name: Shabina Khatri
Age: 22
School: University of Michigan-Ann Arbor
Major or Area of interest: Business and Spanish
Hometown: Troy, Michigan
Inspiration for the piece: I am alarmed by the growing indifference of my generation. Apathy begins with helplessness, and I wrote this piece to remind my peers that we are nowhere near helpless. We are rising stars, easily some of the most educated, powerful and privileged groups in the world. We'd do well to remember that reality, and one more: The time for excuses is over, the time for play has past and the time for establishing our place has come.

Name: Stephen Schwartz

Name: Takeo Rivera

Name: Thom Gray
Age: 19
School: University of Tennessee, Knoxville
Major or Area of interest: English (Rhetoric and Writing), minors in Religious Studies and Secondary Education
Hometown: Elizabethton, TN
Inspiration for "Political Geek:" General frustration over the false dichotomy of the "two-party system."

Name: Timothy O'Brien
Age: 20
School: State University of New York at Albany
Major or Area of interest: Psychology/Political Science
Hometown: Staten Island
Inspiration for "Openly Gay:" A constant flow of things going unnoticed is what keeps me thinking and keeps me writing.

Name: Timothy Schuermer
Age: 20 years old
School: Rutgers University
Major or Area of interest: Anthropology and Economics
Hometown: Spokane, WA
Inspiration for "Race and Affirmative Action:" Affirmative Action is an attempt to give all humans, regardless of race, sex, nor creed the opportunity to live equally. However, within higher education Affirmative Action has failed. Too much emphasis is placed on race and not on economic opportunity. My hope is people better understand the goal of Affirmative Action and will rightfully apply it in the future so every student is at least given the chance to receive an education.

Name: Tom McSorley
Age: 20
School: Harvard University
Major or Area of interest: Government
Hometown: Warminster, PA
Inspiration for "Identity:" Mr. John Buettler and Dr. Patricia Sisca Pace, two extraordinary mentors who not only taught me how to think critically and have faith in my abilities, but also how to approach the world with hope and optimism.

Name: Tony Torres
Age: 25
School: Virginia Tech
Major or Area of interest: History and Classical Studies
Hometown: Fairfax, VA

Inspiration for "Young Voters Should Look to Libertarians:" I am a strong supporter of the Libertarian Party and the Constitution of the United States and believe passionately that we need to return to a limited and decentralized government where the primary role of government is to protect our lives, liberty, and property and little else.

Name: Tyrone Nelson Collier
Age: 20
School: University of Cincinnati

Major or Area of interest: Philosophy/Pre-Law
Hometown:
Inspiration for "Impassioned by a Famous Photograph…:" Tommie Smith and John Carlos.

Name: Veronika Penciakova
Age: 18
School: George Washington University
Major or Area of interest: International Affairs
Hometown: Wichita, Kansas
Inspiration for "Dear Candidate:" For as long as I can remember various professors and adults have told me that young people can't appreciate the political process. I know that the opposite is true, and wanted to express some of the reasons why many individuals, both young and old, choose not to vote.

Name: Zach Foster
Age: 19
School: University of Michigan, Ann Arbor
Major or Area of interest: Sociology and Political Science
Hometown: West Bloomfield, Michigan
Inspiration for "Fictitious Image of Race:" This piece was originally written for the purpose of a seminar I took at the University of Michigan. Since its submission, however, I have spent countless hours reworking the essay to lend itself for a broader audience.

Bibliography

NOTE: We were diligent in our efforts to bibliographically reference as necessary. However, not all submissions included biographical citations. Consequently, some phrases, sentences, and paragraphs may remain unreferenced. The following bibliography includes all submitted bibliographical information.

Fictitious Image of Race

Hartigan Jr., John. 1997. White Trash: Race and Class in America. "Name Calling: Objectifying "Poor Whites" and "White Trash" in Detroit. Edited by Matt Wray and Annalee Newitz. New York: Routledge. (p. 40-56)

Kottak, Conrad. 2004. Anthropology: The Exploration of Human Diversity (10th edition). New York: McGraw-Hill. (p. 545-569).

Lamont, Michele. 2000. The Dignity of Working Men: Morality and the Boundaries of Race, Class, and Immigration. New York: Russel Sage Foundation. (p. 1-96)

Linnaeus, Charles. 1758. General Systems of Nature. (10th edition). (p. 425-426).

Lopez, Ian F. Haney. 1996. White By Law. "Racial Restrictions in the Law of Citizenship". New York New York University Press. (p. 37-107).

Paige, Jeffery. "Toward an Integrated Theory". Sociology 105. University of Michigan. Ann Arbor, MI. December 8, 2003.

Paige, Jeffery. "Abstract Subjects, 'Class', 'Race', 'Gender' and 'Modernity'. Department of Sociology. University of Michigan. Racialized Identity and Disciplined Self. (p. 8-12).

Vaughan, Alden T. (June 1982). The American Historical Review. 87, no. 3. "From White Man to Redskin: Changing American Perceptions of the American Indian". (p 917- 953).

Weber, Max. 1958. The Protestant Ethic and the Spirit of Capitalism. New York: Charles Scribner's. (p. 155-183)

How to Make Your Vote Count

Benditt, Sarah. Personal Interview. 18 February 2004.
Berman, Dennis K. "The Young and the (Still) Listless." Business Week 27 November 2000 Proquest Online accessed 14 February 2004.
Young Voter Turnout Diminishing at Polls. 3 November 2003. FOX News Channel Online. 14 February 2004
<<http://www.foxnews.com/printer_friendly_story/0,3566,102014,00.html>>

Immorality of Conscription

[1] Ronald Reagan, Letter To Mark O. Hatfield, May 5, 1980.
<http://www.cato.org/pubs/pas/pa086.html>
[2] Ayn Rand, "The Wreckage of the Consensus," in Ayn Rand, Capitalism: The Unknown Ideal. Italics added.
[3] A.J. Muste, "Conscription and Conscience," in Martin Anderson (ed), with Barbara Honegger, The Military Draft: Selected Readings on Conscription (Hoover: Stanford, 1982), p. 570.
[4] David Mayer, "Interpreting the Constitution Contextually," Navigator, October 2003. <http://www.objectivistcenter.org/navigator/articles/nav+dmayer_interpreting-constitu-tion-contextually.asp>
[5] The New Hampshire state license plate puts it even more succinctly: "Live free or die."
[6] Harry Roberts, Comments on Arthur Silber, "With Friends Like These, Continued—and Arguing with David Horowitz," LightofReason.com, November 19, 2002. <http://coldfury.com/reason/comments.php?id=P58_0_1_21>
[7] William Jefferson Clinton, Letter To the Senate, May 18, 1994. <http://www.chin-fo.navy.mil/navpalib/people/recruit/whs0518.txt>
[8] "Statistics about the Vietnam War," Vietnam Helicopter Flight Crew Network. <http://www.vhfcn.org/stat.htm>
[9] Burton Stevenson, The Home Book of Quotations (New York: Dodd, Mead, 1952), p. 2114.
[10] Ronald Reagan, First Inaugural Address, January 20, 1981. <http://www.reagan-foundation.org/reagan/speeches/first.asp>
[11] For years people have quoted these eloquent words—either "People sleep peace-ably in their beds at night only because rough men stand ready to do violence on their behalf," or, "We sleep safely at night because rough men stand ready to visit violence on those who would harm us"—and attributed them to George Orwell. Yet neither the stan-dard quotation books, general and military, extensive Google searches, the Stumpers ListServ (http://domin.dom.edu/depts/gslis/stumpers), nor the only Orwell quotation booklet, The Sayings of George Orwell (London: Duckworth, 1994), cites a specific source.
[12] Nathaniel Fick, "Don't Dumb down the Military," New York Times, July 20, 2004, p. A19.

<http://www.nytimes.com/2004/07/20/opinion/20fick.html?ex=1091413780&ei=1&en=c
992def4f5c9f67d>

[13] Nathaniel Fick, "Don't Dumb down the Military," New York Times, July 20, 2004,
p. A19.
<http://www.nytimes.com/2004/07/20/opinion/20fick.html?ex=1091413780&ei=1&en=c
992def4f5c9f67d>

[14] William Broyles Jr., "A War for Us, Fought by Them," New York Times, May 4,
2004. <http://www.nytimes.com/2004/05/04/opinion/04BROY.html>

[15] Lawrence F. Kaplan, "Apocalypse Kerry," New Republic Online, July 30, 2004.
<http://www.tnr.com/doc.mhtml?i=express&s=kaplan073004>

[16] Jean-Jacques Rousseau, Discourse on the Moral Effects of the Arts and Sciences.

[17] George W. Bush, Statement by the President in His Address To the Nation, White
House, September 11, 2001. <http://www.whitehouse.gov/news/releas-
es/2001/09/20010911-16.html>

[18] Ayn Rand, "The Wreckage of the Consensus," in Ayn Rand, Capitalism: The
Unknown Ideal.

Let Us Not Be Oridinary Intellectuals

1 The Book of Ammon by Ammon Hennacy, see also http://ah.lovarchy.org/
2 Is There No Other Way? The search for a nonviolent future by Michael Nagler
3 Political Structuring of the Institutions of Science by Charles Schwartz, in Naked
Science: Anthropological inquiry into boundaries, power, and knowledge by Laura
Nader, see also http://ist-socrates.berkeley.edu/~schwrtz/SRS.html

Metamorphosing Hours in Ramallah

Morris, Benny. Righteous Victims, A History of the Zionist Arab Conflict 1881-2201.
Vintage Books, a division of Random House. New York: 2001

New York Times. U.N. Estimates Israeli Barrier Will Disrupt Lives of 600,000.
        November 12, 2003.

New York Times. Myre, Greg. Israelis Approve $22 Million For Settlements on West
Bank. February 18, 2004

New York Times. Burns, John F. Palestinian Ends Defense in Murder Trial. September
30, 2003

Perry-Castañeda Library Map Collection. Israel Maps.
        http://www.lib.utexas.edu/maps/middle_east_and_asia/israel_pol01.jpg

Shehadeh, Raja. Strangers in the House, Coming of Age in Occupied Palestine. Penguin
Books. New York: 2002

World Bank. World Bank Report Highlights 60 Percent Poverty Level In Palestinian
Territories. March 5, 2003.
        http://web.worldbank.org/WBSITE/EXTERNAL/NEWS/0,,contentMDK:20095
849~menuPK:34463~pagePK:34370~piPK:34424~theSitePK:4607,00.html

World Policy Institute. Arms Trade Resource Center. U.S. Arms Transfers and Security
Assistance to Israel. May 6, 2002
http://www.worldpolicy.org/projects/arms/reports/israel050602.html

Probing Terrorism

Annan, Kofi; Gowers, Andrew; Chomsky, Noam; Kirkpatrick, Jeane; Hehir, Bryan; Ogata, Sadko; Bello, Walden; Appadurai, Arjun; Wedgwood, Ruth. What is the International Community? Foreign Policy. September / October 2003. Issue 132

Bernstein, Douglas A. and Nash, Peggy W. Essentials of Psychology. Houghton Mifflin Company. Boston: 1999

Power, Samantha. "A Problem from Hell", America and the age of Genocide. Harper Collins Books. New York: 2003

Singer, Peter. One World, the Ethics of Globalization. Yale University Press. New Haven: 2002

The Fundamental Attribution Error
        http://www.sage.edu/divisions/psych/courses/p301ch03.htm

September 11th in the Classroom

"American studies Urged as Focus." The New York Times 7 Oct. 2001: B4.

Bush, George W. Speech. Vital Speeches of the Day 24 (2001): 760-763.

Clayton, Mark. "Learning Arabic is a long–term investment." The Christian Science Monitor 2 Oct. 2001: 15.

--- "Standing Room Only." The Christian Science Monitor 2 Oct. 2001: 13+.

Cox, Ana Marie. "The Changed Classroom, Post-September 11." Chronicle of Higher Education 26 Oct. 2001: A16-A18.

Dorsey, Gary. " The TEACH-IN." The Baltimore Sun 13 Oct. 2001. 27 Nov. 2001 < http://nl4.newsbank.com/nl-search/we/Archives?paction+list&p _topdoc=176>.

Leo, John. "Don't Tread on Free Speakers." U.S. News and World Report 5 Nov. 2001: 59.

Lord, Mary. "Real World 101." U.S. News and World Report 5 Nov. 2001: 56.

Mikhaylova, Alexandra. Personal Interview. 27 Nov. 2001.

Sergi, Thomas. Personal Interview. 28 Nov. 2001.

War on The Home Front and Other Renegade Warriors: The Power of One

Advocates for Youth. (January 1995). Child Sexual Abuse 1: An Overview. Retrieved August 11, 2004 from http://www.advocatesforyouth.org/publications/factsheet/fsabuse1.htm

Babington, Charles. (July 7, 2004). Senate Confirms Controversial Nominee to Federal Court. Retrieved August 10, 2004, from The Washington Post. Website: http://www.washingtonpost.com/wp-dyn/articles/A32206-2004Jul6.html

Bush, George. (March 12, 2004). Remarks by the First Lady and the President on Efforts to Globally Promote Women's Human Rights. Retrieved August 9, 2004, from

Bibliography

The White House. Website: http://www.whitehouse.gov/news/releases/2004/03/20040312-5.html

Earlham College. (Fall 2002). Statistics. Retrieved August 9, 2004, from http://www.earlham.edu/~aar/stats.html

George Mason University. (September 2004). Effects of Sexual Assault. Retrieved August 11, 2004 from http://www.gmu.edu/facstaff/sexual/effects_of_assault.html#top

Higher Education Center for Alcohol and Other Drug Prevention. (July 2002). Infofacts Resources: Sexual Assault and Alcohol and Other Drug Use. Retrieved August 11, 2004 from http://www.edc.org/hec/pubs/factsheets/fact_sheet1.pdf

National Organization for Women. (Summer 2001). Men Organize to Stop Sexual Assault. Retrieved August 11, 2004 from http://www.now.org/nnt/summer-2001/sexualassault.html

Pravda. (November 12, 2003). Dead Woman Who Accused Bush of Rape. Retrieved August 11, 2004 from http://english.pravda.ru/world/20/91/368/11257_scandal.html

Resources for Women. (September 2004). Domestic Violence. Retrieved August 11, 2004 from http://www.resourcesforwomen.com/domesticviolence.htm

University of Rochester Student Association. (February 20, 2003). Men Against Sexual Assault. Retrieved August 11, 2004 from http://sa.rochester.edu/masa/stats.php

Afterword
by Justin Padley

Frozen Burritos and a Dream. It's campy, I know. But as I reflect on the infancy of this project, I can't help but wonder what else kept Rob and Dean going on those hot summer nights. I've never been around an inspirational force as gripping and magnetic as watching those two work late into the night, devising strategies for reaching more and more young people and sharing in the excitement that comes with making a palpable difference. Their vision of bridging the generational gap in our common discourse snowballed at a stunning rate. The press attention was almost immediate; a torrent of submissions followed in short order. And as the passionate resolve for change held by so many young Americans flooded through the wires, I saw the future being distilled from an illusory ideal (or worse yet, a threat) to a much more pliable thing – an opportunity. What doubts I had about the social and political drive of my contemporaries were soundly defeated by the earnest ambition of the works in this book. The future is undoubtedly a weighty responsibility, but it's a responsibility I now feel we are equipped to take on.

Many thousands of hours and a few more frozen burritos later and the voices of our peers coalesced into the compendium you hold today. The unbridled enthusiasm Rob and Dean held for this book is undoubtedly indicative of a similar (but largely ignored) zeal coursing through the hearts and minds of the oft-quoted "34 Million." After reading the pieces that made the cut and the many fine entries that did not, I am confident that this generation's well of passion runs deep and true, no matter what the distant and disaffected pundits may say. For years, we've been told that we just don't care. In point of fact, we were stating our case all along.

But in the end, this reflection is not about me. And it's not really about our generation's driving aspiration to forge a better America. It's about the tireless efforts of two young men who strove to affect a substantive change. I cannot stress enough just how unshakeable their resolve was. There was a look in Rob's tired eyes as he asked to take a quick shower following a night's sleep on the floor of his office (amazingly, it was still there when he later informed me that a total lack of hot water had made it a quick shower indeed). I saw the same look in Dean's eyes as he organized papers at the tail end of a marathon session reviewing submissions. It was determination and it would not rest.

Let it never again be said that our generation is so nested in torpidity as to waste our years in a glut of self-indulgence and indifference. I have seen the dedication of two bright minds turn an unlikely ambition into a full-service franchise in the trade of ideas. My thanks and the thanks of 34 million of my closest friends go out to Rob and Dean for realizing the dream we didn't know we had.

Acknowledgements

Rob would like to acknowledge:
My mom - for being my greatest advocate and teacher. This is also a belated thank you for the labors of love endured on July 12, 1981. My brother Tim - for great insights and for having a hot, intelligent wife-Mia I love you, girl. My brother Chris - for his hours of editing, and companionship up Livingston Peak. Dean Robbins - Congratulations buddy! Shannon Odell, you're amazing! No Shannon, no book! Justin Padley - You're my boy! Leave Keira alone. Kelly Antoncich - the most clever sob I know. The Robbins' Family - Thank you for all your support and advice. The Bresnahan Clan - dinners, Christmas parties, use of shower and most of all the support and hospitality. Walter and Eleanor Rodgers. Lesley Bresnahan - You're my girl - Amazing hummus! Brigid O'Brien - good luck in Swaziland! Nina Stern - our friend and amazing publicist. Paul Belknap. Jamie and Cara - for the best fake-dates of my life. Sarah Flett - for keeping it real! We'll always have Greece! Ryan Bell, Dan Garitty, Nissa, Nathan Bryant, Richie Campana, Shannon Rice, Preston Anonuevo, Jo and Paul Stephens, Patti Boyden, Julia Wehner, Familie Menzel, The Beierles, The Baetzings and all my buddies in Germany, Danielle Cendejas, Paul Schaeffer, Josh Kurz, Norm Leatha, Kim Bunkers, Mrs. Titus, the custodial staff of Schoenberg, Bo from the computer lab, the ghost of Gonzaga - I respect you! Finally and most importantly the submitters and everyone else involved in creating a heeded voice for the next great generation!

Dean would like to acknowledge:
I want to thank: my parents for an education in life's principles; my older brother Jack for challenging me; my younger sister Alice for her intriguing insights, my Grandma and Grandad for giving me the chance to see the world, my Nana and Papa for their active involvement in my life's interests, my cofounder Rob for a "cogent and undergirding" presentation of the other side of things; Logan for the advice and sagacity only a fellow man of Scottish blood could give, Mike (a.k.a. 'Wall') for being a great friend; Ryan, RC, Jeff, John, and Mike for the year at 327 and the times that will be; Russell and Kim for the year that will be at 908; Paul (a.k.a. 'The A Man') for the continued support; Colette for everything; Morgan for the same;Dan Garitty, New Light Industries (Jeff, Roger, Marcy, Mike, Steve, and Jesse) for the great internship and advice on College Tree; my professors of engineering (Dacquisto, Capobianchi, Appel, and Nowak) for

being great teachers; my senior design group (Seth, Patty, and Dustin); Professor Steverson; Shelley Daugherty and Dale Goodwin for helping us get started; Nissa for being patient with our demands; Sally and Shelley at Global Credit Union for being my financial legislators; Professor Helgeson for paying our phone bills so we could call our moms; all my cousins especially Marg and Liz for informing their friends; my God Parents Uncle Doug and Aunt Donna; my Welsh Corgi Bobby for eating anything that dropped on the floor; my tortoise Manny who died an early age at the paws of Bobby who likely buried him alive somewhere I have yet to find; my old Giant Schnauzer Max who set the bar to high for Bobby; Gorlow for providing a recurrence of events that were absolutely uncertain by the laws of physics and chance; to all the people who have given time and advice on our project, its successes are attributed to you; and finally Thomas Jefferson and Benjamen Franklin for intriguing me to no end with your genius, wisdom, vision, and connectedness to the realm of the human spirit that was so well echoed in your writing and letters.

Who we together should acknowledge:
Tony Bamonte - Thanks for giving us the necessary direction, and challenging us to make our deadlines.
Shannon Odell - You were sensational and your joy and kindness will never go unnoticed by us.
Rosie Porter - Your confidence in our project inspired us to dream big. Thank you!
Sheryn Hara - You're publishing savvy made this a logistically possible.
Jenna McManus - You were destined to join our team thank you for all your help.
Dale Goodwin - Thanks for getting this project off the ground and believing in it
Shelly Daugherty - Thanks for all your help and time.
Gonzaga University - Thank you for providing us with an amazing education that went beyond the classroom and into the realm of the human mind and spirit.
James Helgeson - Thanks for paying for our phone bills so we could call our moms - and great input.
Justin Padley - Thanks for your great ideas, time, political insights, and pizza!

Everyone Who Submitted - This book is yours!

Coming Soon...

What *We* Think *II*
&
What *We* Think: *About God*

For information on how to submit, please visit:
www.collegetreepublishing.com